IMAGES
of Aviation

LIBERAL ARMY AIRFIELD

ON THE COVER: Standing proudly in front of one of their flying classrooms, the first set of instructors are ready for the next class of future commanders. These men had varying tasks of teaching the advanced twin-engine-rated pilots every aspect of the B-24 and had only nine weeks to do it. (Courtesy of the Mid-America Air Museum.)

IMAGES
of Aviation

LIBERAL ARMY AIRFIELD

Lidia Hook-Gray and Connie Gray-Bowman

ARCADIA
PUBLISHING

ISBN 978-1-4671-6228-9

Published by Arcadia Publishing
Charleston, South Carolina

Printed in the United States of America

Library of Congress Control Number: 2024947540

For all general information, please contact Arcadia Publishing:
Telephone 843-853-2070
Fax 843-853-0044
E-mail sales@arcadiapublishing.com

Visit us on the Internet at www.arcadiapublishing.com

We dedicate this book to all who served at the Liberal Army Airfield.

Contents

ACKNOWLEDGMENTS

We would like to thank several people who helped immensely in writing this book; firstly, the Mid-America Air Museum's staff. Thank you to Bob Immell, museum director; Peggy McCulley, archivist; and Cari Sallee and Krisi Anderson, assistants. Without their friendliness, expertise, and enthusiasm, this book would not have been possible.

A big thank-you also goes to Bob Keating, Gary Classen, Carol Feather Francis, Karen Martin, Rita McManus, Dr. April Bowman, Tim Strickland, the Jean Randall family, and John T. Smith for their contributions. Also, thanks to the City of Liberal. When we went to them with the idea of a history of the Liberal Army Airfield, they did not hesitate to help.

Our final thanks go to our families. They did not mind that our dining-room tables became covered with photographs, books, and notes and that we had become obsessed with the stories of the people who served our great nation.

The majority of the images in this book are courtesy of the Mid-America Air Museum's archives. Any other images are credited to the appropriate source. Any errors are the sole responsibility of the authors.

Please note that within the text, Liberal Army Airfield has been abbreviated as LAAF.

INTRODUCTION

After Pearl Harbor was attacked, the farm community of Liberal, Kansas, wanted nothing more than to contribute to the war effort. The Liberal Chamber of Commerce proposed to citizens the idea of establishing an air training base. With an average of 246 sunny days per year, flat terrain, and a good supply of food and water, Liberal was ideal. With the backing of his board of directors, H.A. Kinney, chamber secretary, contacted military officials and politicians to consider Liberal for a military airfield.

In the spring of 1942, Gen. William Ord Ryan, US Air Force (USAF), and a British Royal Air Force officer came to Liberal to see if the area would work for a Royal Air Force bombing area. The men chose two sites west of town.

In May 1942, the Corps of Engineers arrived to survey both sites. This survey was finished in July 1942. On July 20, 1942, Liberal officials received notice the project had been dropped.

Devastated, the chamber of commerce board made another appeal to Army Air Corps officials. This time, the Liberal men were heard.

On December 1, 1942, Murray A. Wilson and Company completed the layout of the 1,900-acre site. Peter Kiewit Sons Company was selected as the prime contractor. On a spur built to the airbase site by the Rock Island Railroad, concrete, lumber, hardware, and men started arriving. Construction had begun.

Plans were designed for an aviation training school. The base and school could accommodate 3,356 personnel. Initial plans called for two 4,000-foot landing strips with an estimated cost of $2,675,000. Interestingly, in an area that contained one of the largest natural gas fields in the world, coal was the authorized official fuel.

March 1 brought changes to the original plans. Four runways 150 by 7,000 feet were to be built along with two additional runways and two taxi strips. The largest change was the decision to use local natural gas. An extra mess hall, post-exchange, more barracks, and a woman's dormitory rounded out the additional changes. Personnel now numbered 4,772. This more than doubled the size of Liberal. Since some men brought their families, every travel court, spare room, garage, and converted chicken coops opened to welcome the new arrivals.

In May 1943, the National Public Housing Administration brought trailers in to relieve the housing shortage. These were for civilians employed at the airfield and were located adjacent to town. In July 1943, construction began on Blue Bonnet Courts. The courts consisted of 120 family units built of concrete blocks featuring natural gas heat. Units rented for $30–$40 per month.

The main function of the LAAF was to train efficient, knowledgeable B-24 commanders. The difference between a pilot and commander was a commander was trained to know his four-engine aircraft from nose to tail. He must understand the construction, the components, systems, and all duties of his crew. The commanders needed the ability to think quickly, be physically fit, and have the confidence of a leader.

The LAAF training program covered a nine-week period. The incoming students received 105 hours of flying, 30 hours of navigation, 15 hours of Link training, 26 hours of bomb approach ground school, 54 hours of physical training, and 146 hours of technical instruction. Officer students were also required to perform maintenance on the flight line and received additional hours in meteorology, first aid, and radio operation. Halfway through the training cycle, another class began. When the field was deactivated, the LAAF had graduated 4,468 four-engine commanders plus 1,025 pilots who had graduated from a pre-transition course.

The airfield was not without problems. Two tornadoes, several blizzards, and the ever-present wind took a toll on both personnel and equipment. When construction began, skilled workers were difficult to find, along with the scarcity of raw materials. Lack of housing was an ongoing problem. When the B-24s started flying, getting extra parts and supplies caused delays in keeping the programs on track. And though the training was intense with little time to waste, homesickness and boredom infected the men who were not accustomed to the treeless plains of southwest Kansas.

The first Liberator landed on June 20, 1943, and the base was officially deactivated on October 5, 1945. What a whirlwind of activity the airfield brought to Liberal! The field was turned over to the Army's District Engineer in Omaha, Nebraska, who assumed command of the field. Excess buildings, equipment, and other surplus items were sold to the public. The entire airfield, which cost $8 million to build, was sold to the City of Liberal for $1.

The B-24, "Bag of Bolts," "Agony Wagon," "the Flying Boxcar," "the Widow Maker," or whatever it was called, was a difficult plane to fly. Inexperienced pilots hastily built planes, and an intense, short instruction process led to accidents. Approximately 111 crashes were recorded in the Liberal area alone. Tragically, 55 men lost their lives in these accidents. Men and women from every corner of the United States came to give their best to their country. At the LAAF, their duty was to get those bombers to the scenes of war.

This book features images of life on and off the airfield, but most importantly, the book wants to honor those who did not survive. These brave men and women put themselves in harm's way for the love of country and freedom. May they never be forgotten. They are:

September 4, 1943
Lt. William J. Beckham Jr.
2nd Lt. Oren L. Sparks
Cpl. Zenog Mooshoian

October 28, 1943
2nd Lt. Laurice G. Axen
Maj. James V. Mesita
2nd Lt. Harold Connerly
2nd Lt. Thomas R. LeCompton
Sgt. Homer L. Walker

November 25, 1943
Cpt. Douglas Milligan
2nd Lt. Herbert M Briley
2nd Lt. Lloyd G. Handy
S.Sgt. Chester McCreary
S.Sgt. Elton Y. Dizbang
Pfc. Charles E. Jacobs Jr.
2nd Lt. Robert W. Tupper
2nd Lt. Ralph E. Pierce
2nd Lt. John B. McConnell
Cpl. James W. Kell
Pfc. John J. Haggerty

December 21, 1943
2nd Lt. James S. O'Toole
2nd Lt. Robert N. Spinelli

December 30, 1943
1st Lt. Morris J. Gendron
2nd Lt. Raymond E. Melinder
2nd Lt. Robert T. Johnson
2nd Lt. Ellwood L. Meyer
FO Warren D. Goodwin
Cpl. James R. Nolte

March 31, 1944
2nd Lt. J.B. Bolyn
Pfc. Frank Ganz
FO Roger Hance
2nd Lt. Chester H. Henson Jr.
2nd Lt. Blanchard J. Horne Jr.
2nd Lt. George W. Medley
2nd Lt. Jack L. Harland
2nd Lt. William Joseph Hunter Jr.
Sgt. Edward T. Sax

June 2, 1944
1st Lt. Julius C. Macho

June 14, 1944
Sgt. Cecil I. Read

July 25, 1944
1st Lt. Maurice L. Forrey
2nd Lt. Charles H. Post

August 1, 1944
2nd Lt. Martin J. Hanson
2nd Lt. John W. Scott Jr.
Pfc. Leonard Satzman

August 21, 1944
1st Lt. Frank S. Cash
2nd Lt. George J. Copa
2nd Lt. Richard G. DeVoe
FO Louis W. Frangos
2nd Lt. Wayne Y. Corse
S.Sgt. Charles Ray Basham
2nd Lt. Alexander N. Mogill

November 16, 1944
2nd Lt. Edward C. Bailiff
2nd Lt. Raymond V. Johnson

March 21, 1945
FO David J. Nixon

May 6, 1945
1st Lt. Rubin Indik
1st Lt. Archie B. Caraway
Pfc. Aloysius Freiburger Jr.

June 14, 1945
2nd Lt. Claude T. Aiken Jr.
2nd Lt. George T. Bright
S.Sgt. Walter M. Martella

One

Early Air History

Liberal, Kansas, has always been a proud community since its founding by Seymour Rogers in 1885. Liberal is located in the southwest corner of Kansas along US Highway 54. The generally mild winters, flat terrain, and dry climate made it an appealing location for the big B-24 bombers to train and land. Liberal also had an eager community with lots of land. The base was officially only here for 27 months but left a legacy that is still important to the community today.

Like so many communities across America, in the 1930s, Liberal was also looking for economic recovery. The Great Depression and the Dust Bowl years were particularly hard on rural Kansas. The City of Liberal submitted plans to the military in 1941 at the start of World War II to construct a training base. LAAF became the Army 2nd Air Force and was officially opened on May 13, 1943, to train pilots and engineers on the B-24 heavy bomber.

Several units were merged into the 2525th AAF. In addition, there were 15 major airfields in Kansas during World War II, all of which played a significant role in the training and manufacturing of planes. Gage, Oklahoma Auxiliary Field, 80 miles from LAAF, served as Liberal's alternate landing field.

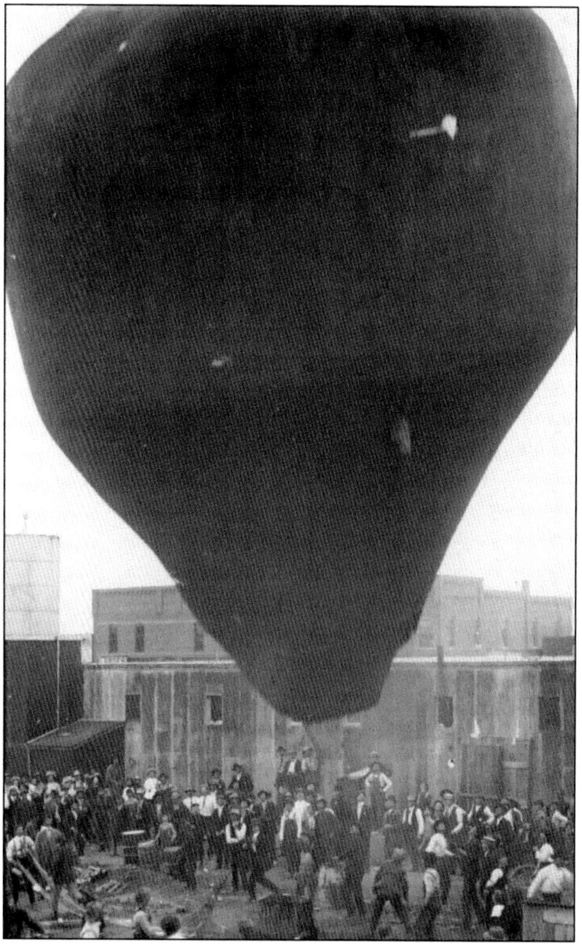

Liberal's first taste of things to come was May 10, 1910. As a promotion by local retailers, a professional balloonist was hired to draw a crowd. The feat almost backfired. When the massive balloon made of 2,000 yards of black silk was inflated and lifted off, people ran. (Courtesy of Lidia Gray.)

Glenn L. Martin, his parents, and his sister moved to Liberal in 1888. As a young boy, Glenn developed an interest in the new thing called aviation and invented a box-type kite that could withstand the ever-present winds of Kansas. He sold kites to his playmates for a quarter each. Glenn, pictured here (front) in 1912 with friend Joe Brown, in his push monoplane, went on to build an aviation empire, eventually becoming Lockheed Martin. (Courtesy of Lidia Gray.)

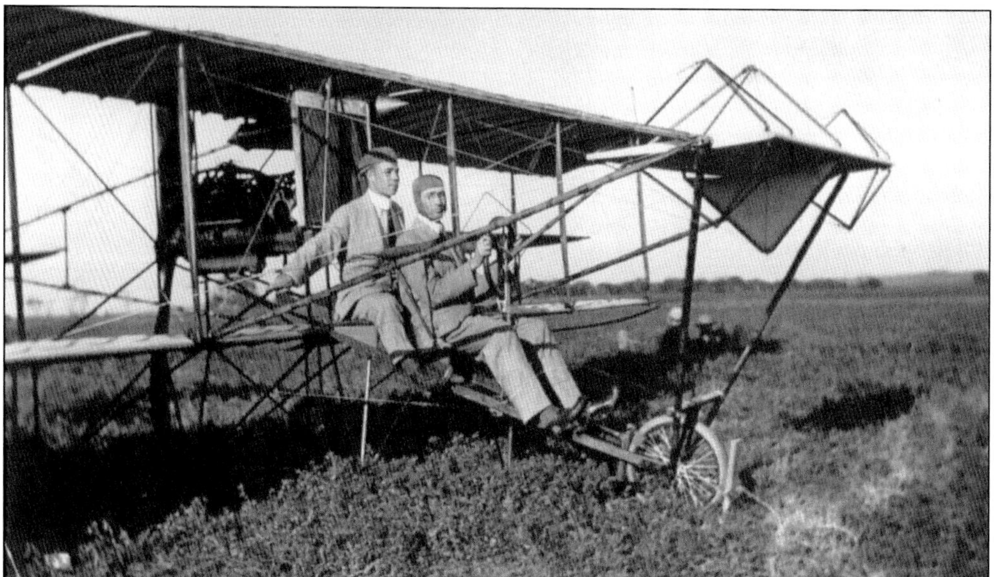

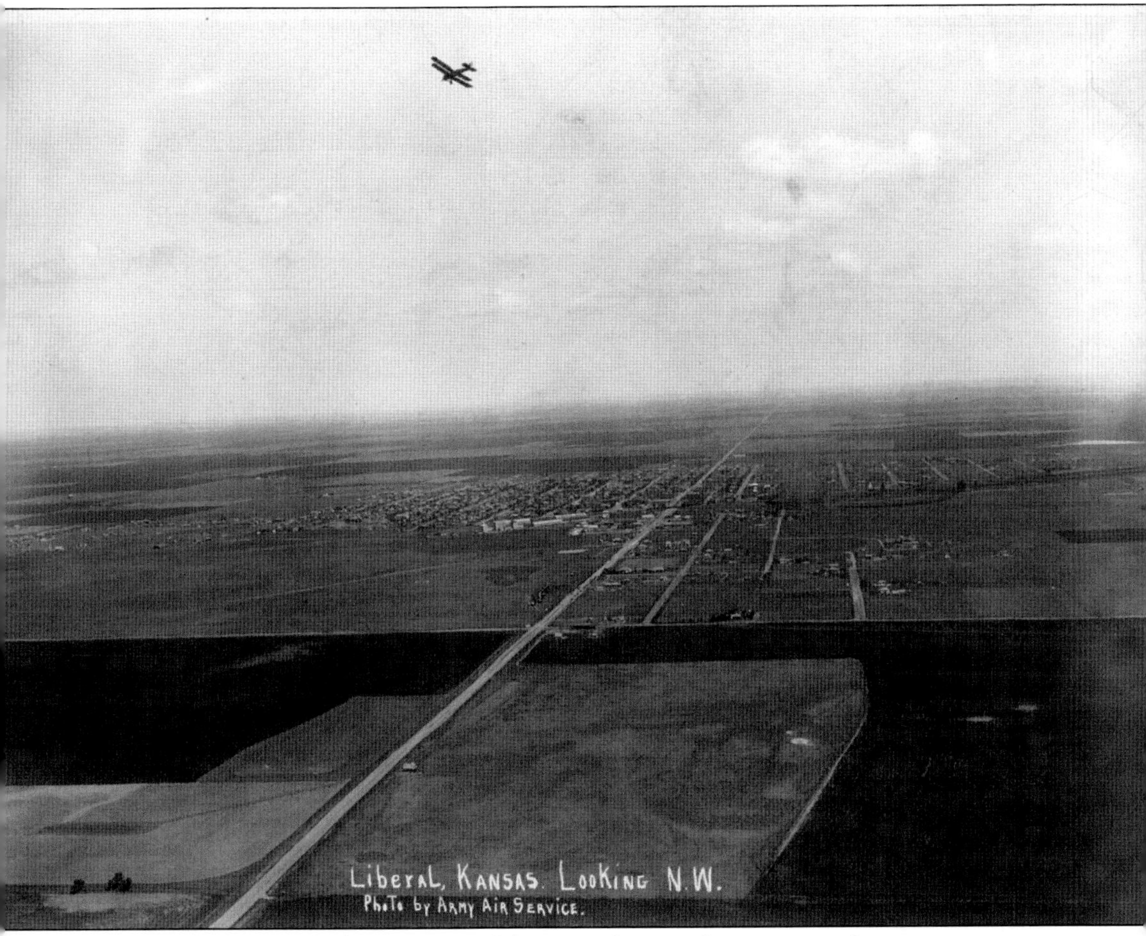

An early aerial photograph shows a view of the town that was fascinating to the average person. More than likely, the image was taken after 1912 from an open cockpit plane. Notice the biplane in the upper center of the image. Interestingly, the photograph was taken by the Army Air Service. (Courtesy of the John Baughman estate.)

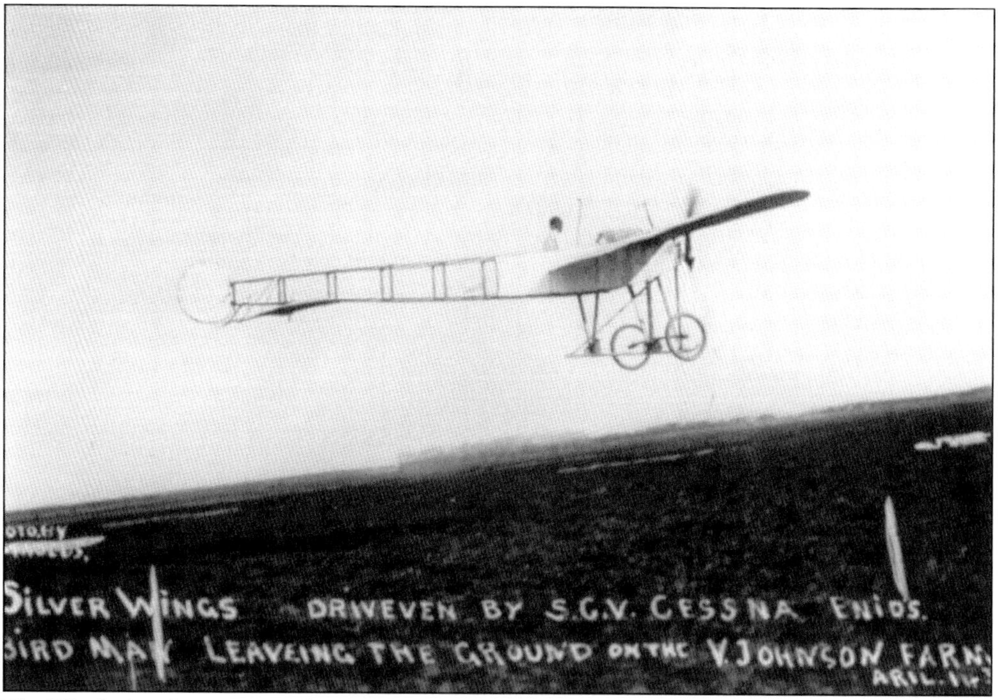

The Wright brothers were such a success that the Southwest Fair Association hired Clyde Cessna and his *Silver Wings* for the event in 1913. Cessna had found in his early flying days; exhibitions netted him more money than the actual building of the plane. The two images show Cessna's 1911 *Silver Wings* taking off from a field in Kansas (above) and joining the boosters of nearby Beaver, Oklahoma. (Both, courtesy of Lidia Gray.)

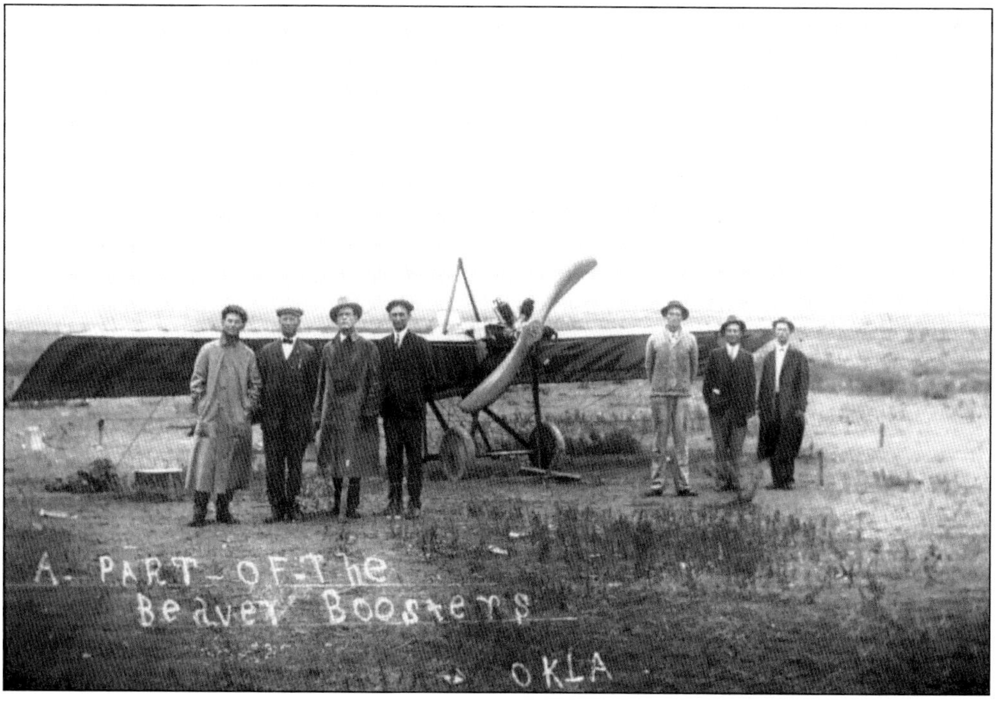

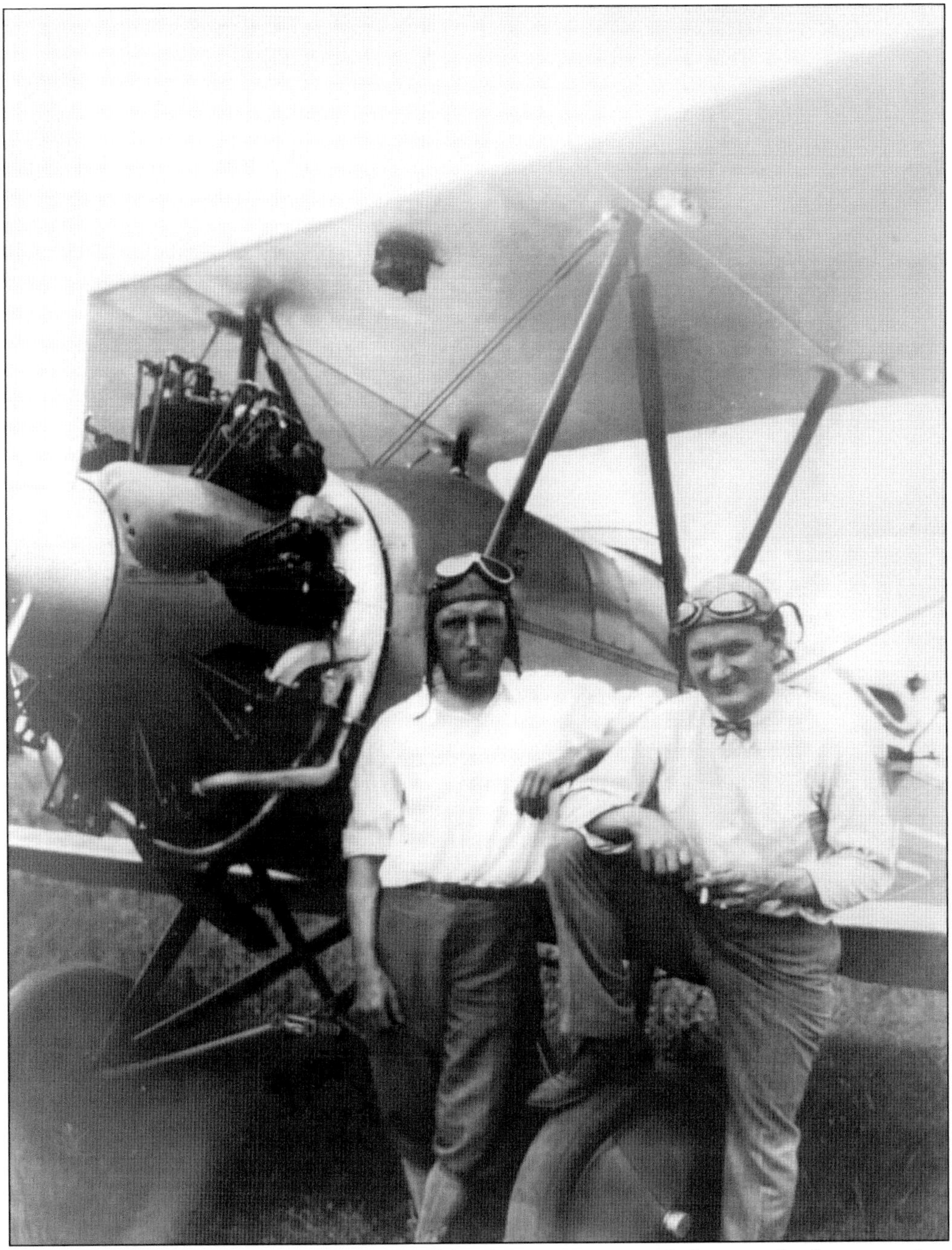

Like Clyde Cessna, Walter Beech financed his burgeoning aircraft business by barnstorming, exhibitions, and racing. Walter came to Liberal on November 12, 1921, to enter "the Flying Frolic" hosted by Liberal businessmen. He earned a third-place finish in the aerobatic contest and $75 for first place in the spot landing contest. Pictured here are Beech (left) and Brice Goldsborough. (Courtesy of the Kansas State Historical Society.)

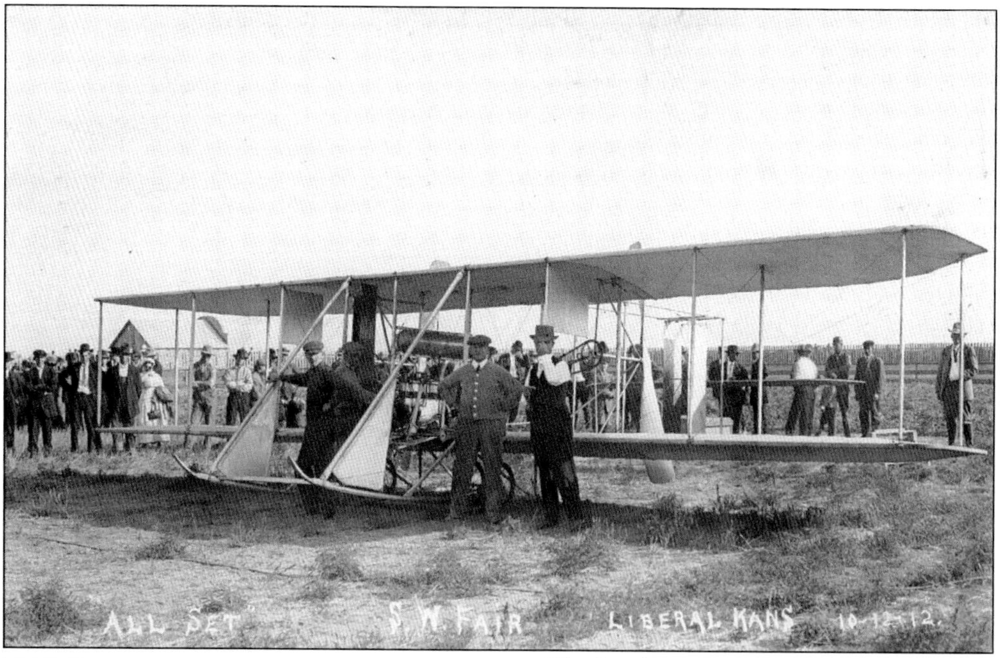

The Southwest Fair Association wanted something exciting to boost attendance at the 1912 fair. The association hired two Wright Flyers and their pilots to land, perform aerial tricks, and give locals a ride. The event was held in front of Seward County's grandstand, with planes landing and taking off within a few feet of the onlookers. The crowd was stunned by the newfangled aero ships. (Courtesy of Lidia Gray.)

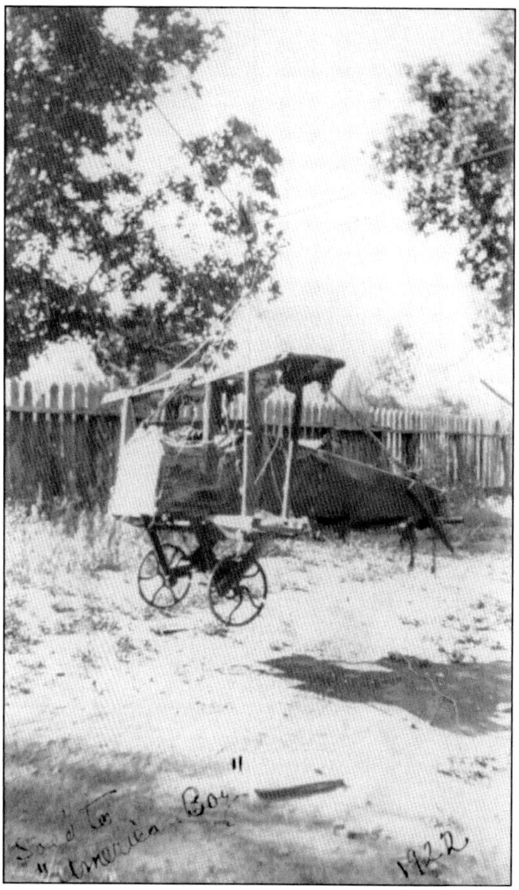

Everyone was getting into the curiosity of airplanes and their flights. Taken by local photographer Emma Jaquins, this model airplane suspended by a series of ropes was built by a young enthusiast in 1922. (Courtesy of Lidia Gray.)

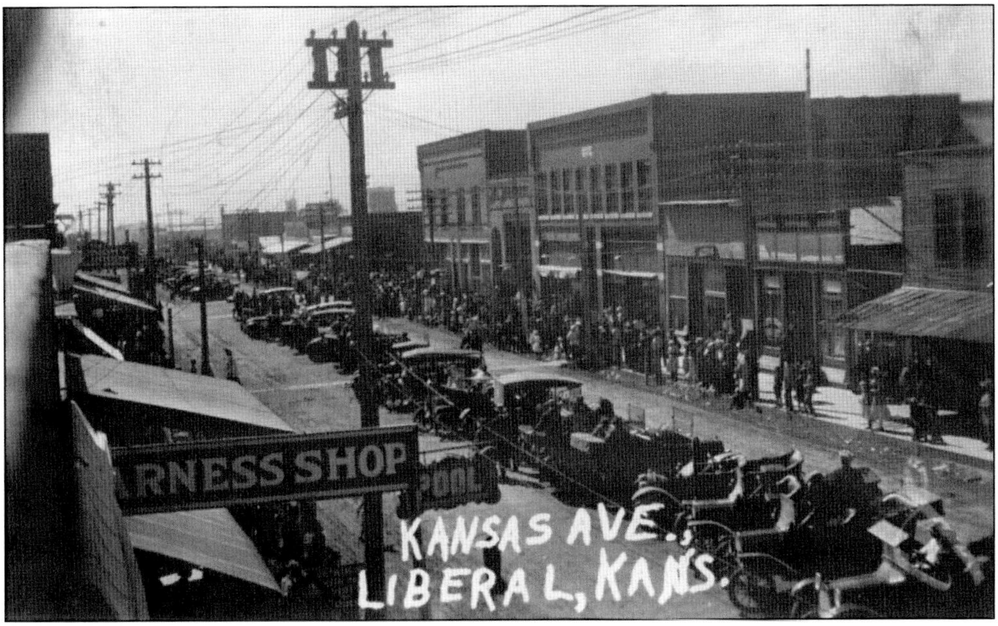

Recovering from the drought years of the 1890s, Liberal was growing. Good wheat prices, new businesses, and even an airport on the east edge of Liberal were signs of a healthy community. From this image taken from the corner of Fourth Street and Kansas Avenue, things were hopping on this 1920s shopping day. (Courtesy of Lidia Gray.)

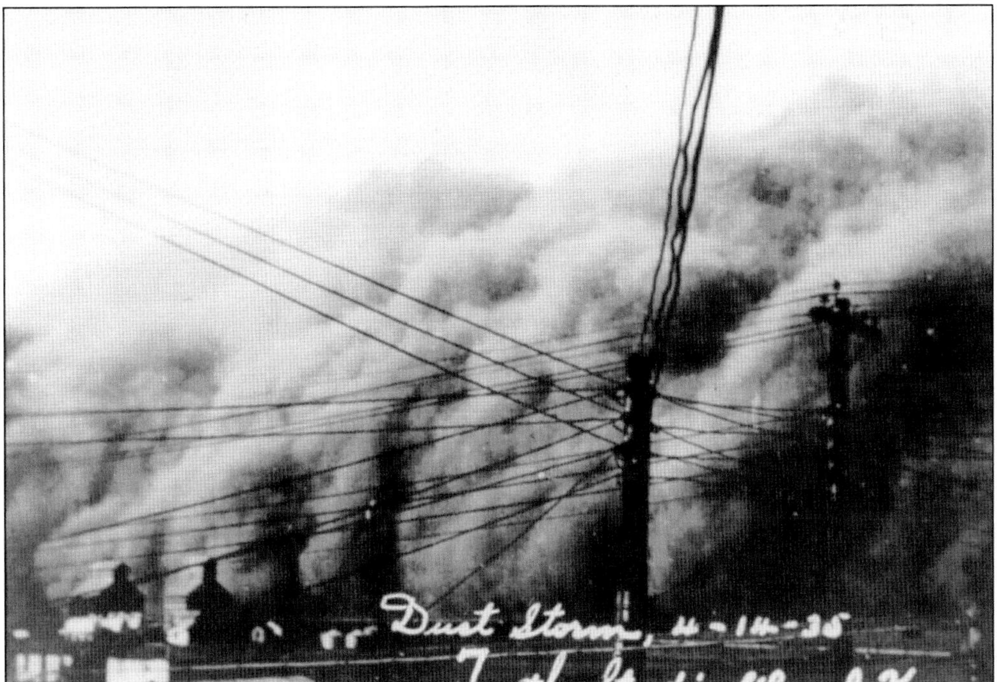

The prosperous days of the 1920s came to a halt after the stock market crash, tumbling wheat prices, and a drought that would last 10 years. Topsoil took to the air, destroying crops, animals, and people. (Courtesy of Connie Bowman.)

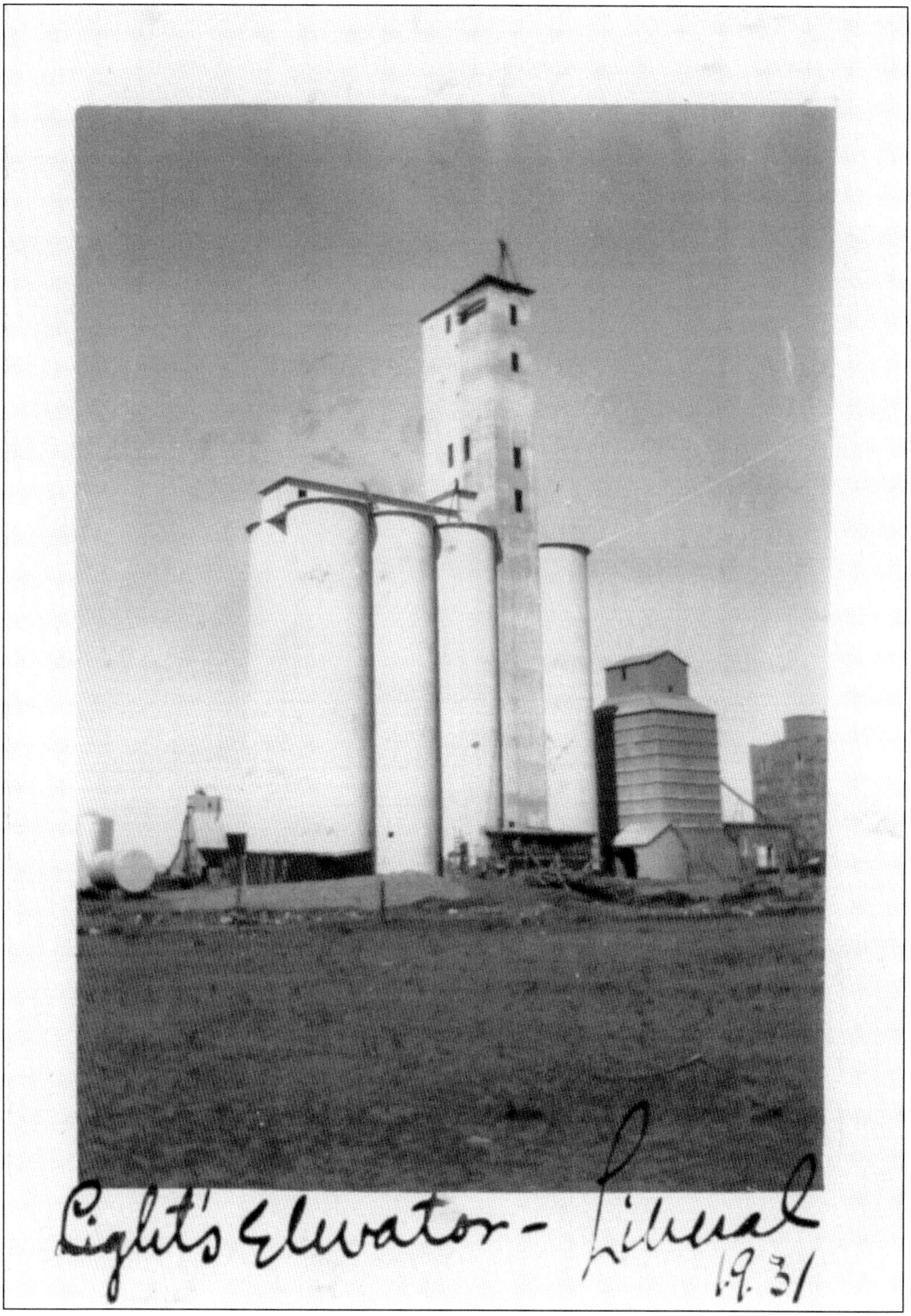

Charles Moses Light began in the grain business in 1915. Expanding his properties, Light built a flouring mill in Liberal in 1918, continuing into the 1970s. This photograph is of his elevator near the center of town, which is still in operation today. (Courtesy of Lidia Gray.)

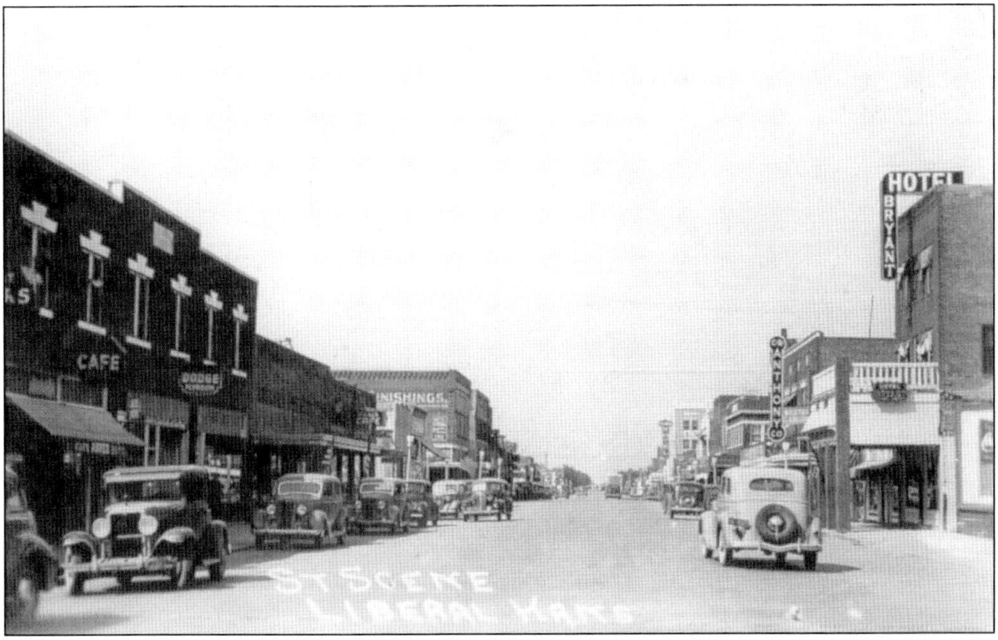

With returning rain, better crop prices, and land conservation, Liberal was on the rebound. Several large projects had helped the economy, but the project that would turn the farm community on its heels was just on the horizon. (Courtesy of Lidia Gray.)

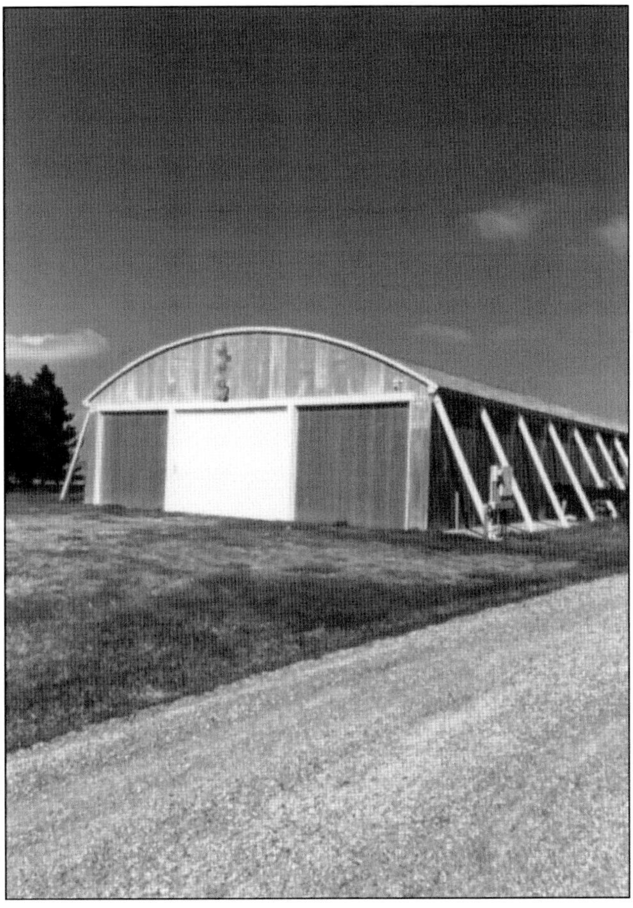

Liberal's first official airport was southeast of town. With only one grass airstrip, which ran east and west, the airport still managed to hold several fly-in events as interest in aviation grew. Pictured here is the remaining hangar located on private property.

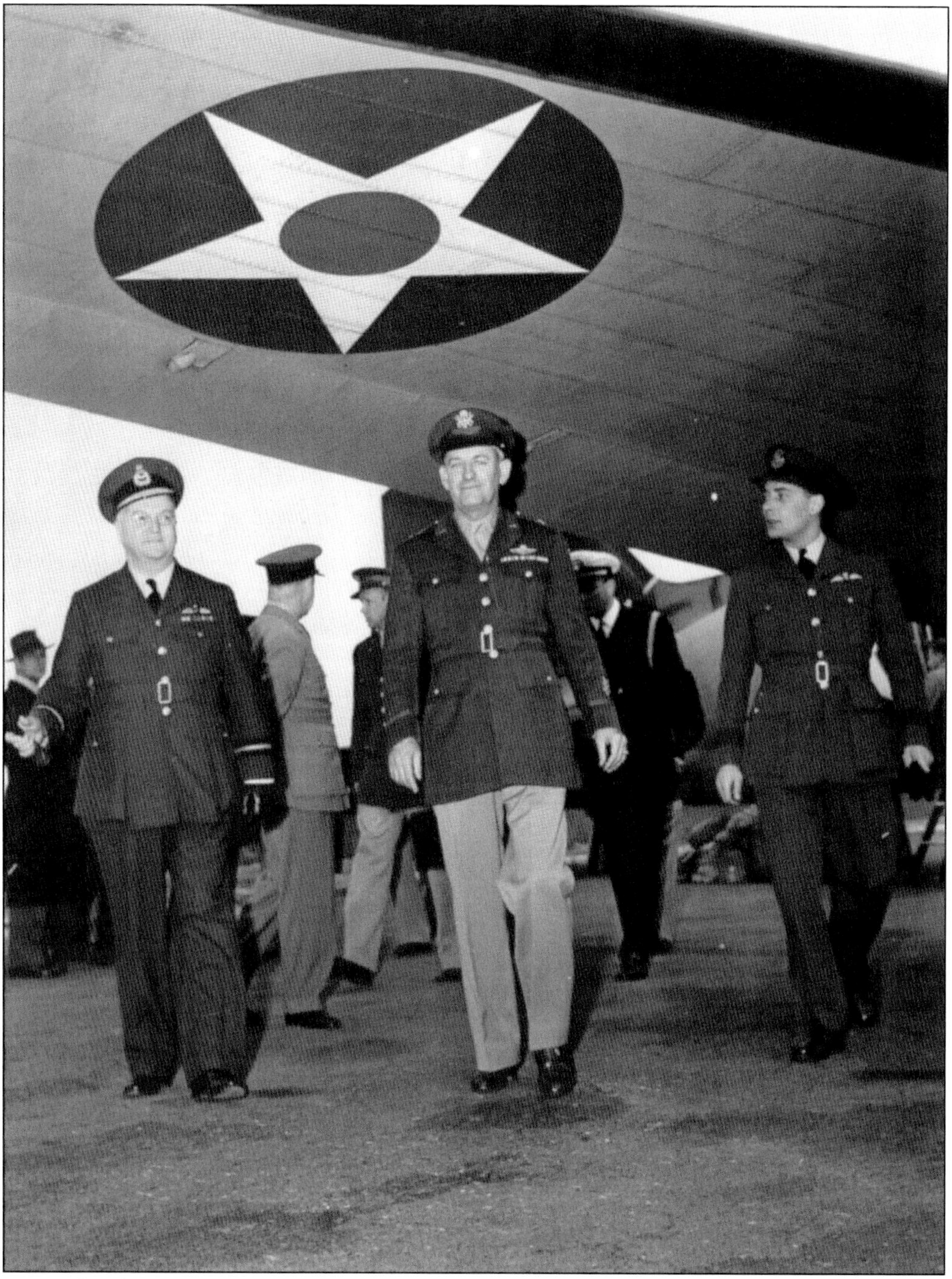

Pictured in the center is Maj. Gen. William Ord Ryan, USAAF (US Army Air Forces), who scouted the area with Liberal city officials to determine if the site would be suitable for an airbase. He was born in Texas in 1891 and had a very distinguished military career, earning the Silver Star in May 1924. He became a brigadier general in 1941, shortly before coming to Liberal. Career assignments included various duties as field grade officer, chief of staff of the Hawaiian Air Force, commanding general of the Pacific Division, and air transport command from 1942 to 1946. He retired shortly after the war ended in September 1946. (Courtesy of Connie Bowman.)

Two

Operations and Training Begin

Operations and training began in earnest once the first B-24 landed on June 20, 1943. It was an exciting time, but not without complications. The training was intense and very fast. Pilots and engineers were pushed through training and graduated in only nine weeks. They were young and inexperienced but always eager. At one point in the war, LAAF turned out one-quarter of all B-24 pilots. It is well known that the B-24 was mass-produced to keep up with the demand for bombers, and safety was often compromised. Pilots were pushed to learn quickly. Imagine flying a four-engine aircraft loaded with bombs and nine crew members in a war after nine weeks of training. Mishaps happened even here; sometimes it was the weather, and other times, poor judgment was to blame for the 111 crashes that occurred around Liberal. Some resulted in fatalities or complete destruction of the aircraft. One such incident happened near Satanta, Kansas, 32 miles north of Liberal. On October 28, 1943, a B-24 went down on Charles Young's farm. The accident killed Maj. James V. Mesita, 2nd Lt. Laurice G. Amen, 2nd Lt. Thomas R. LeCompte Jr., 2nd Lt. Harold W. Connerly, and Sgt. Homer L. Walker. S.Sgt. Edward R. Skoza survived. In 1997, a flagpole and plaque were erected in the field at the site of the crash.

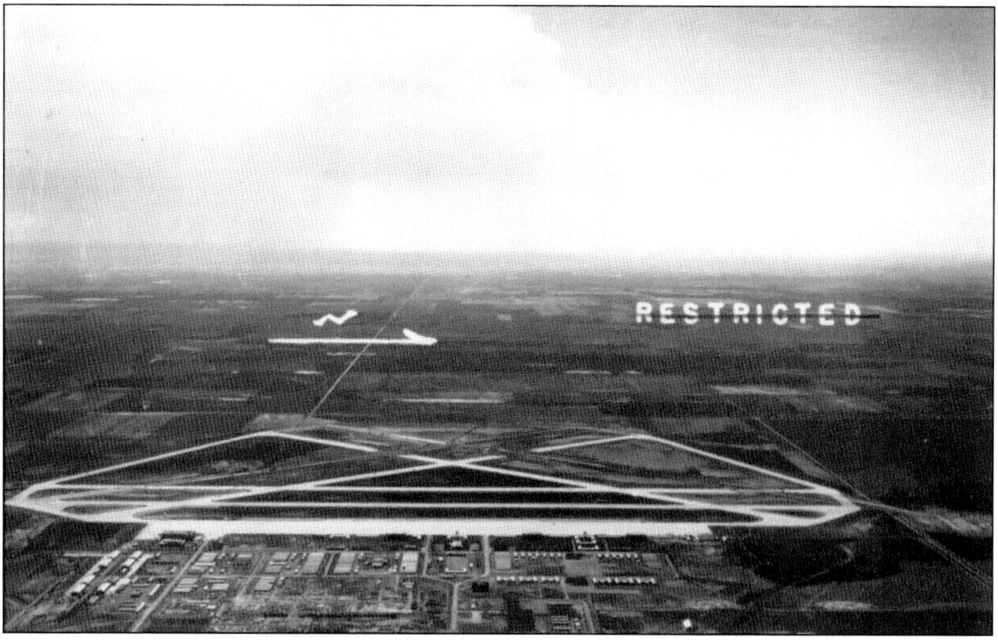

One of the last Army airfields in Kansas to be constructed was the LAAF. Even before the survey and layout were completed, Peter Kiewet Sons began construction on January 15, 1943, on the 1,946-acre site adjacent to town. After a massive effort at top speed and $8 million, an entire city grew out of the plowed ground, doubling the population of Liberal. The photograph above shows the finished project. The image below shows additional runways and taxi strips that were added to assist in the training.

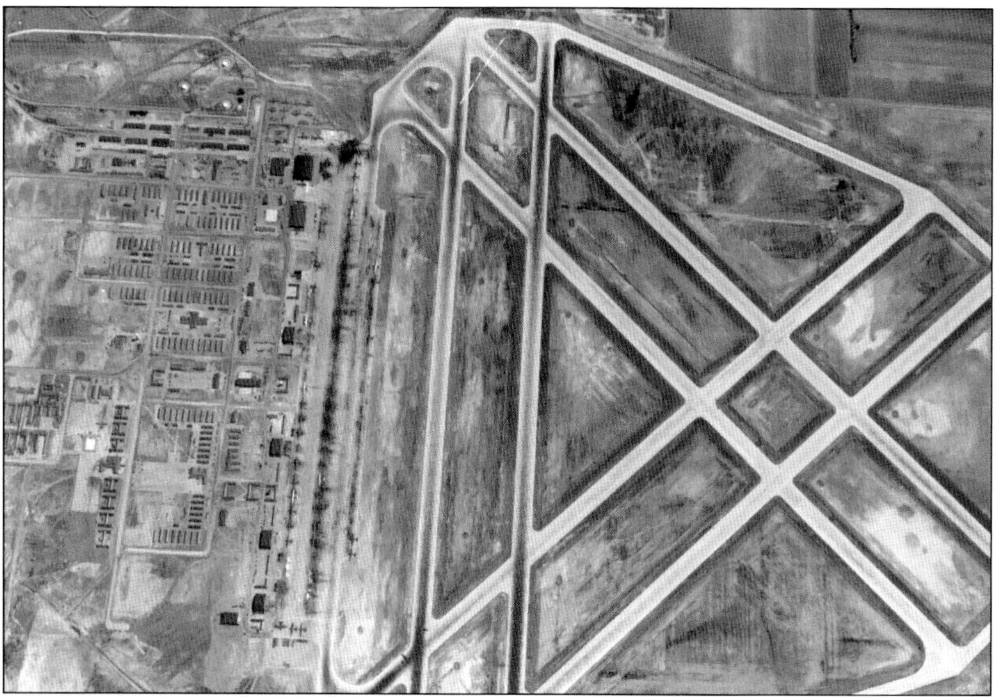

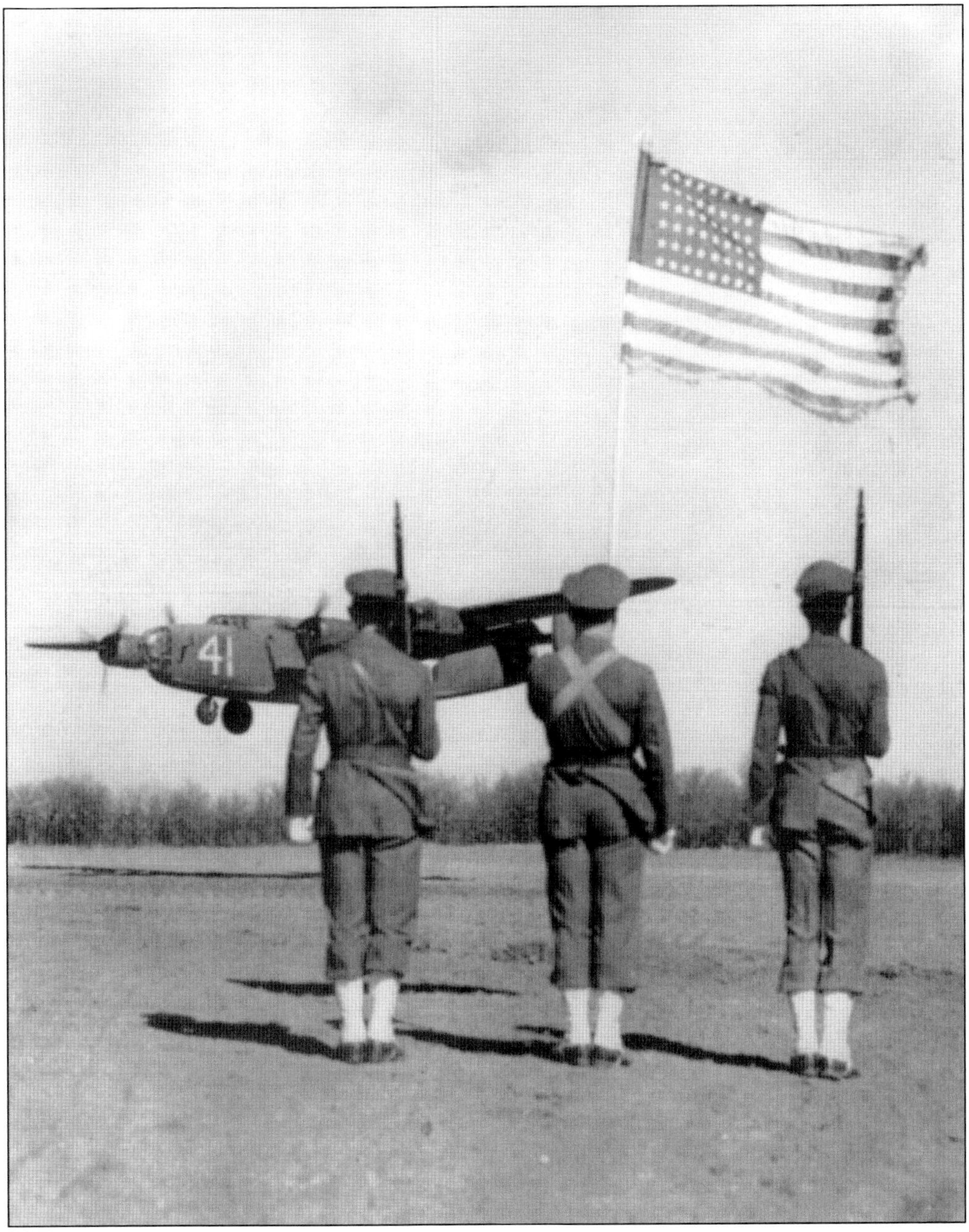

Staffing of the field was in high gear. Mechanics, cooks, instructors, ground crew, clerks, and physicians now called Liberal home. It was not until June 20, 1943, that the first B-24 circled the field and landed. Until then, the only plane had been a UC-78.

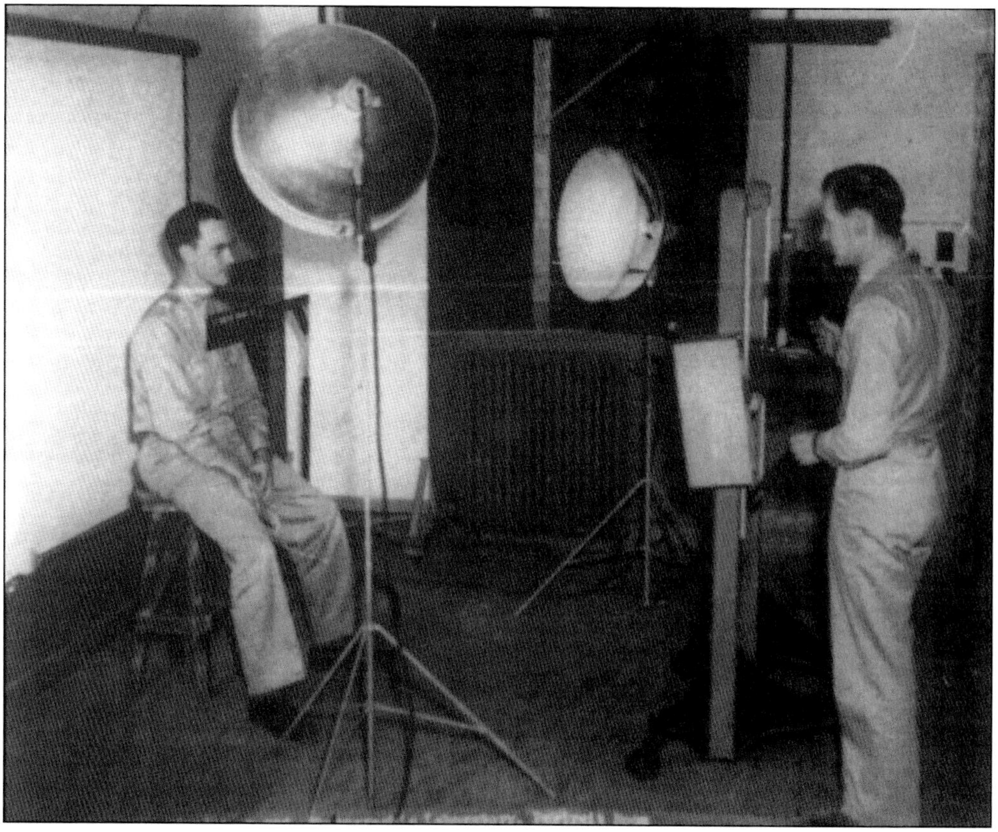

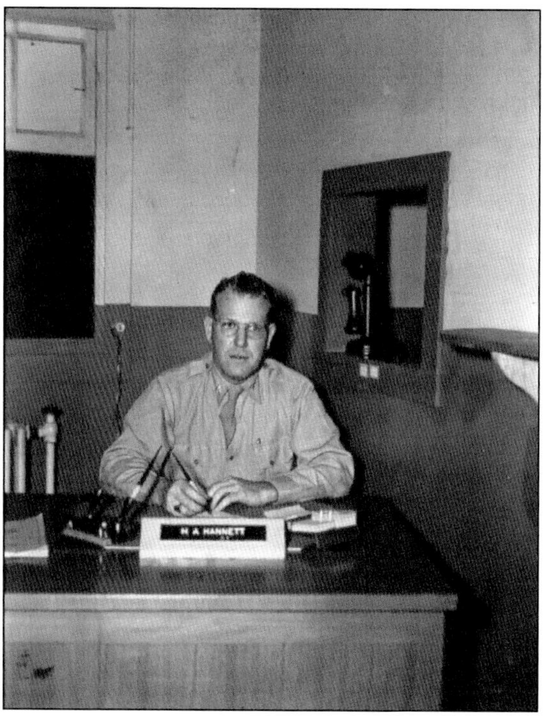

Personnel started arriving at the new airfield even before the base was completed. Officers were on base in April 1943, including the first base commander, Col. Arthur L. Bump. The first fellow the men and women saw was base photographer Whitney Williams. He took everyone's ID photograph, gathered a bit of information, and sent them to the next stage.

Maj. Hildreth "Sonny" Hannett was part of the medical staff at the airfield. Dr. Hannett, a former college baseball player, graduated from the Chicago School of Dentistry. Although in his mid-40s, when he arrived in Liberal, he elected to do his part for the war effort by keeping personnel in top condition.

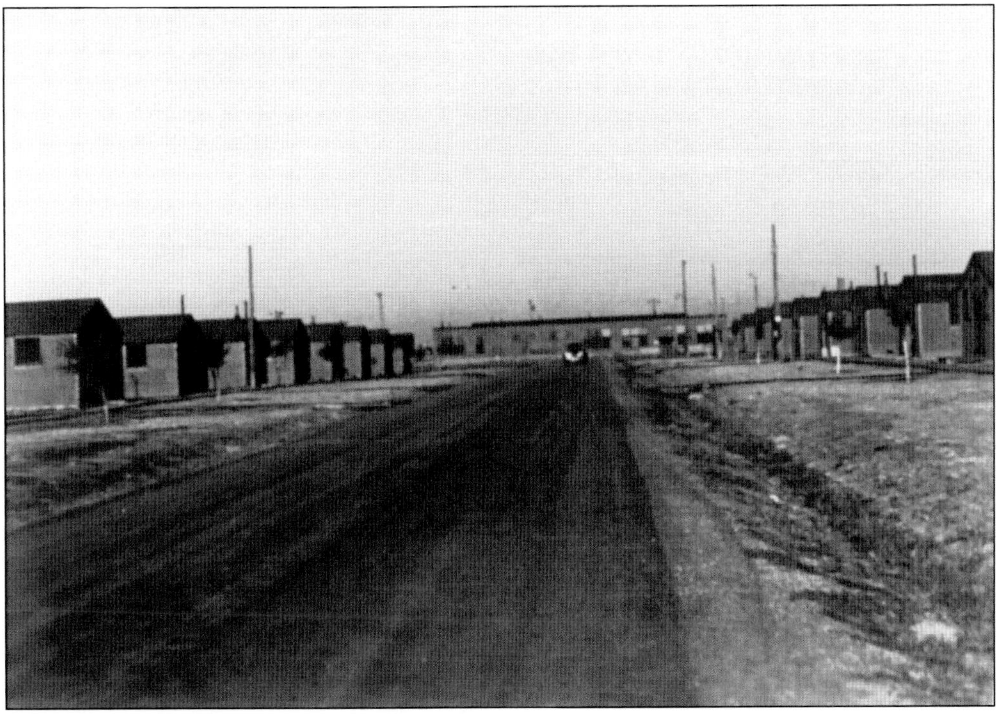

Using standardized plans, prefabricated components, locally resourced materials, and an efficient construction style, entire buildings could be raised in a matter of hours. Between rows of barracks were rough wooden planks to make a sidewalk between the barracks and latrines. Barracks were heated using natural gas stoves. The latrines were in separate buildings. The rough dimensions of each barrack were 28 feet wide by 89 feet long.

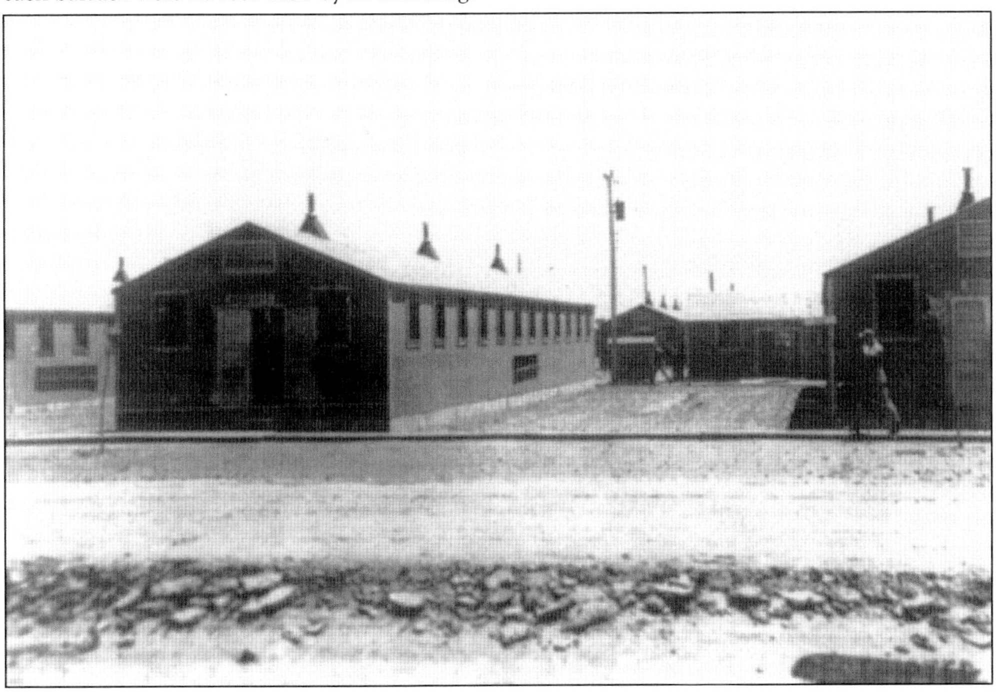

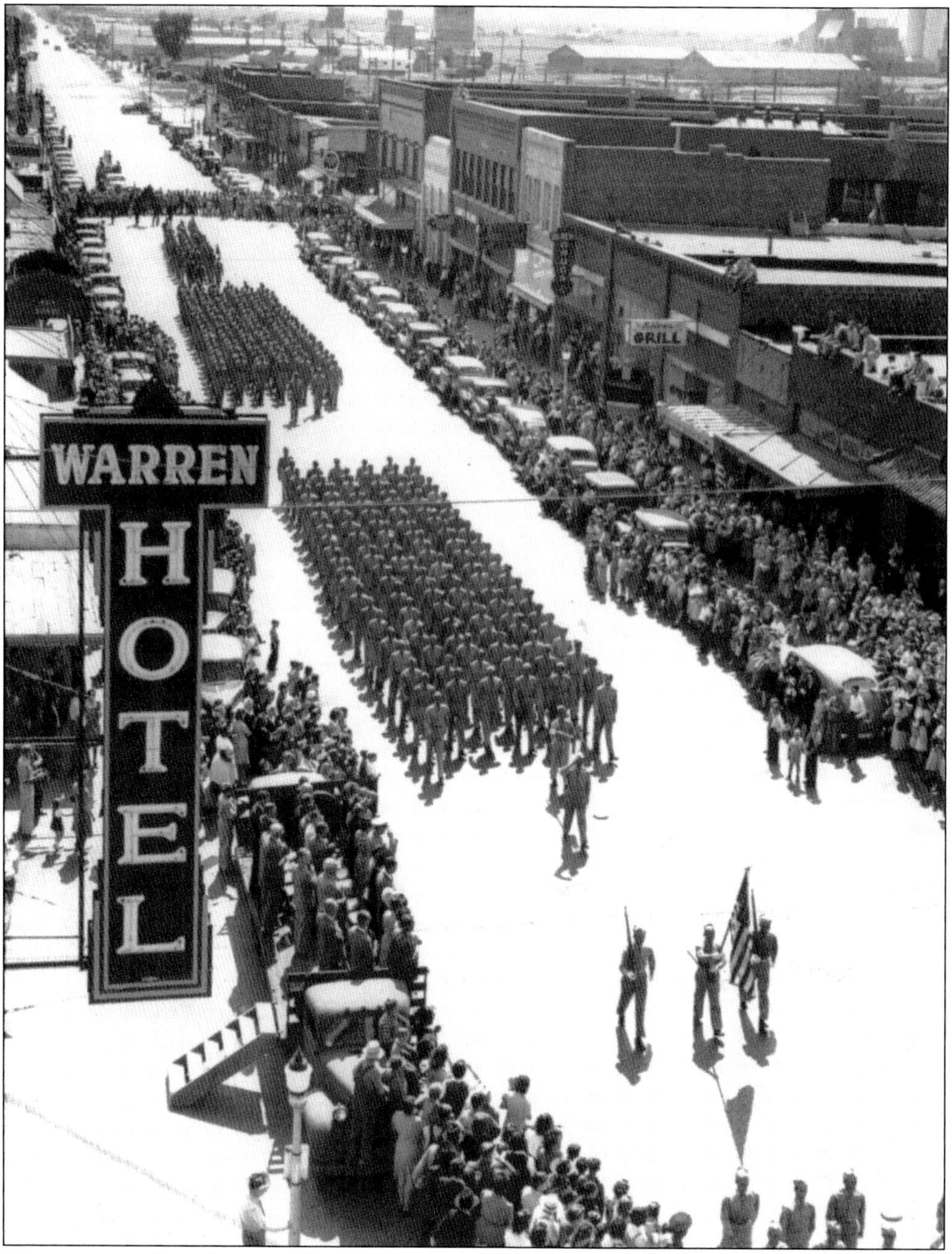

This great view from the top of the Warren Hotel at Third Street and Kansas Avenue in downtown Liberal shows precision marching units as they proceed towards Seventh Street and return to base. The parade encouraged the purchasing of war bonds. Turning out en masse, the people of Liberal were always ready to cheer, support, and purchase bonds. In September 1944, the townsfolks had bought enough war bonds to pay for an entire B-24.

Learning the oil system of the B-24 was crucial to the Commanders as well as the mechanics. B-24s were equipped with either 33- or 39-gallon tanks for oil. These tanks were located in each engine nacelle. This 1943 image shows attentive students learning the complex system.

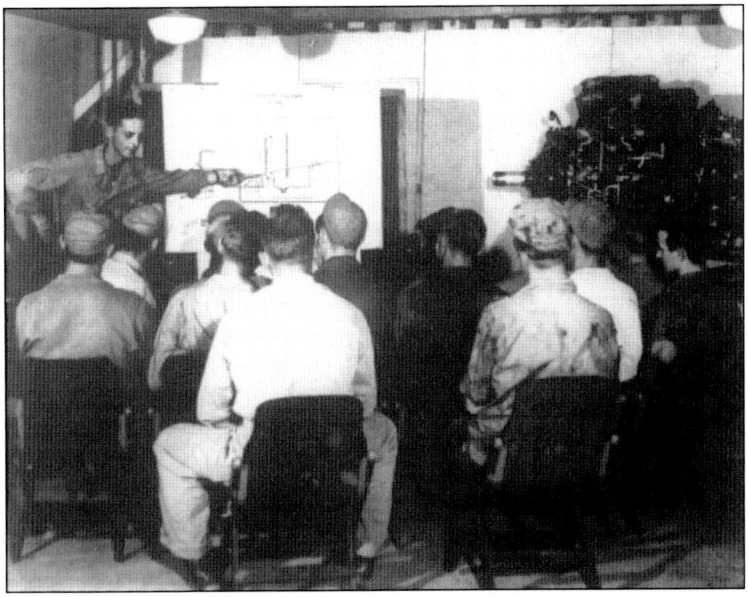

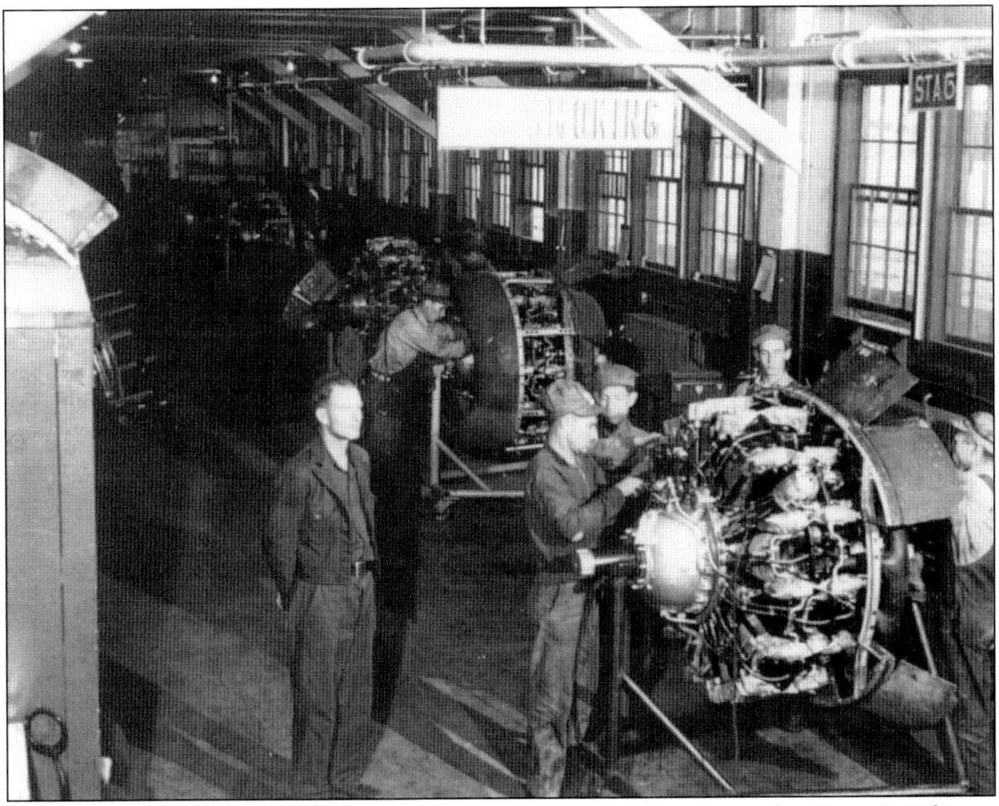

Under the watchful eye of the instructor, mechanics attempt to get another Pratt & Whitney engine repaired to be put back in service on the B-24. During training, the bombers were put to heavy use by inexperienced pilots. Adding to the problem was the scarcity and slow delivery of extra parts and lack of experienced mechanics.

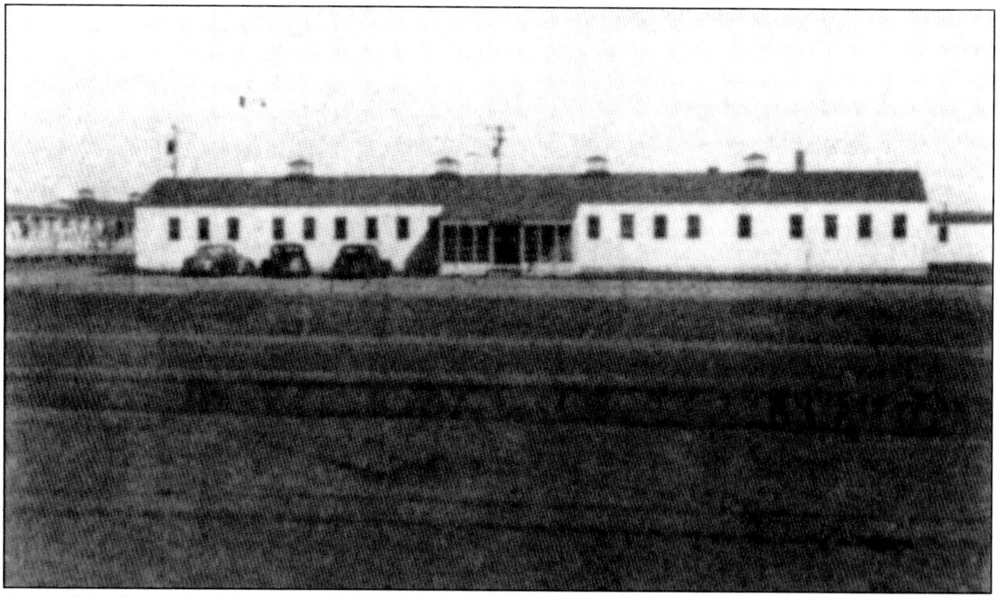

One of the larger buildings on the LAAF was the 142-bed hospital. Four surgeons, five dentists, two lab techs, eight RNs, an X-ray tech, an ENT (ears, nose, and throat) doctor, a pharmacist, and a veterinarian made up the staff. The hospital kept busy with day-to-day illnesses but was especially needed when planes crashed.

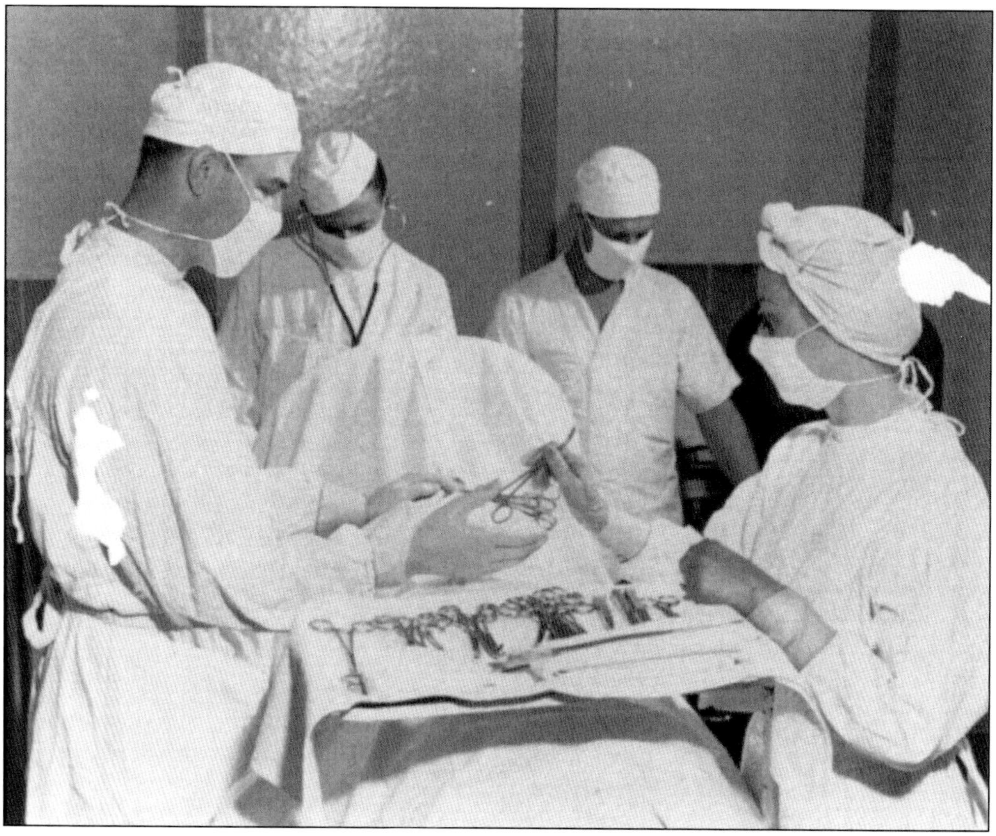

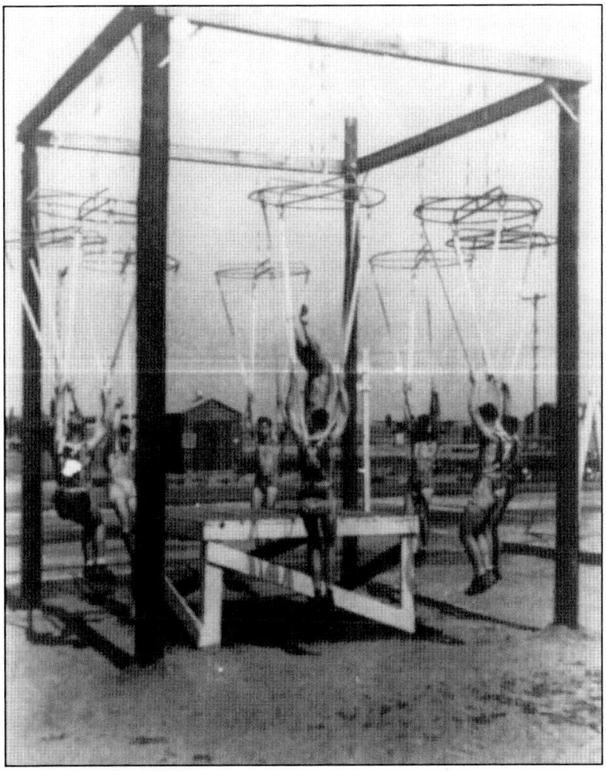

Airmen were trained for the worst-case scenario. If the B-24 had to be abandoned, the men were advised to parachute out, hopefully out of harm's way. The men in this image are learning control and proper methods of landing.

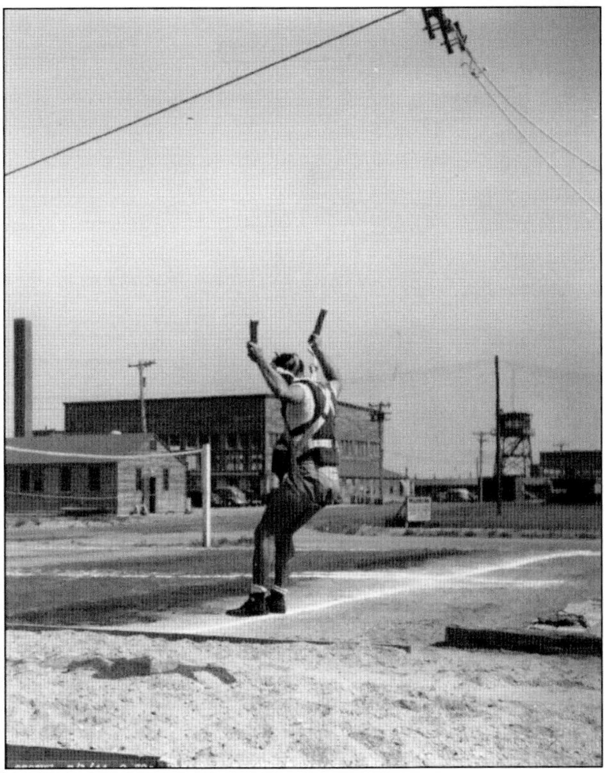

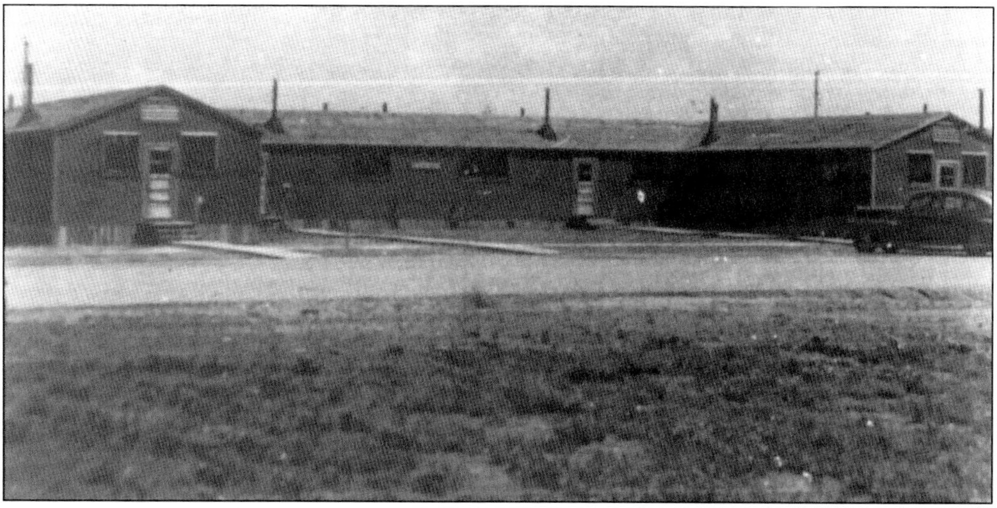

These bachelor officers' quarters were a bit better than the long 50-man barracks but still sparse. They may have had a small private room with a single-sized bed, a small desk with a chair, and a small open cabinet. Even officers had to share the latrine with other officers. Men spent little time in their quarters except to sleep and study at night.

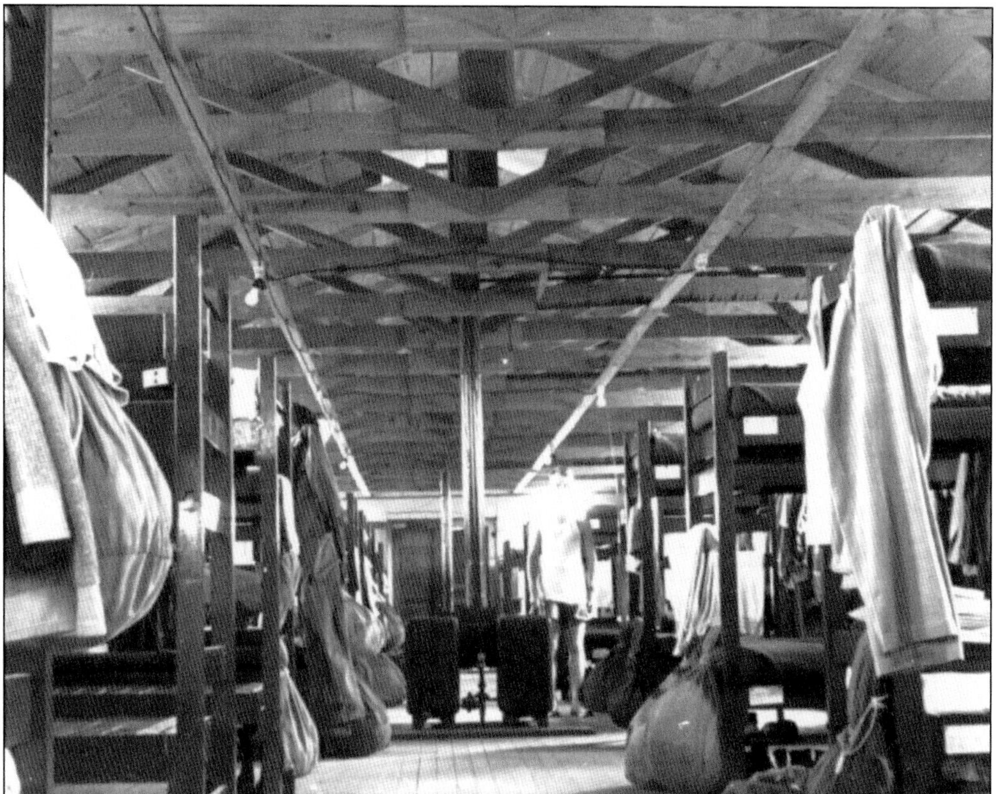

Barracks were spartan and offered little privacy or room for personal belongings. Bunks were stacked, and there were 50 men per barrack. With over 4,000 personnel to house, housing was at a premium. Looking at the base map of LAAF, there are over 100 barracks.

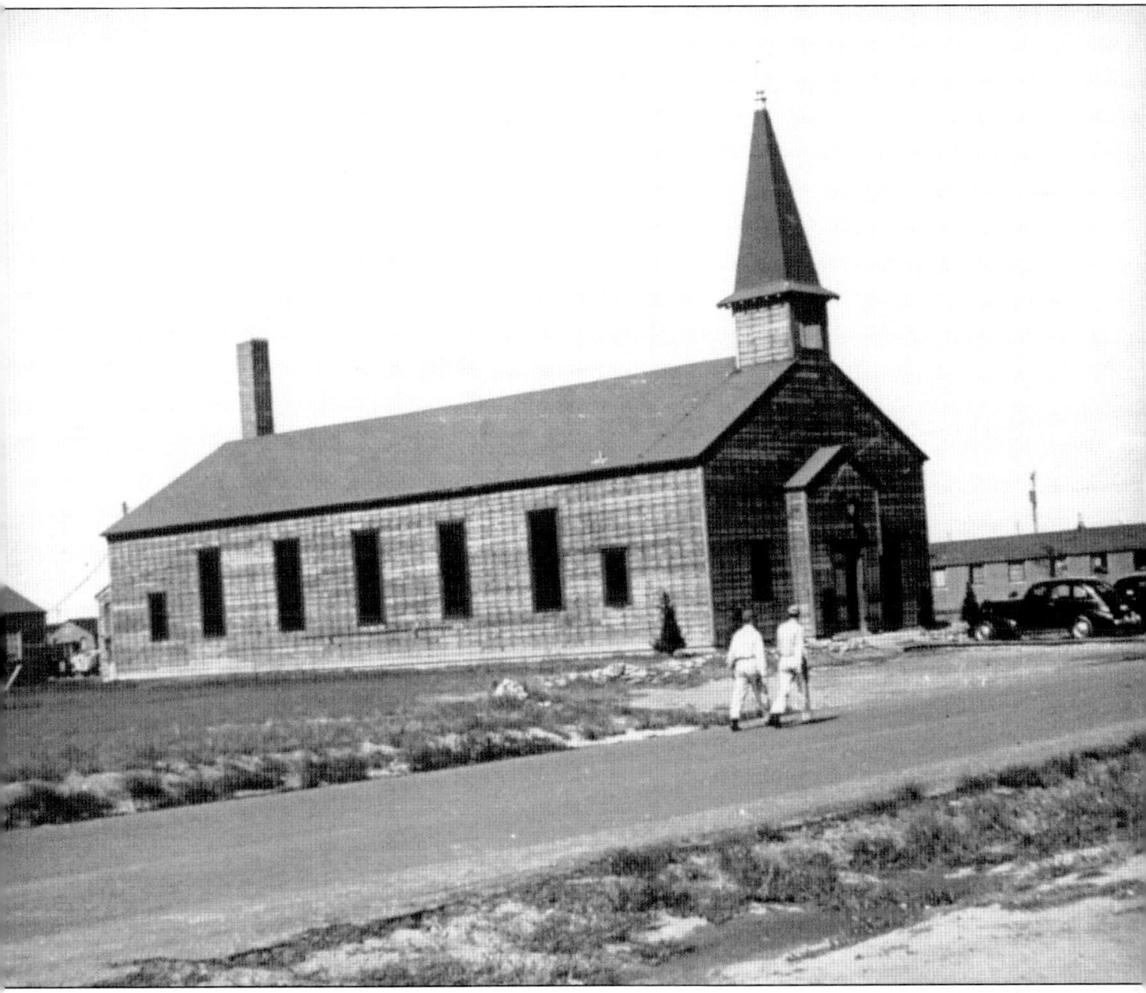

The post chapel was located on the corner of A Street and Seventh Street and was different from the other series 700 temporary buildings. The exterior still featured raw wood, but the chapel featured a finished interior, steeple, and just a touch of landscaping. Designed to be multi-denominational, chaplain Rex A. Harmon officiated over Sunday services, marriages, and funerals and gave comfort to those in need.

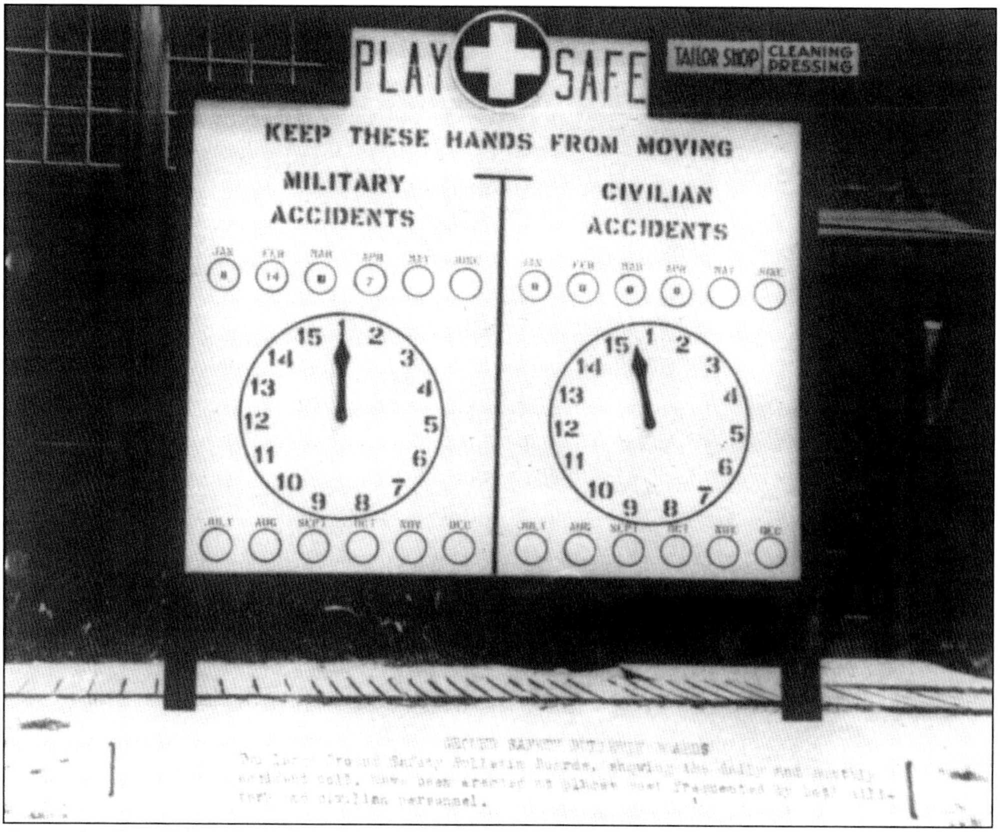

Ground safety bulletin boards and war information boards were erected so both civilians and military personnel had access. It was important to keep people informed about the "goings on" in base life and war news. Notices about a dance, a movie, town activities, or other types of entertainment could be found here. Boards like these were effective ways to inform in addition to a base newspaper, like LAAF's the *Air Scoop*. They were good reminders to practice safety and reduce accidents.

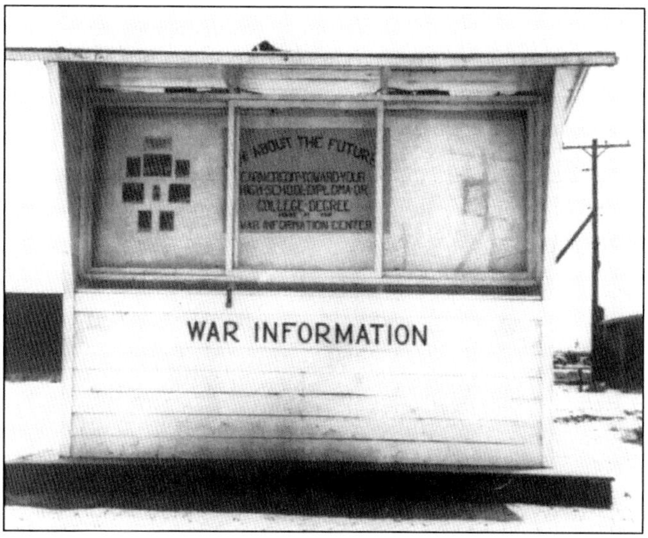

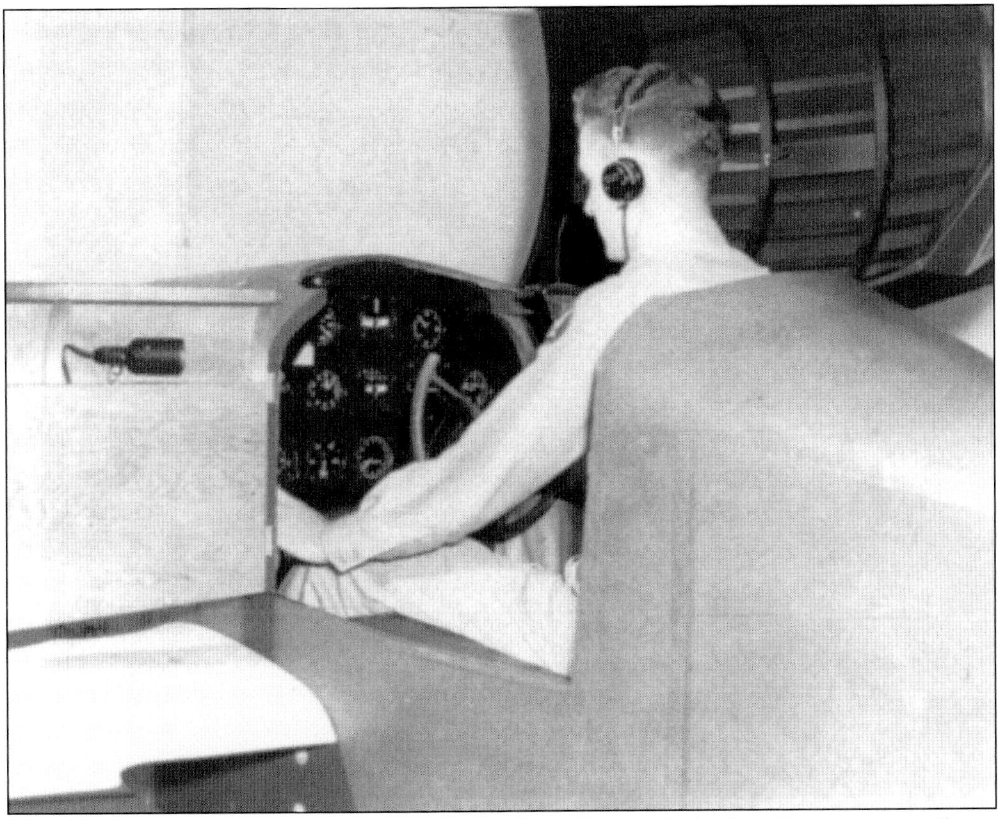

The all-important Link Trainer was a flight simulator that readied pilots for instrument flying. Most Links were painted blue and yellow with short wings and tails. The main component was the box that resembled the cockpit, containing a pilot's seat, controls, and instruments. The second component was the external instructor's desk with a large map, a twin set of the pilot's instruments, and the "Crab." The Crab moved across the map, plotting the pilot's track. The Link was powered by air bellows that simulated movement and vibration. Ethel B. Barnham was in charge of the Link.

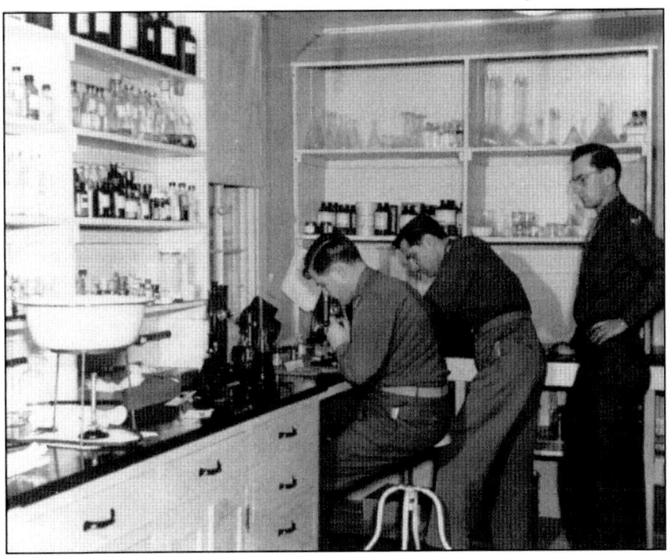

The lab was crucial for the 142-bed base hospital. It was staffed by doctors and technicians who aided in the testing and health of base personnel. During World War II, the Army built many hospitals to support its troops. General surgery was available, so the lab was kept busy analyzing tests and helping pharmacists.

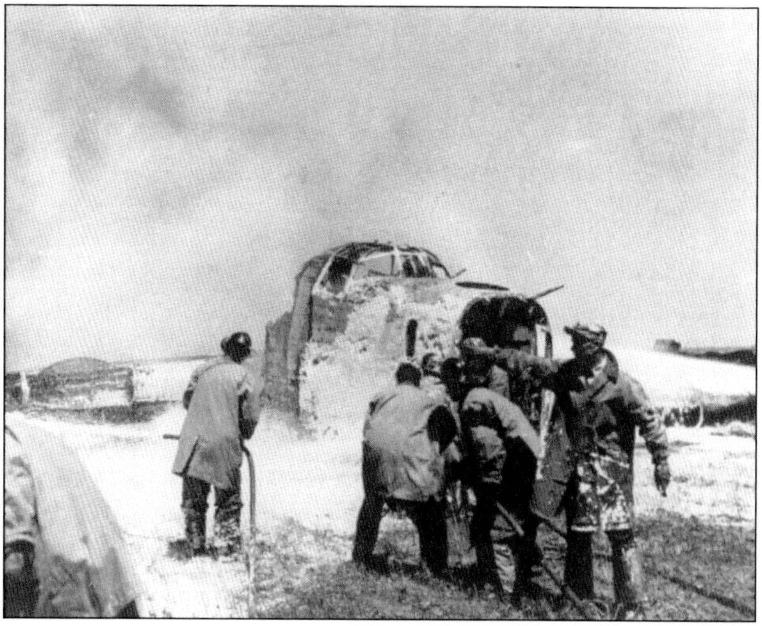

Essential exercise in firefighting was important in everyday life on the airfield. Using a fire-retardant foam, the men are practicing on a previously wrecked B-24.

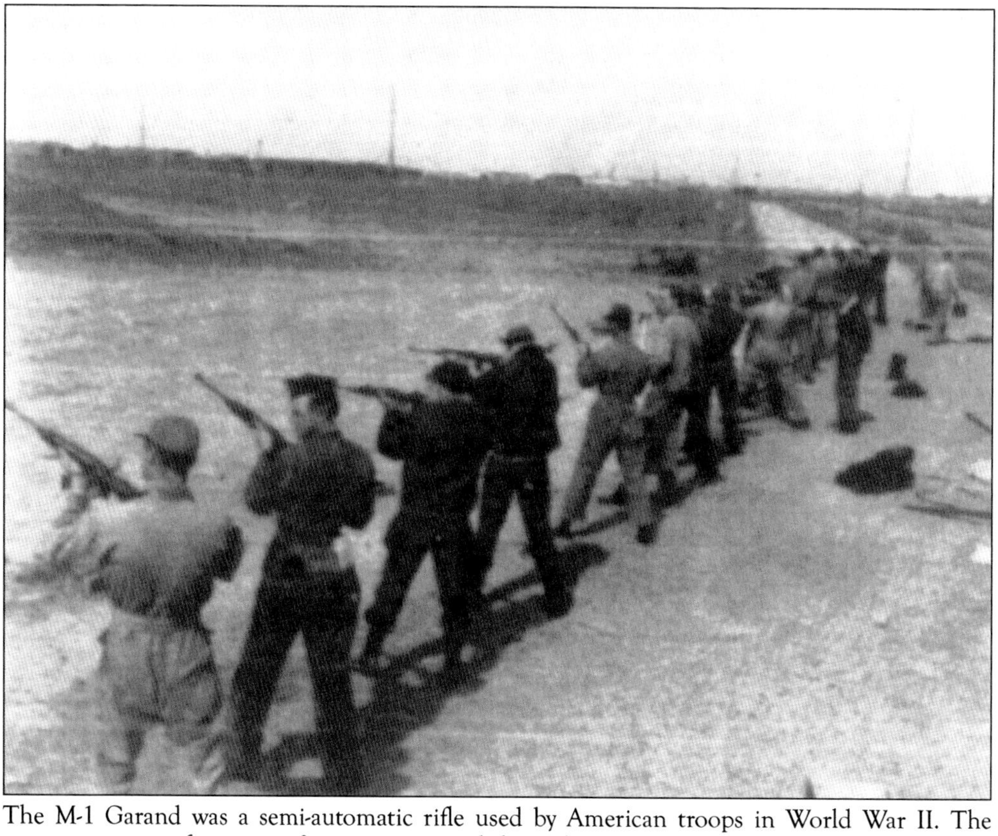

The M-1 Garand was a semi-automatic rifle used by American troops in World War II. The average amount of time at a firing range varied depending on the airman's specialty. All officers and enlisted personnel had to qualify in basic training with rifles, handguns, and other military weapons. The men are shooting at targets at the very south end of the base.

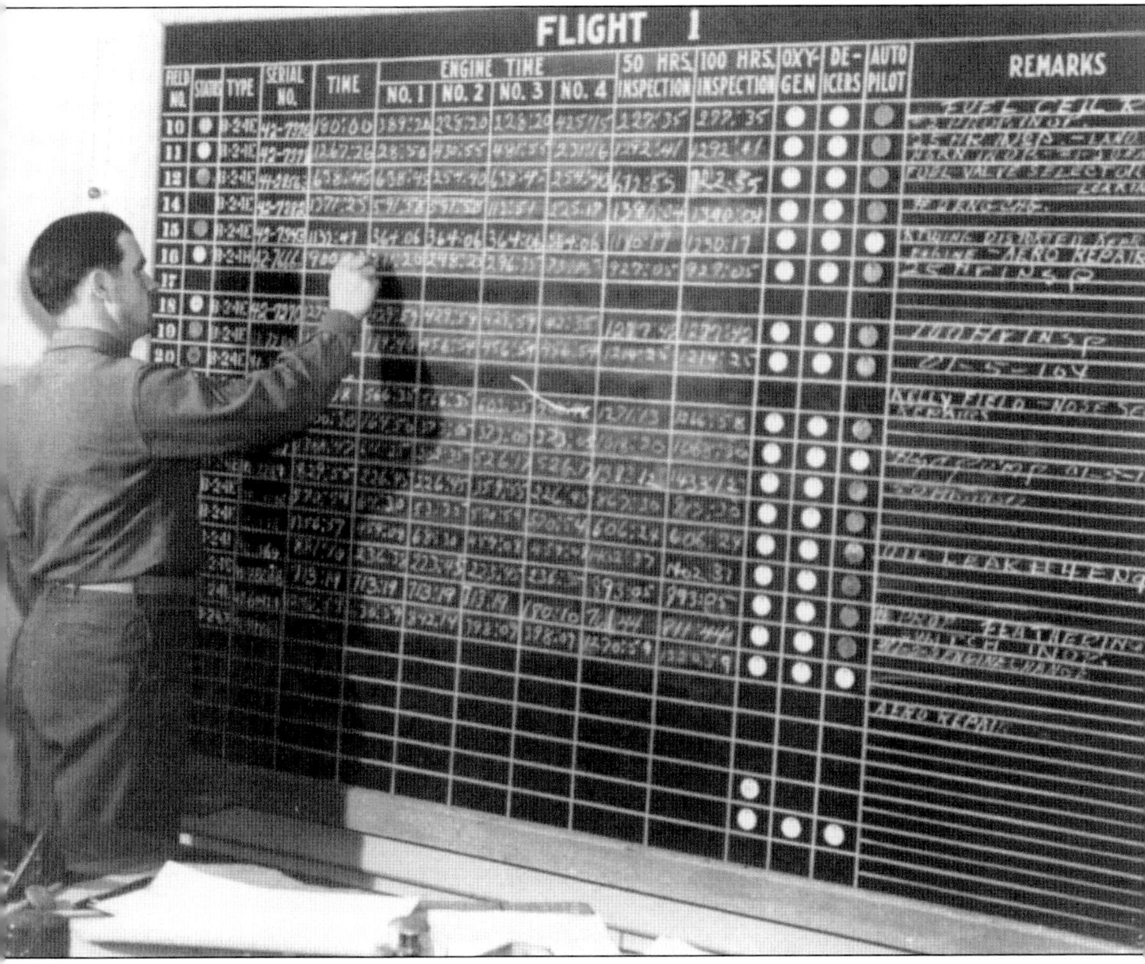

To keep track of each plane's maintenance record, this board was updated on a frequent basis. Serial numbers of the planes, each of the four engines times, 50- and 100-hour inspections, oxygen, deicers, and auto-pilot availability, as well as a place to note problems with each B-24, gave the pilots a chance to see the condition of the planes. This board has survived the years and is on display at the Mid-America Air Museum.

HEADQUARTERS
LIBERAL ARMY AIR FIELD
ARMY AIR FORCES PILOT SCHOOL (SPECIALIZED 4-ENGINE)
Office of the Deputy for Training and Operations

WJC:lp
Liberal, Kansas
4 August 1944

TRAINING MEMORANDUM)
NO 90-3)

CONTROL TOWER

LANDING INSTRUCTIONS

1. Effective immediately, when pilots call the control tower for full stop landing instructions, they will notify the tower whether they have completed their mission or not by saying "Mission Completed". If the pilot is going to make a full stop landing and taxi back and take-off again, he will notify the tower of this by saying "To Take-Off Again" when asking the tower for full stop landing instructions.

2. This will be brought to the attention of all pilots, and will be strictly complied with.

William J. Cain Jr.
WILLIAM J. CAIN, JR
Colonel, Air Corps
Deputy for Training and Opns.

-1-

An August notice to all airmen warned the pilots and instructors to strictly comply with traffic control instructions. Pilots could no longer land without proper clearance.

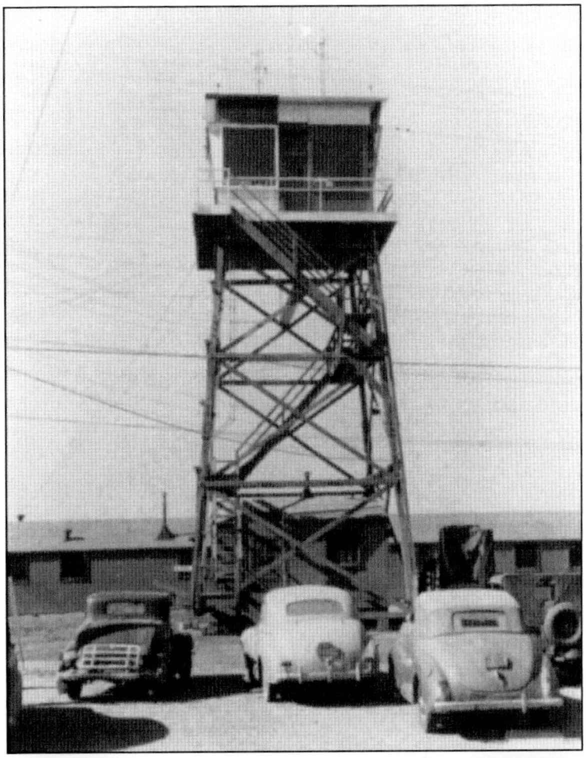

Control towers were an essential part of any airfield. Although hastily constructed, LAAF's tower and its staff provided a safe, orderly, and expeditious flow of air traffic. Accessed by wooden stairs, the tower afforded an unobstructed view of the base and all activities. Manned 24 hours a day, radio contact and weather observation had to be on point. Interestingly, LAAF's tower was fitted with blue glass. The tower's beacon was in use until 2024.

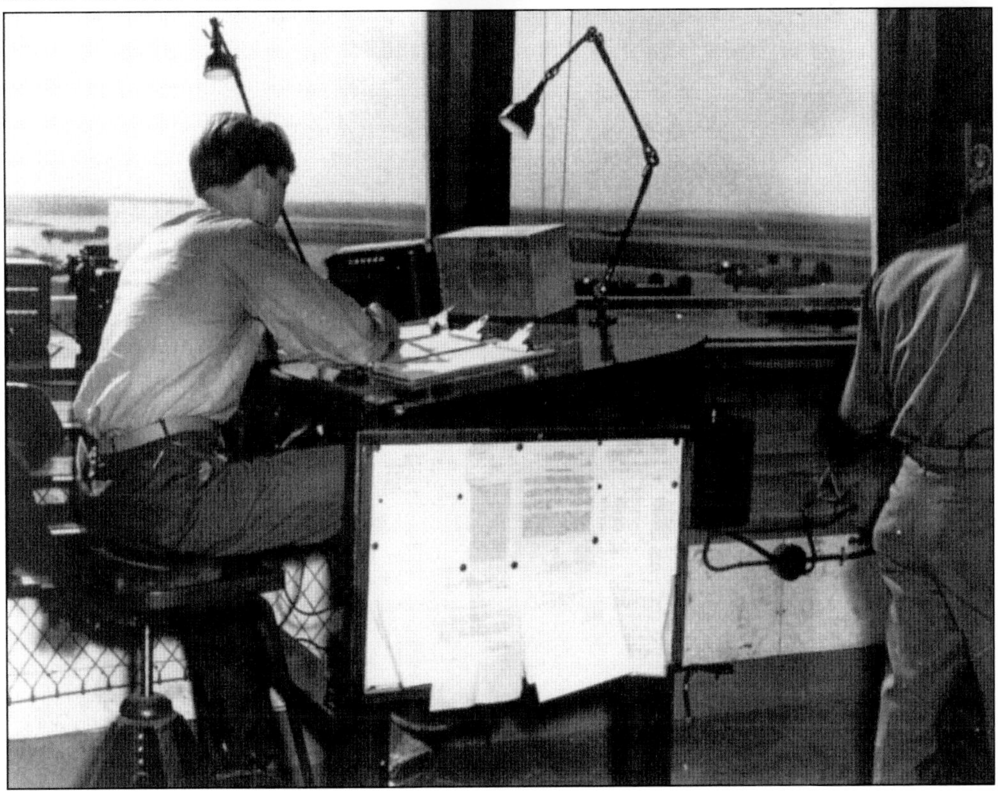

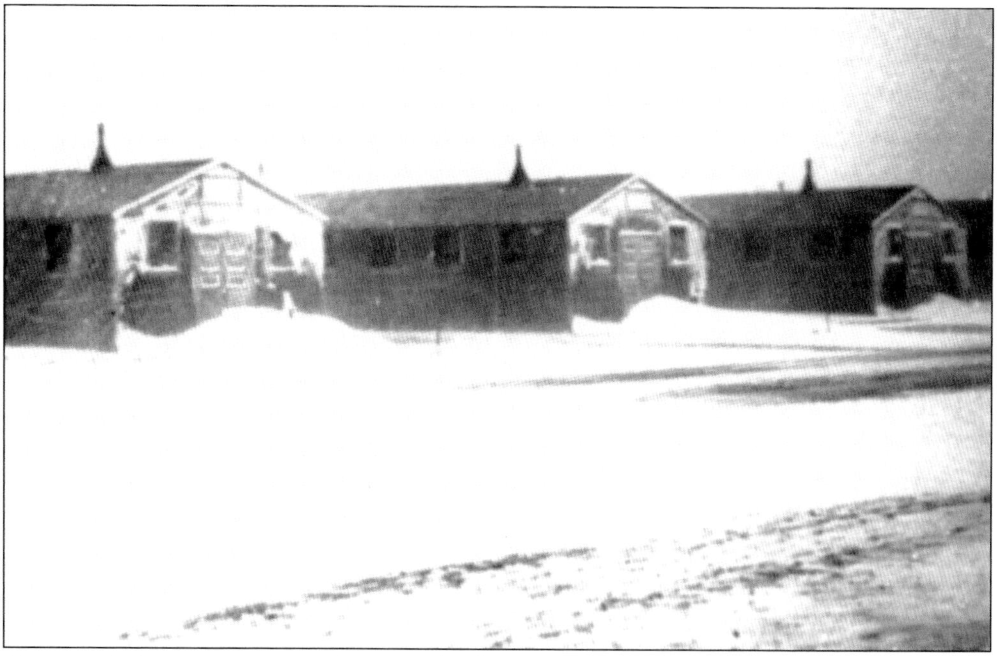

There was little housing on base for married officers who were instructors. This photograph shows the row housing on base for those instructors. Most married training officers' wives had to find housing, usually a single room in a local resident's home.

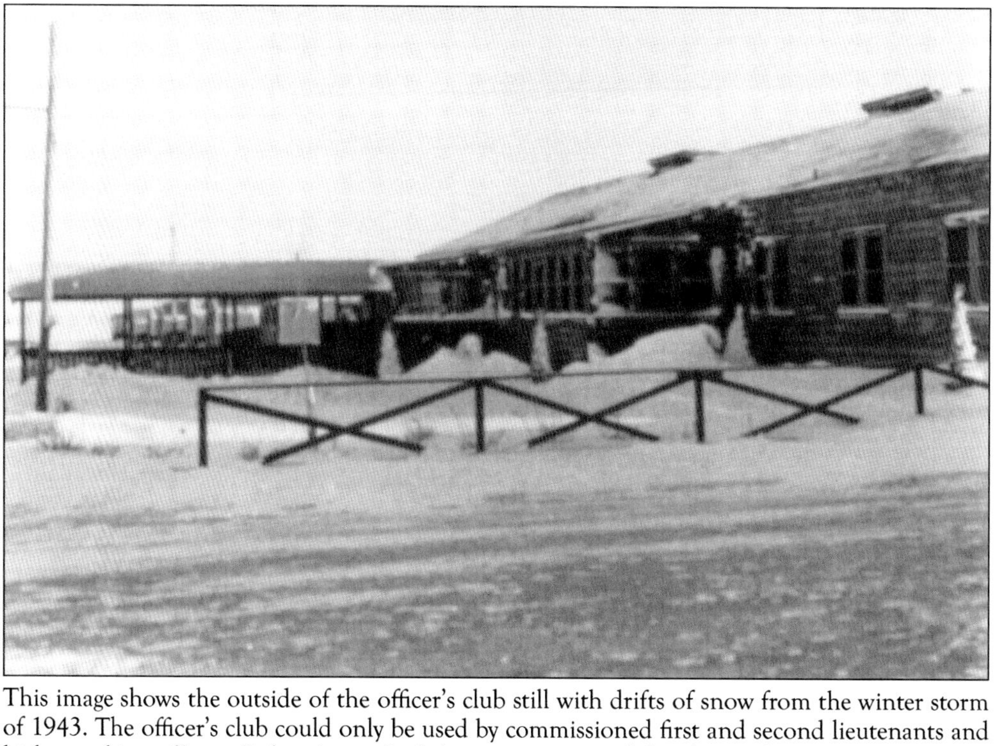

This image shows the outside of the officer's club still with drifts of snow from the winter storm of 1943. The officer's club could only be used by commissioned first and second lieutenants and higher-ranking officers. Enlisted men had their own service club. This tradition of separation of officers and enlisted personnel still exists on military bases today.

Often ignored and unrecorded, women played vital roles during World War II. In the Liberal area, women took over farming, treated the ill, and volunteered for the Red Cross, as well as worked at the LAAF. Here, women test and package parachutes to be used by the airmen.

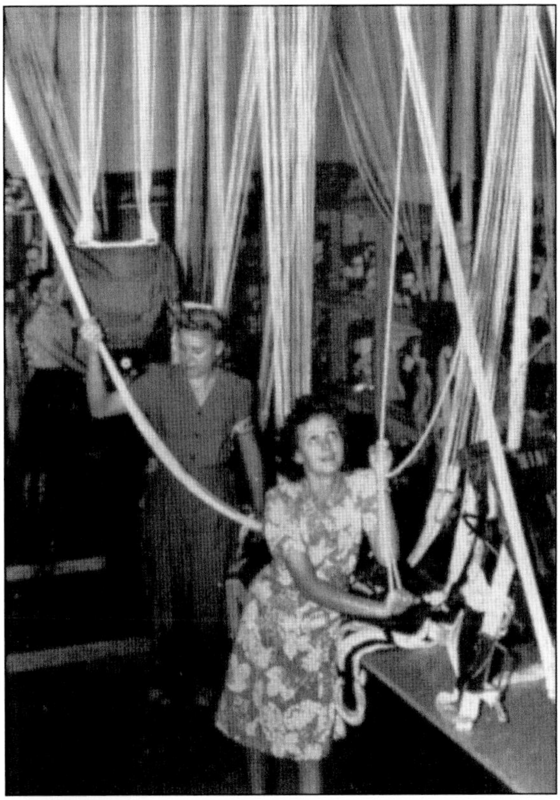

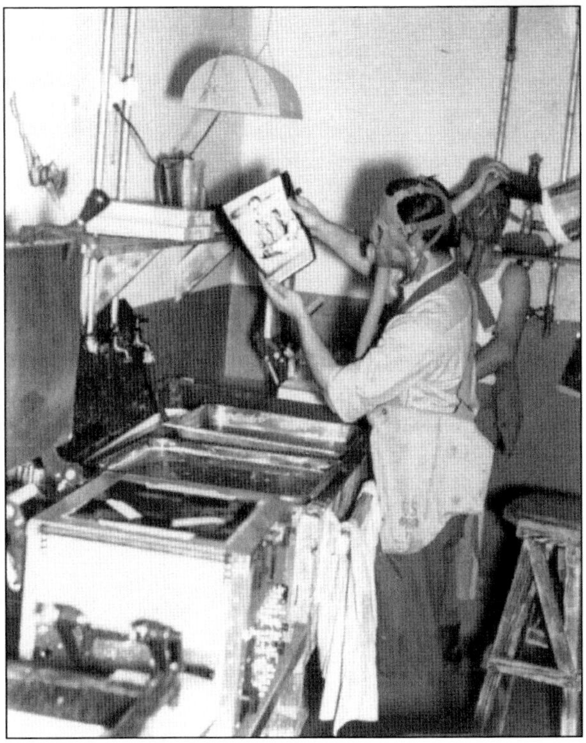

Color film was available during the 1940s, but the armed services usually used black and white film. Black and white film was readily available, cheaper, and easier to develop. Due to the high volume of photographs taken to record base activities, gas masks were used by the lab personnel when developing film. One of the crew has just developed the official photograph of the commander, Col. Arthur L. Bump.

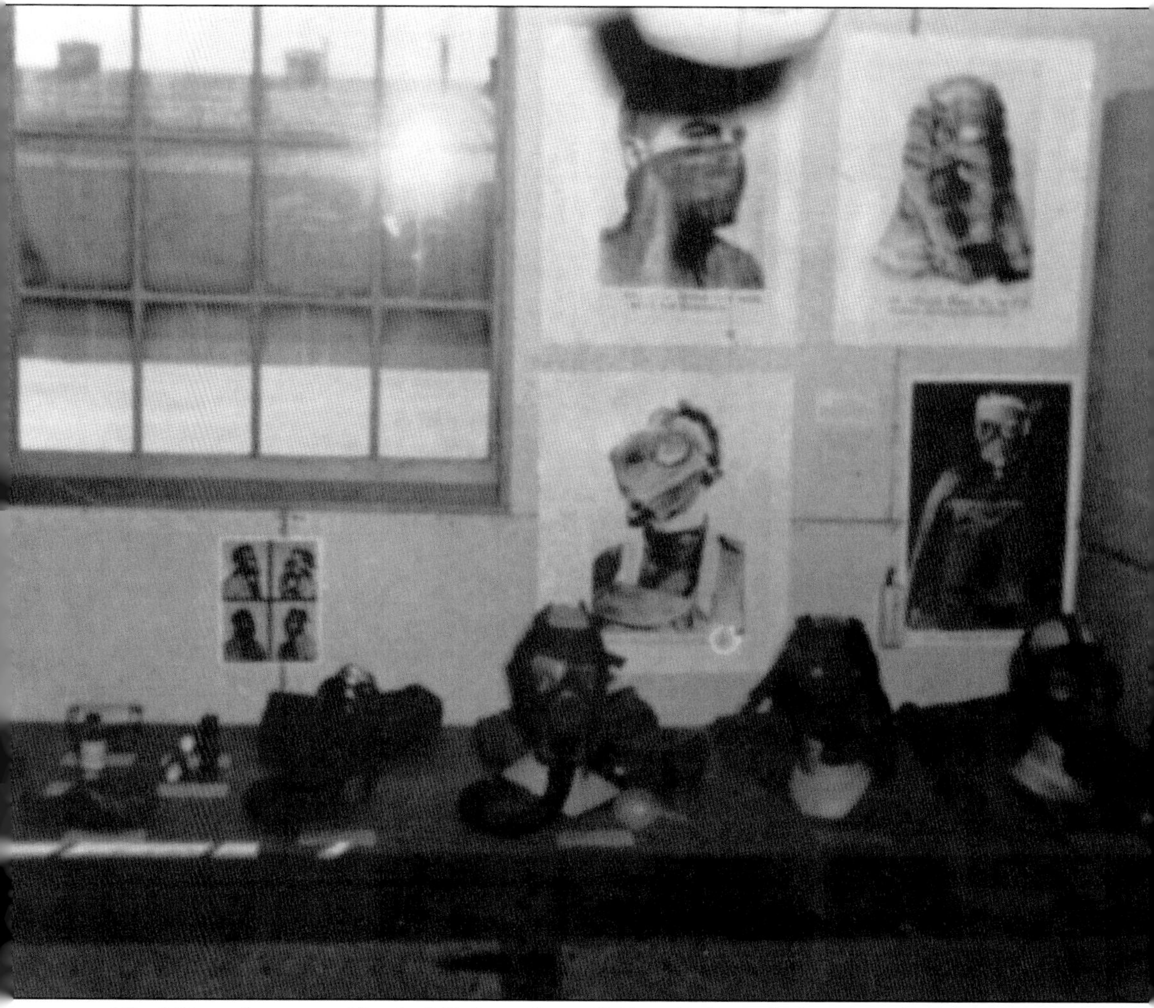

The M-2 mask was used by the US Army from 1941 to 1949. Today's gas masks are the M-50 and M-51, a long way from these crude masks on display. The common phrase by instructors was, "Take care of your gas mask and your gas mask will take care of you." Instructions included how to pack and store it as well as how to put it on and take it off. Just as popular as the posters urging citizens to buy war bonds were posters urging citizens to buy a gas mask. Most people did not, partly because of the cost of $1. Fortunately, there was never a need for them.

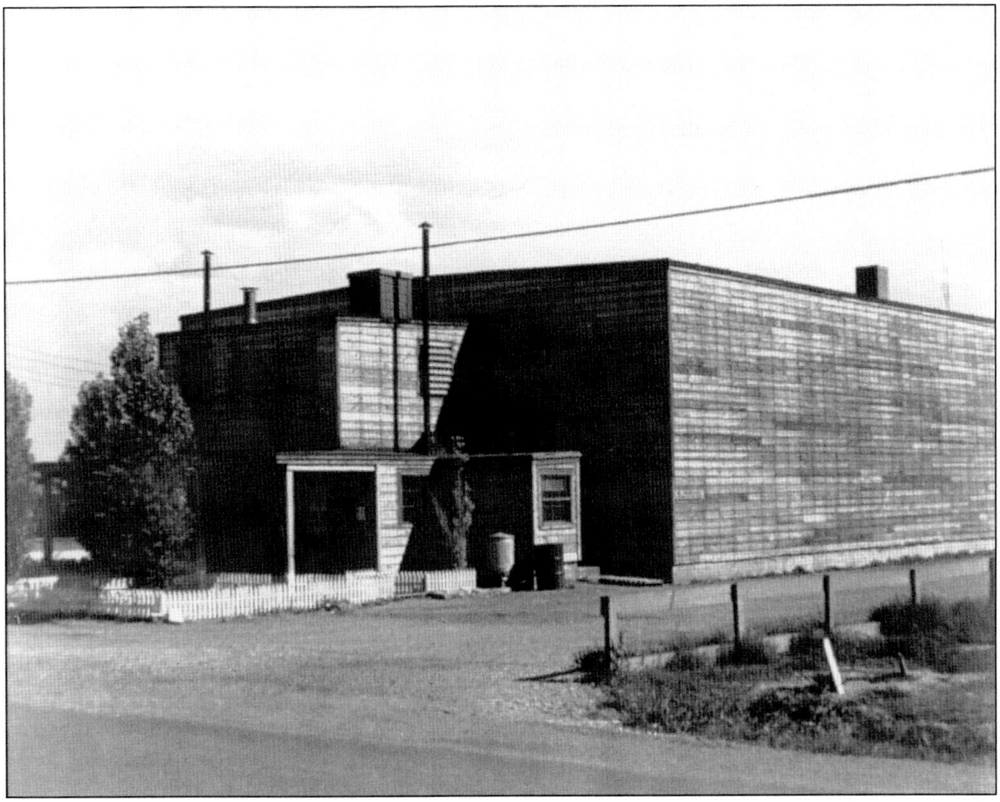

This photograph is of the outside of one of the two base theaters. It also served as a stage for entertainers. Most theaters built on base had a capacity of 100 to 150 seats. Personnel on base took the initiative to beautify the grounds around the theater. Popular movies in 1943 were *Gone With the Wind*, *Northern Pursuit*, and *The Gang's All Here*.

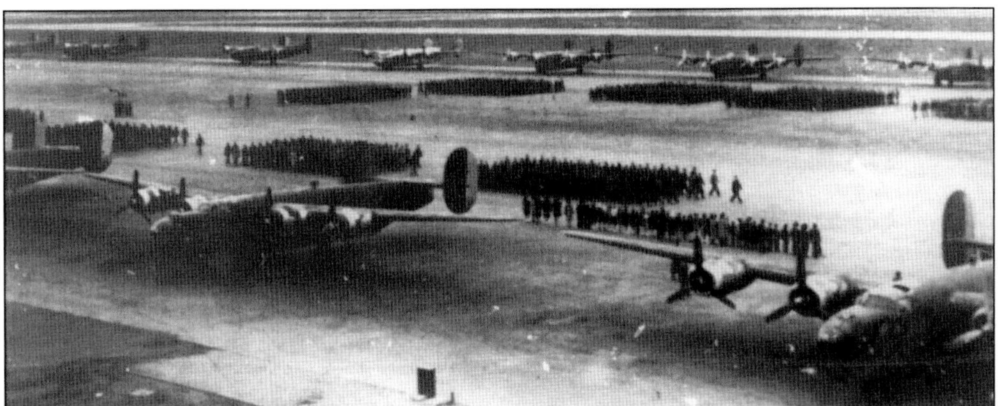

Personnel and planes were in perfect unison in this 1943 drill. The occasion is unknown, but it appears everyone is accounted for. Pass and review were held periodically for visiting dignitaries and other special occasions.

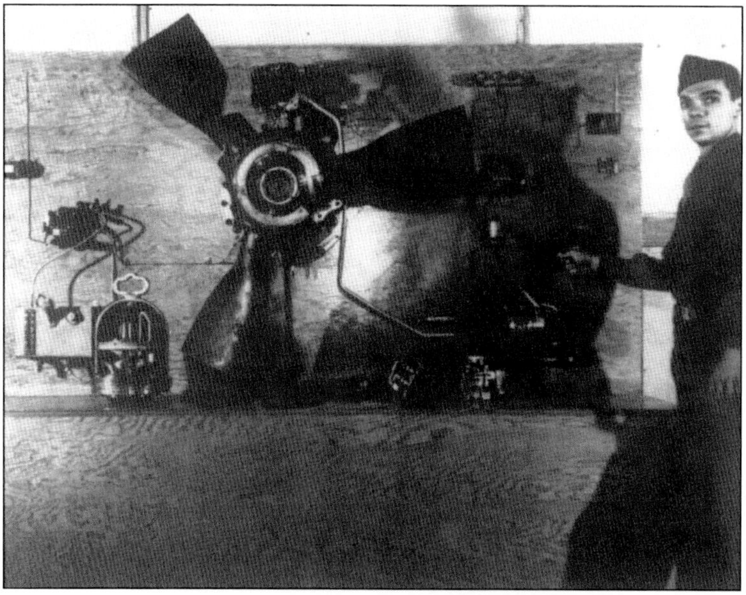

This photograph shows the prop demonstration class. This prop system mockup demonstrates exactly how the B-24 propeller system worked. It taught what problems to expect and the corrections to those problems.

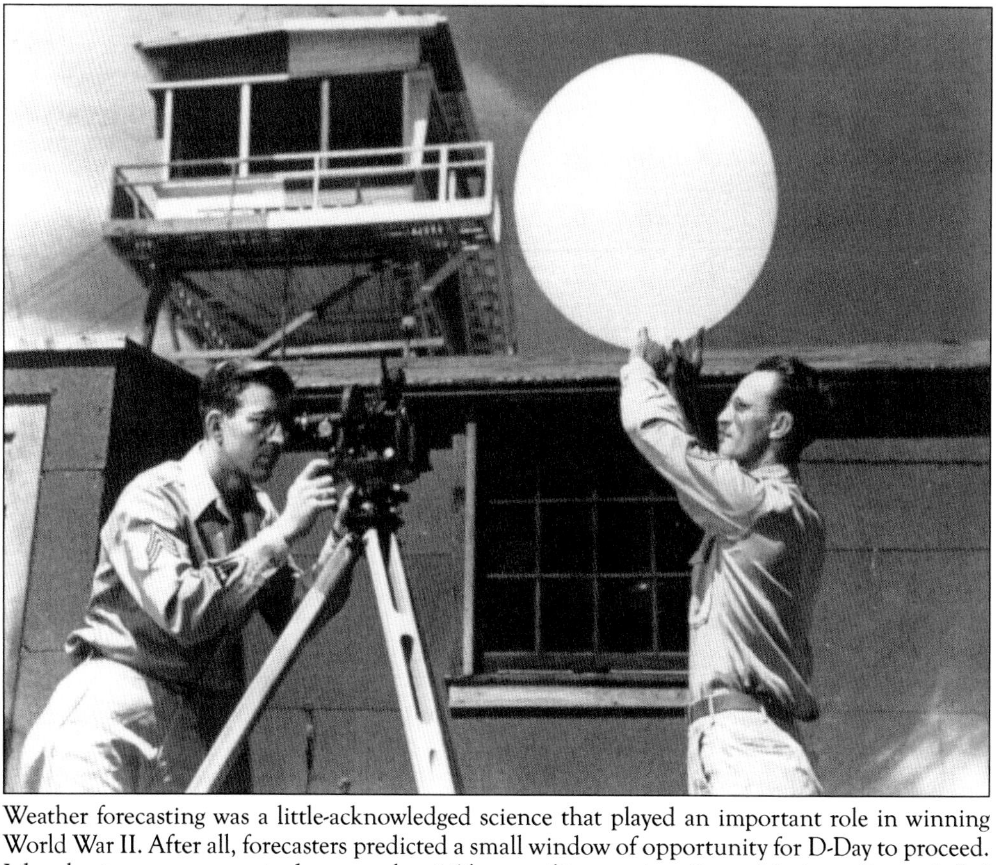

Weather forecasting was a little-acknowledged science that played an important role in winning World War II. After all, forecasters predicted a small window of opportunity for D-Day to proceed. Liberal aviators were required to complete 15 hours of instruction. Part of their studies included releasing hydrogen-filled balloons to measure temperature, humidity, barometric pressure, wind speed, and direction.

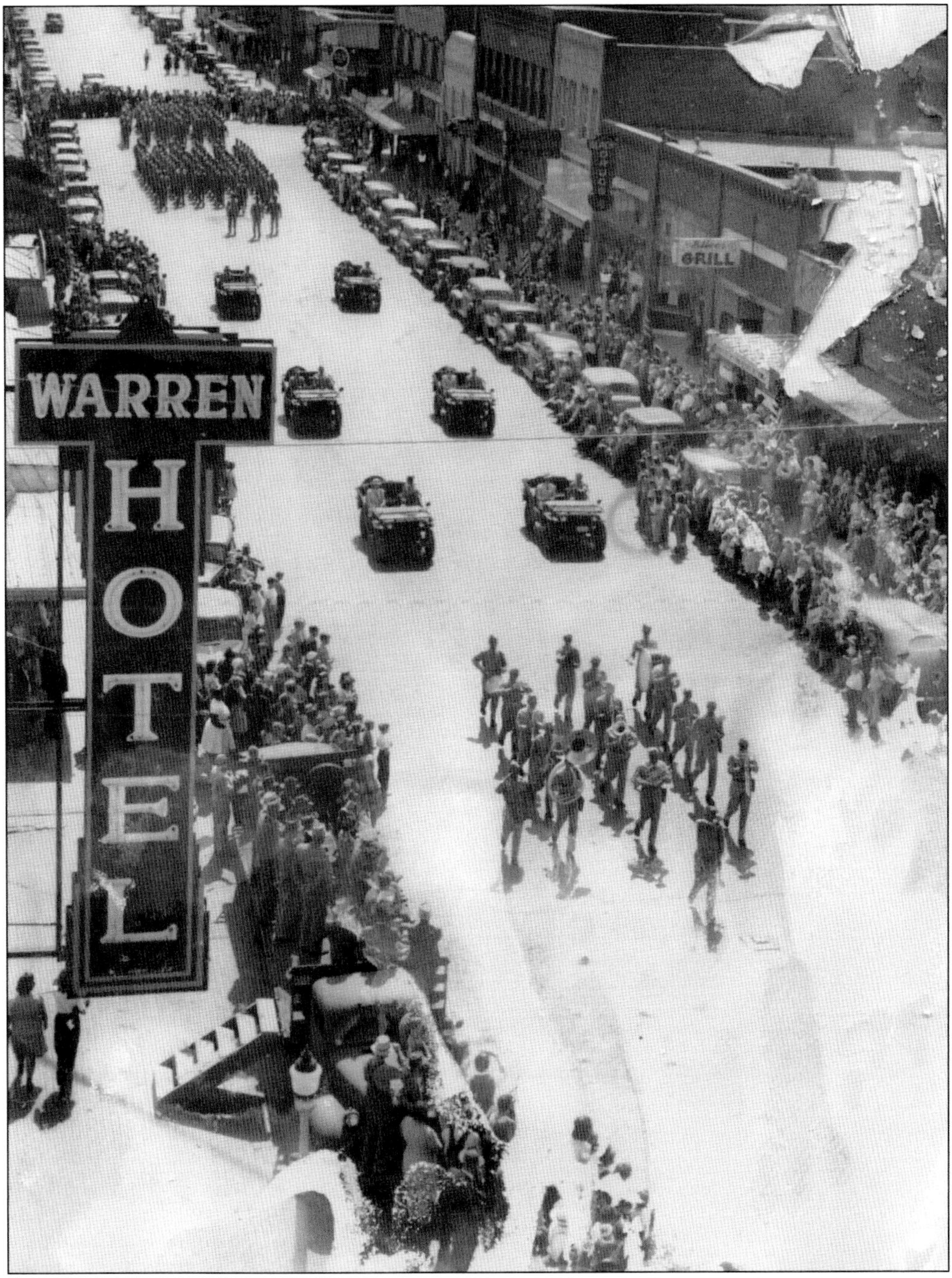

This photograph was taken on September 18, 1943, from the Warren Hotel. All available personnel from the LAAF participated in this Second War Bond Drive Parade. The band playing was the 444th LAAF band, and in the jeeps were 3 WAAC (Women's Army Auxiliary Corps) and Army nurses. Marching in the parade were the 63rd and 60th TEFTS (Two Engine Flying Training Squadron). Also marching was the 1029th and 1030th BFTS (Base Flying Training Squadron). In the mix were also the 527th, 1278th, and the 396th Squadrons.

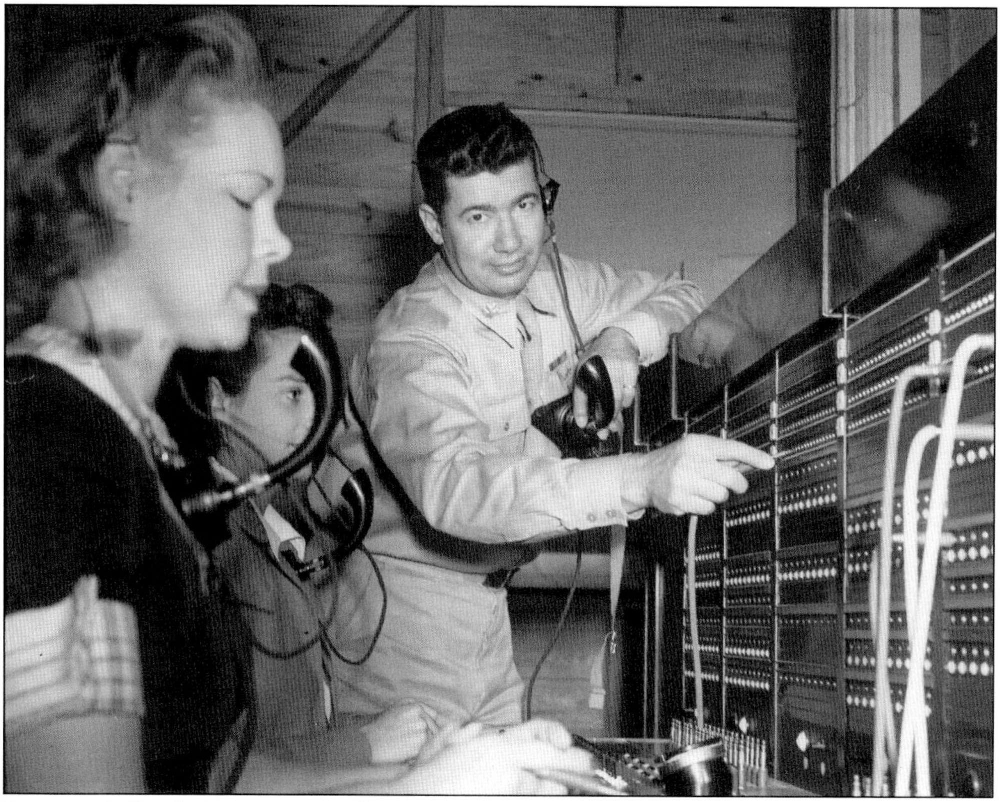

To quote Bell Telephone Systems, "America's telephones are busy with the urgent, vital calls of production and defense." Civilians from Liberal and surrounding communities are being trained by military personnel for what they labeled "non-essential" jobs. With 4,000 personnel on base daily, every job has become essential. The system was always manned to put through calls to command, hospital, or to a GI getting a call from home.

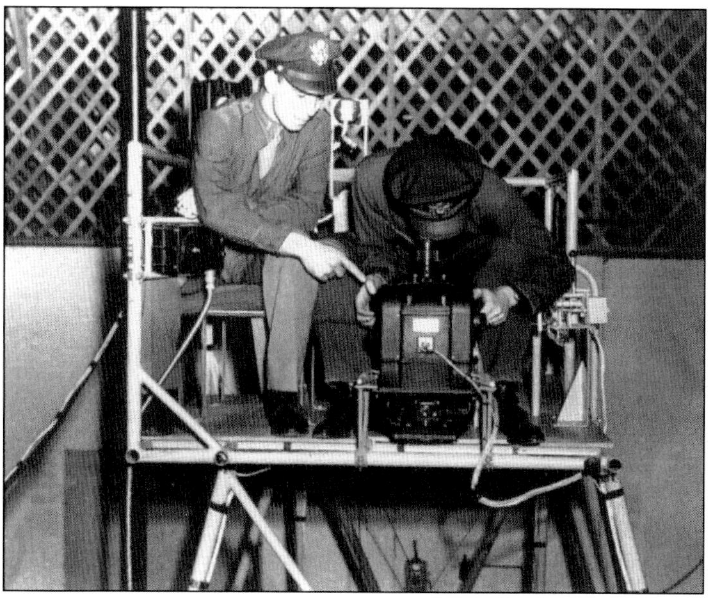

The Norden Bombsight used by the Army Air Force was a tachometer design that measured ground speed, wind drift, and direction. It was up to the bombardier to calculate through a manual process where and when the B-24 bombs were to be dropped. In 1944, an analog computer recalculated changing conditions and allowed the bombardier to fly the plane in the last minutes of a bomb run. Accuracy greatly increased.

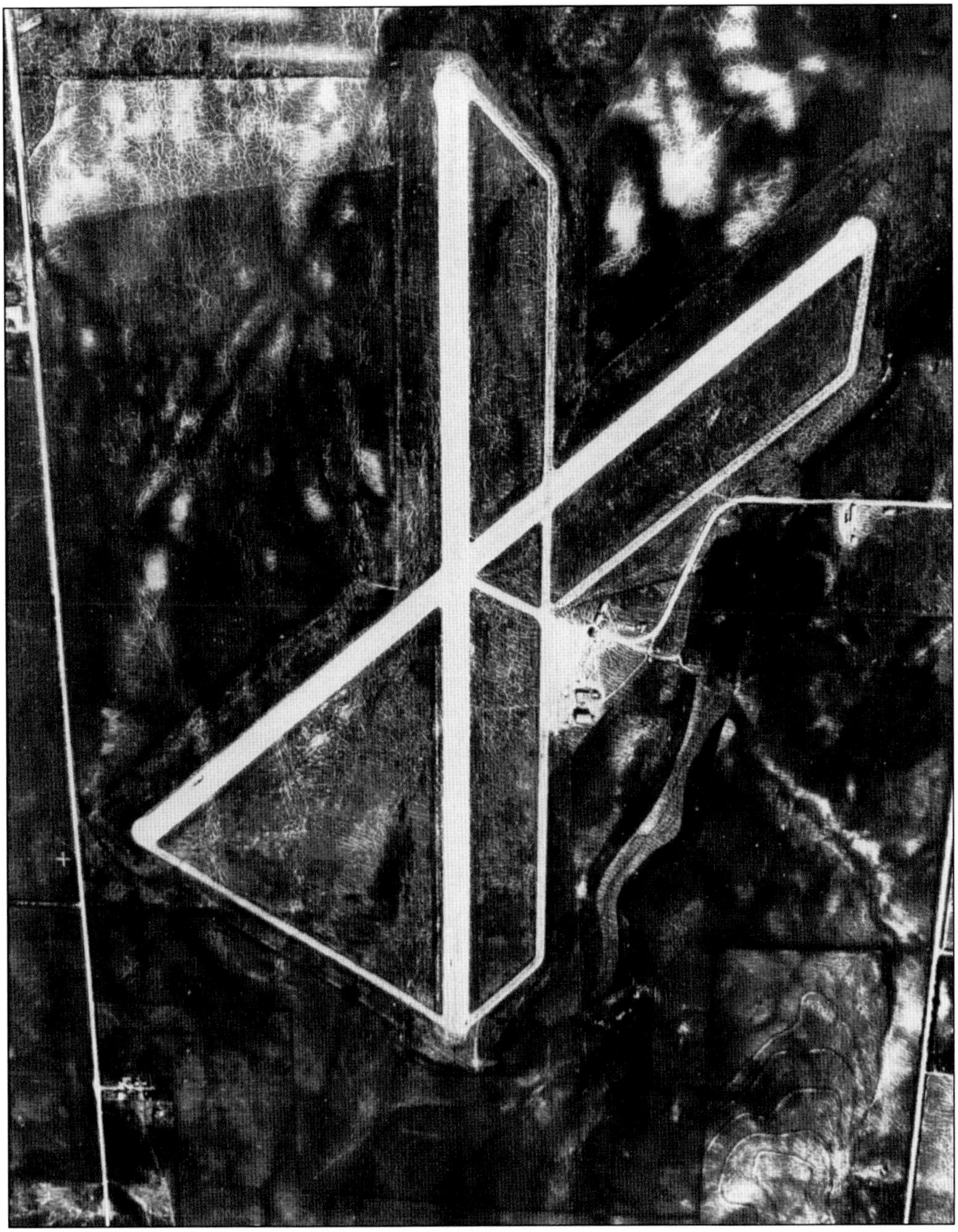

When Woodward and Shattuck, Oklahoma, citizens denied an airfield, fearing their towns would become enemy targets, the Town of Gage, Oklahoma, stepped up. Construction began in 1942 and featured the Army's cross-runway pattern. Already in use by Enid and Woodward Air Bases, Gage became the official auxiliary airfield for the LAAF, mainly to practice landings and take-offs. The airfield experienced one B-24 accident when Lt. James G. Reidy and his crew of six men crashed upon landing. No one was seriously hurt. The airport was deeded to the City of Gage after the war ended. (Courtesy of the Town of Gage, Oklahoma.)

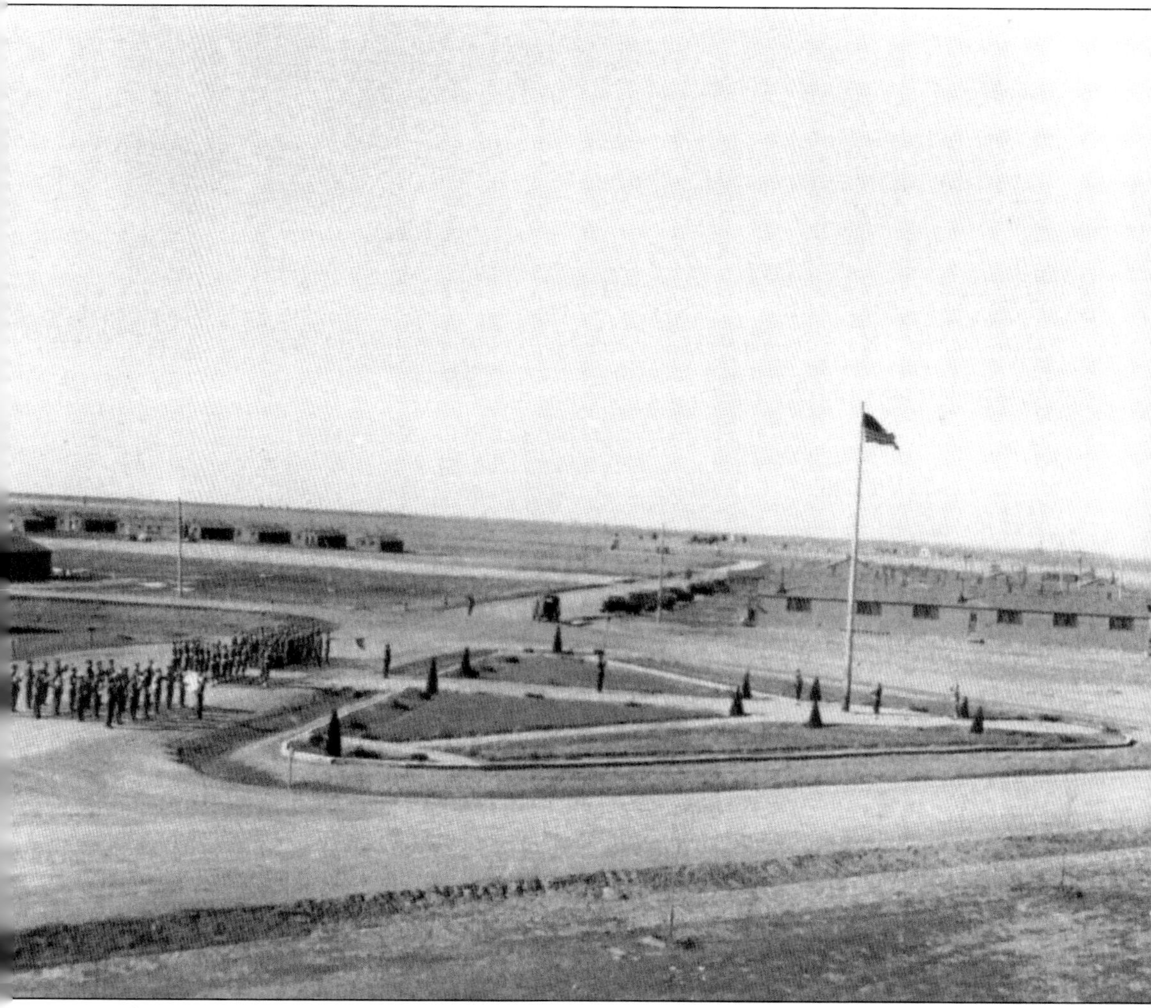

The retreat ceremony was part of airfield life. Looking beyond the flagpole are the barracks, tarmac, landing strips, and wide-open prairie. On the left is the 444th Army Air Force band led by 1st Lt. Richard Ferris, along with troops in dress uniform. To the right are the ground school buildings. Just out of the photograph are the guard shack and gate. The Y configuration is still used today as an entry to the Liberal Municipal Airport.

Three

The B-24 and Commanders

The B-24, also known as the "Widow Maker" and the "Flying Boxcar," was one of the most produced American wartime aircraft, with over 18,000 built. Different models and specifications were constantly being introduced, with many modifications being implemented. The wingspan on all B-24s remained at 110 feet, and the length also remained at 63 feet 9 inches. The height was 18 feet. The maximum speed varied by design between 273 and 313 miles per hour, making it faster than its sister ship, the B-17. Service ceilings were between 28,000 and 31,500 feet, with a combat range of 3,000 to 4,400 miles. The B-24 was armed with six to ten .50 caliber machine guns and carried a bomb load of 8,000 to 12,800 pounds. It was the workhorse of the war. The most distinctive trait was the four 1,200-horsepower Pratt & Whitney engines. A typical crew of 10 men worked in cramped, cold spaces with no pressurization or comfortable seats. Gunners had to sit on the floor for long inactive periods. A narrow catwalk ran between bombs and open waist doors. It took every man to know and do his job well since their lives depended on each other. Pilots worked hard just flying the unruly aircraft since the bomber had no automatic controls. The B-24 took muscle to fly, especially at high altitudes. The difference in comfort between the B-24 and the B-17 is attributed to the fact that the B-24 was mass-produced during the war and the B-17 was manufactured at a slower pace during peacetime. B-17 pilots and B-24 pilots always gave each other a hard time. One of the favorite things for B-17 pilots to say was that the B-24 was the box the B-17 came in.

The base commanders held great responsibility to meet the demands set forth by the Army Air Force. The commanders had to run an efficient base. LAAF's first commander, Col. Arthur Leroy Bump Jr., certainly had his hands full. Overseeing personnel, new instructors, ongoing construction, and lack of skilled mechanics, among other problems, kept Colonel Bump busy. Colonel Bump commanded LAAF from April 27, 1943, to April 1, 1944. After his time in Liberal, he was sent to Indonesia, where he was killed in aerial combat on March 10, 1945. The second commander at LAAF was Col. Edward H. Underhill. He served at the airbase from April 1, 1944, to July 18, 1945. The third commander was Col. Charles Sommers, who served from July 18, 1945, to September 18, 1945. The final commander was Col. Ford V. Lauer, who served from September 18, 1945, to September 30, 1945.

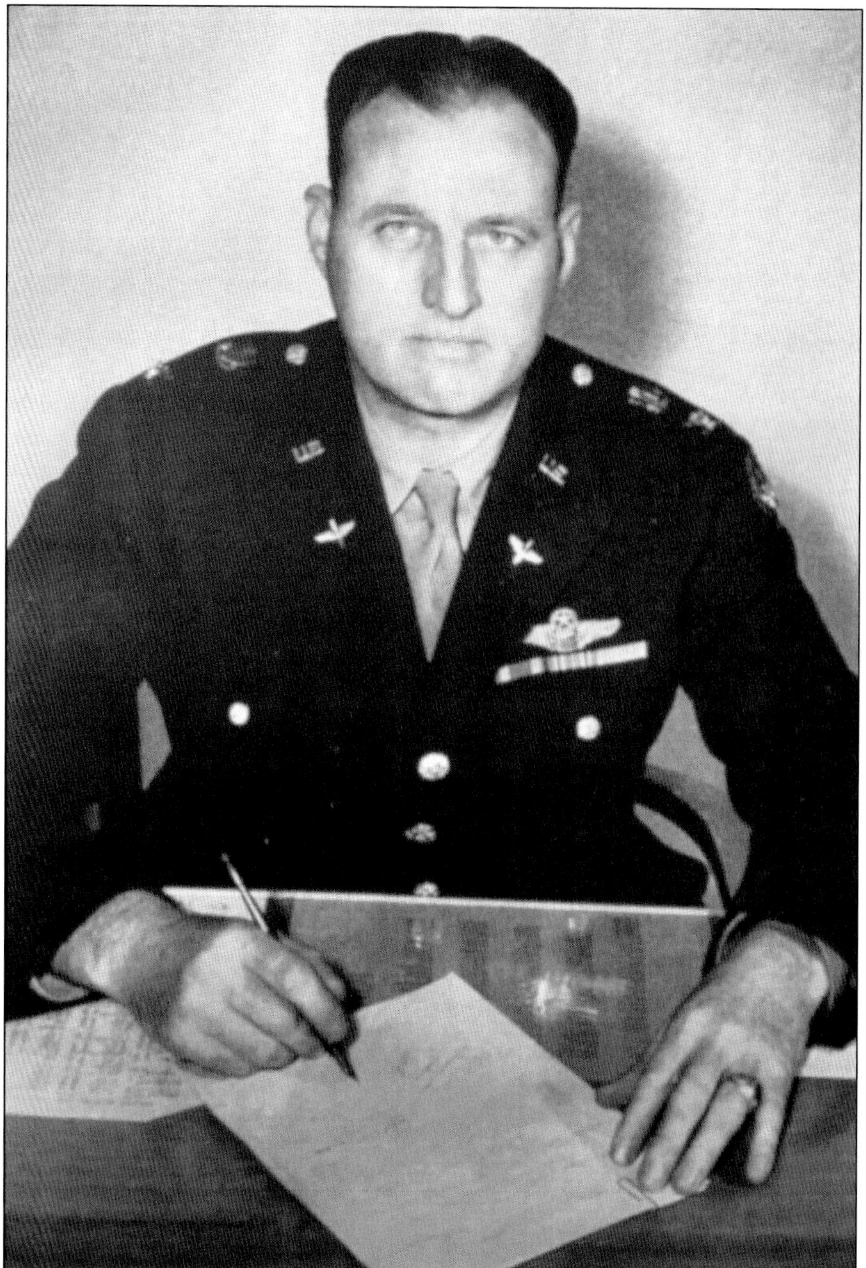

Col. Arthur Leroy Bump Jr. commanded the LAAF from April 27, 1942, to April 1, 1944. He was born in Ohio in 1902 and graduated from West Point, following in his father's footsteps. Bump was sent to both Brooks and Kelly Fields in Texas, graduating in 1926 from Kelly as a flying officer. He was stationed with a pursuit squadron in the Philippines from 1928 to 1930. In 1938, Colonel Bump returned to Kelly Field as an engineering officer. From 1939 through 1941, he became a wing S-4 officer at Albrook Field in the Panama Canal Zone. It was here that Colonel Bump was awarded the prestigious Air Medal for his heroic rescue of a crew that had crashed into the sea, saving three airmen. Colonel Bump died on March 10, 1945, during aerial combat near Maluku, Indonesia. He was buried on March 10, 1949, next to his father at Arlington Cemetery.

Edward H. Underhill was appointed an aviation cadet in 1927 and was soon commissioned as a 2nd Lt. in the Army Air Corps. He spent one year in the Panama Canal Zone as commanding officer of the 24th Pursuit Squad. In 1939, he became director of flying at Brooks Field. In 1942, he assumed command of the Army Airforce Glider School in Dalhart, Texas. The following November, he assumed command of Brooks Field. In April 1944, he became commander of the LAAF. After leaving Liberal, he was assigned to the South Pacific Theater. By now a general, Underhill became chief of staff of the 5th Air Force, then became major general in 1954.

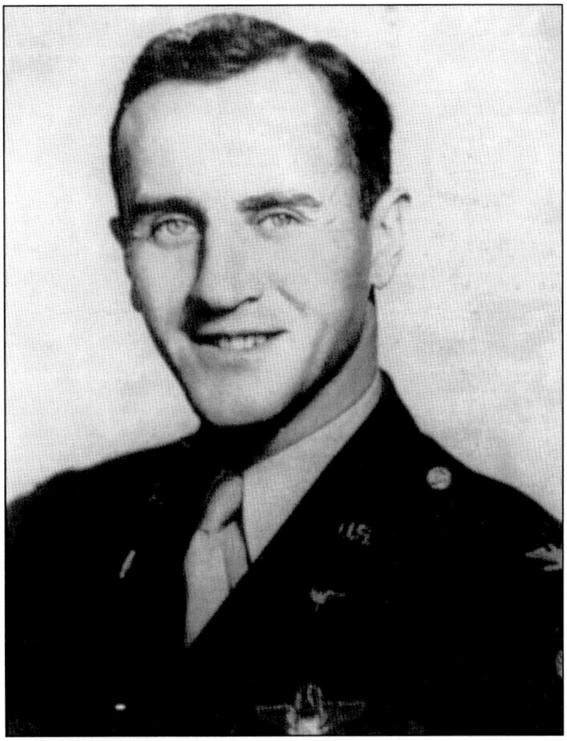

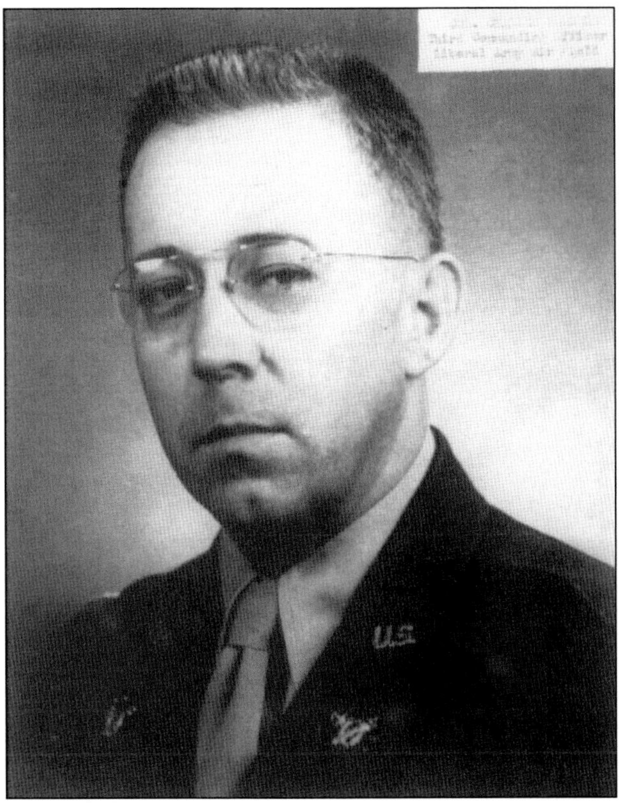

Col. Charles L. Sommers commanded the LAAF from July 18, 1945, to September 18, 1945. Colonel Sommers threw one of the biggest parties the airfield ever hosted. Thousands of people from five states gathered to celebrate the 38th anniversary of the US Air Force. After Colonel Sommers transferred, Col. Ford V. Lauer commanded the base for an even shorter time. Colonel Lauer was in charge from September 18, 1945, to September 30, 1945. He was known as a "stick and rudder" man and a "soldier's colonel."

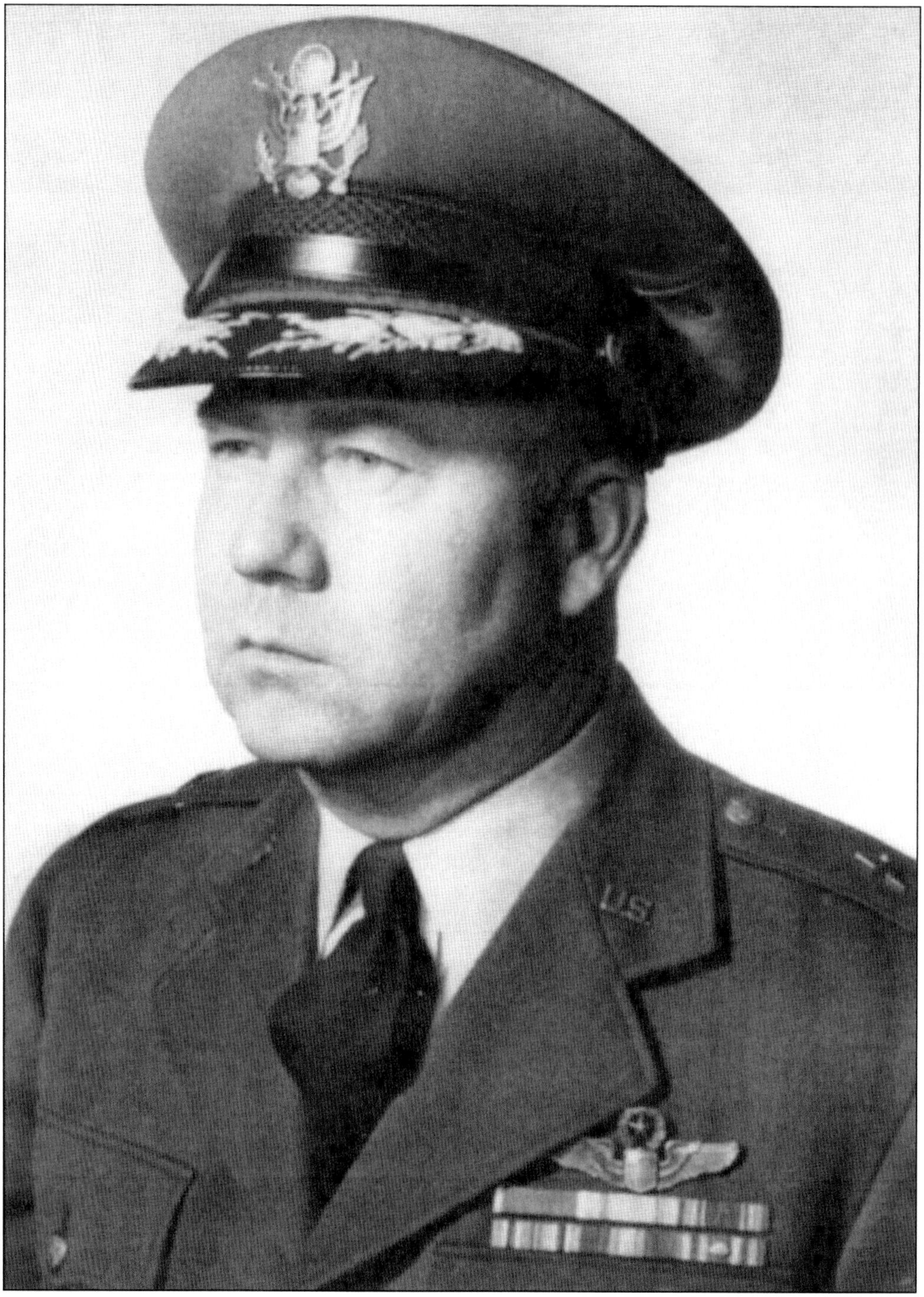

Ralph Rockwood was born in Sapulpa, Oklahoma, and received a mechanical engineering degree from Oklahoma University. He entered the Army Air Force in 1933 and served as a fighter pilot out of Barksdale, Louisiana. He arrived in Liberal in 1943 to serve as director of training. General Rockwood transferred to the US Air Force when it became a separate branch of service. He retired in 1966 as a US Air Force brigadier general.

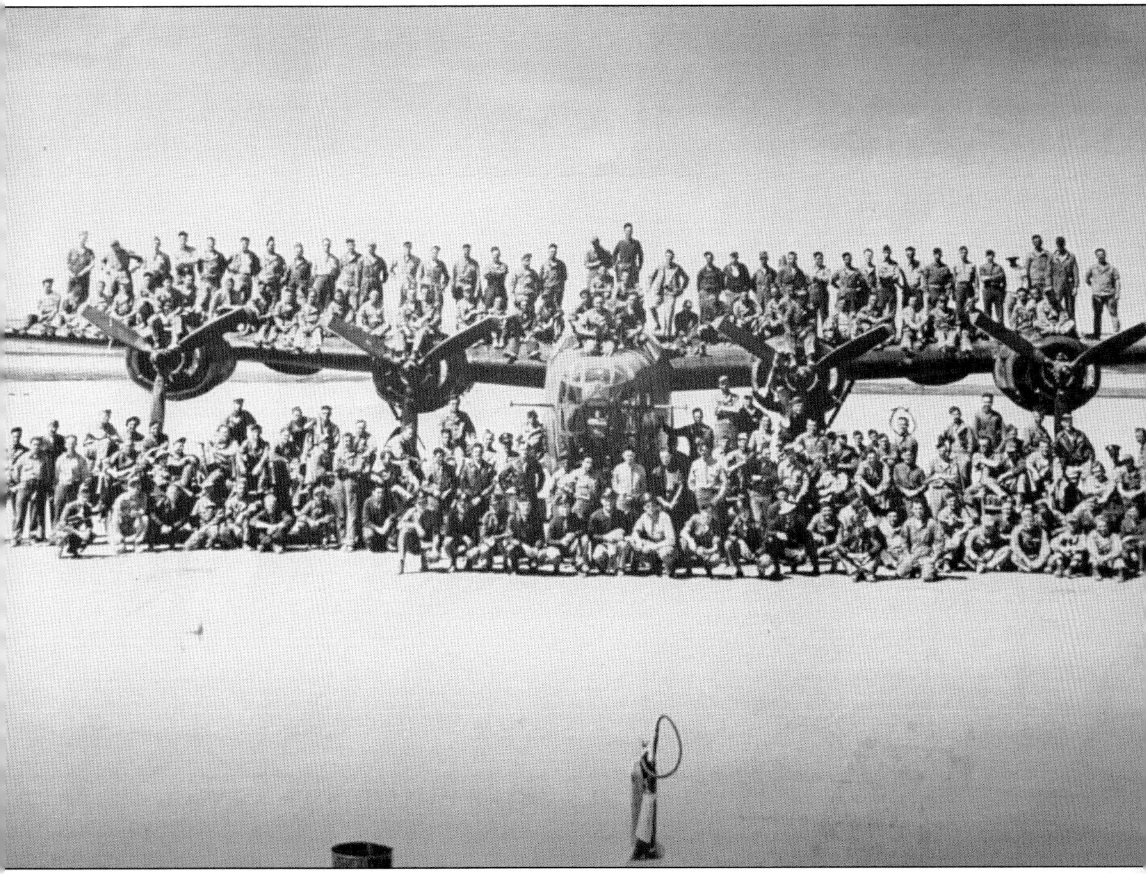

Two hundred airmen, pilots, and ground crew come together from all parts of the United States to work and train. The B-24 could carry a huge amount of weight and fuel for extended missions, so all the men in this 1944 photograph were no strain on the expansive Davis wings of the plane. The smiles and pride shown on their faces truly represent who the 2525th Bomb Group stood for.

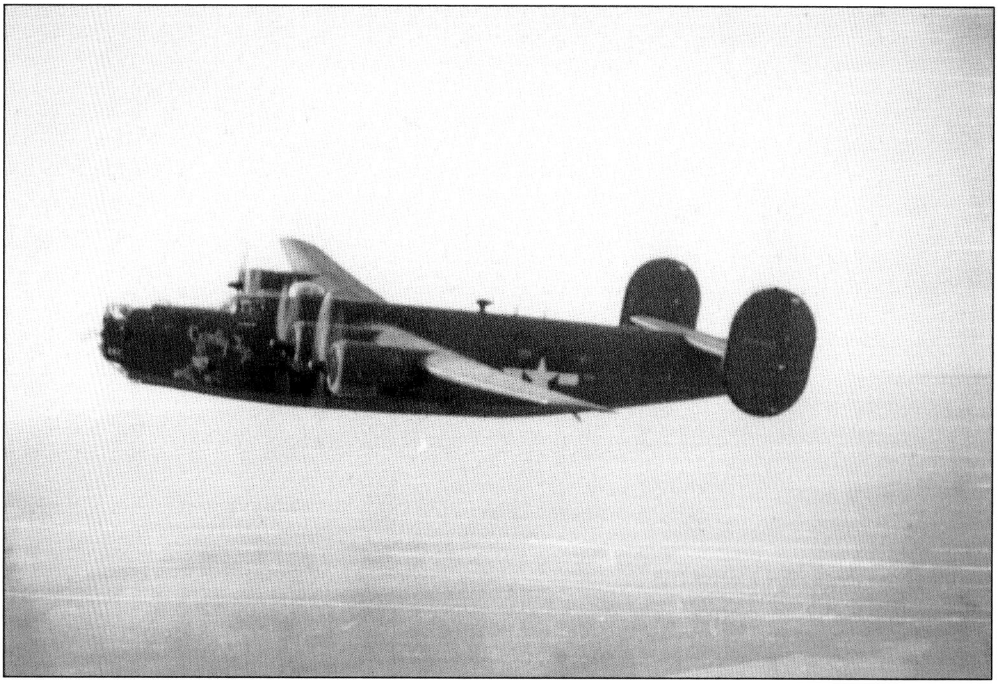

Aviation nose art was as important to the crew as it was to the mechanics and ground crew who took care of the planes. The unofficial art often mirrored the values of the pilot or his crew. Nose art created a powerful bond between man and machine. The art often depicted a voluptuous woman who symbolized their wife, mother, or sweetheart back home. Cartoon characters from Walt Disney were also extremely popular. "Curly Top" and "Stand By" were examples of creativity on B-24s. Whatever the theme or art on a plane's nose, these young crew members always treated it with respect.

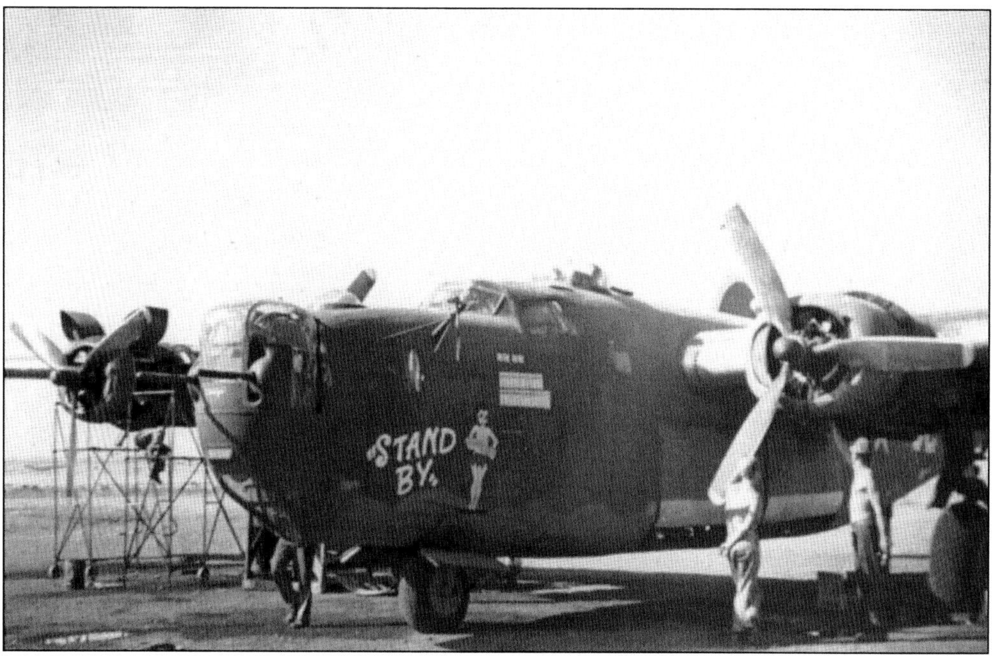

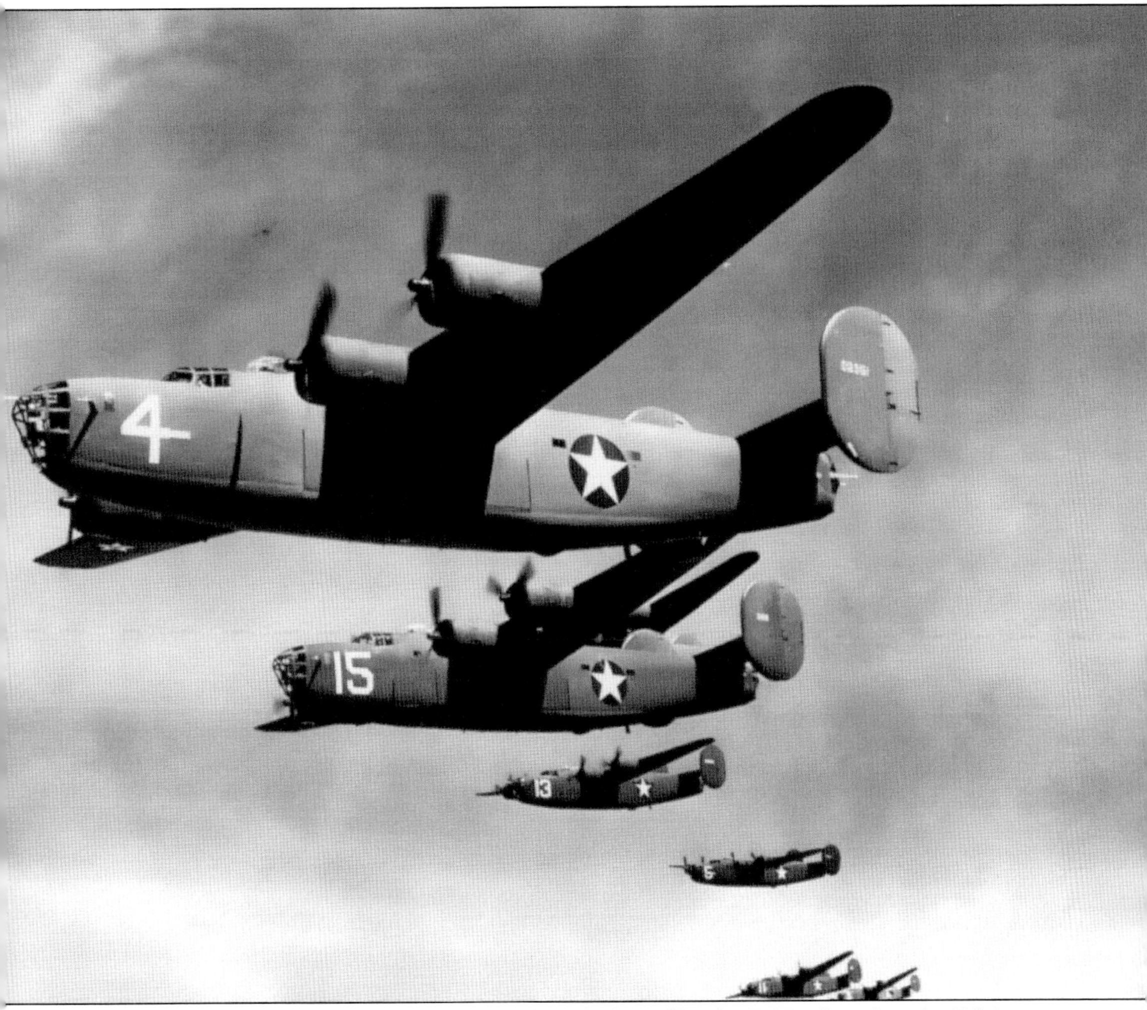

The B-24s were huge, ugly, hard to handle, and made fun of by the B-17 pilots, but the B-24 was well thought out, and what it offered in performance, reliability, durability, and efficiency was equaled by very few planes. Even though most Americans thought they were less than pretty, the British thought they were beautiful.

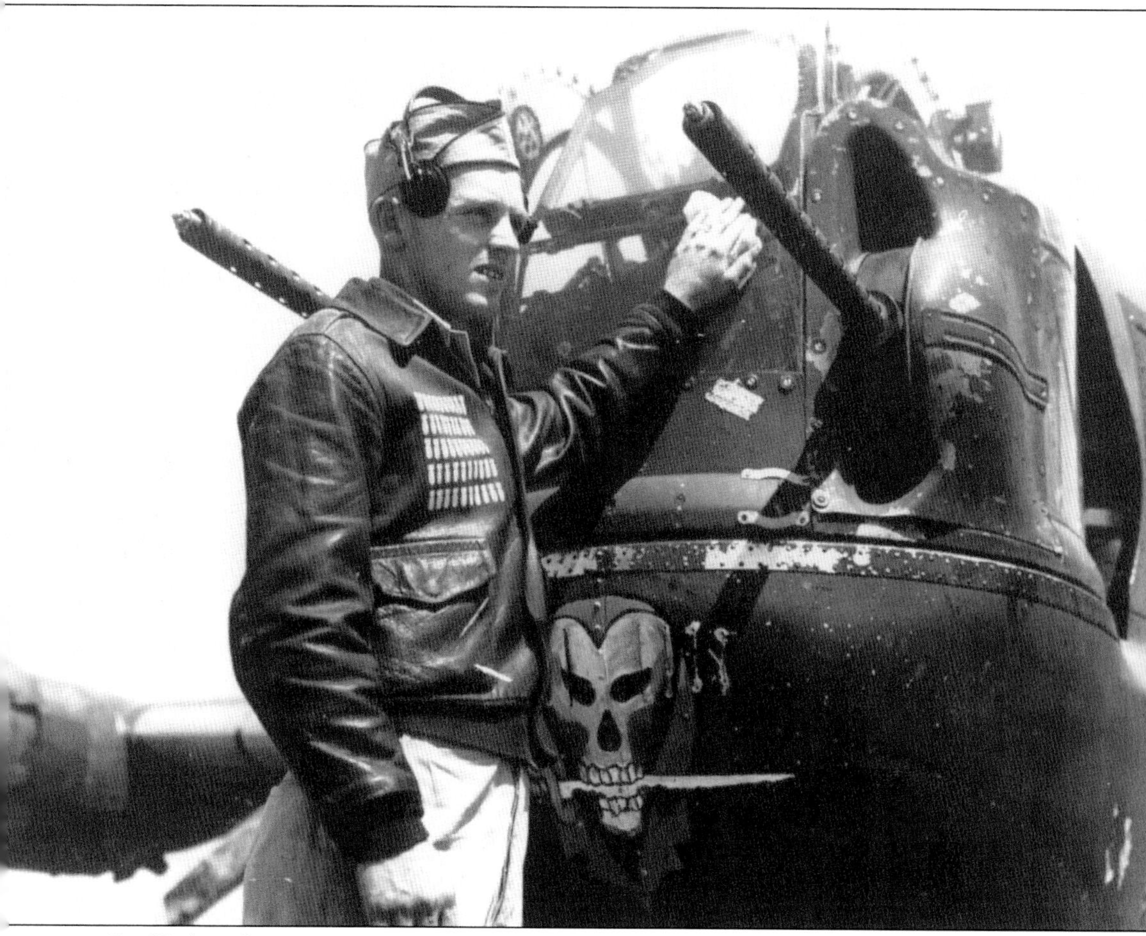

Sgt. Herbert Gray, a B-24 nose gunner, returned home safely from the European theater along with his crew. These crew members flew a remarkable 52 missions, as indicated by his flight jacket and airman's log. Gray, originally from nearby Elmwood, Oklahoma, returned to the LAAF to become an instructor. (Courtesy of Connie Bowman.)

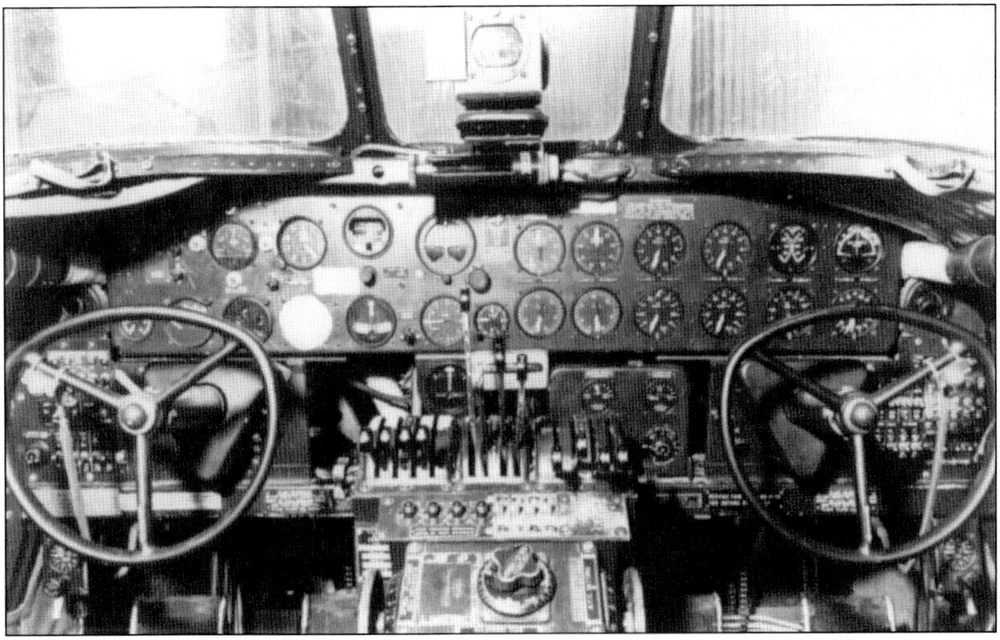

The pedestal of the B-24 flight deck had three sets of four engine control levers, superchargers, throttles, and mixture. The push/pull action on the control wheel worked the elevators and required only a slight movement to have an effect. The cockpit was spacious for both the pilot and co-pilot but required considerable muscle for the other controls. Pilots and co-pilots had to know every aspect of the B-24, not just how to fly them.

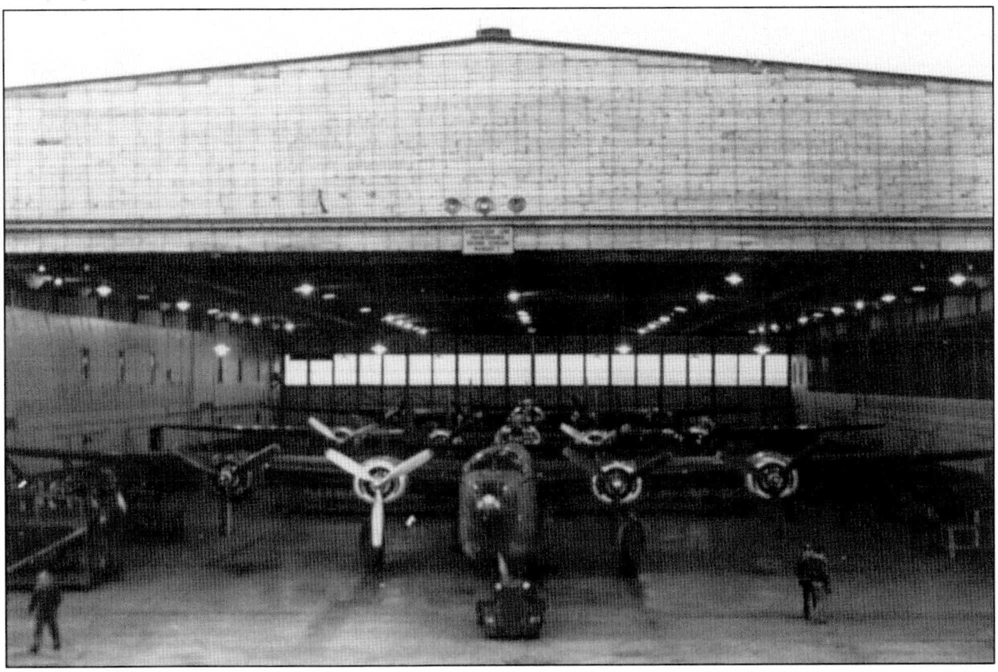

LAAF consisted of three wooden hangars measuring 143 feet by 149 feet and two steel hangars that measured 203 feet by 144 feet. All had round-top roofs, cantilevered sliding doors, one-story sides, and brick chimneys for the boilers. The steel hangars were large enough to easily park three B-24s.

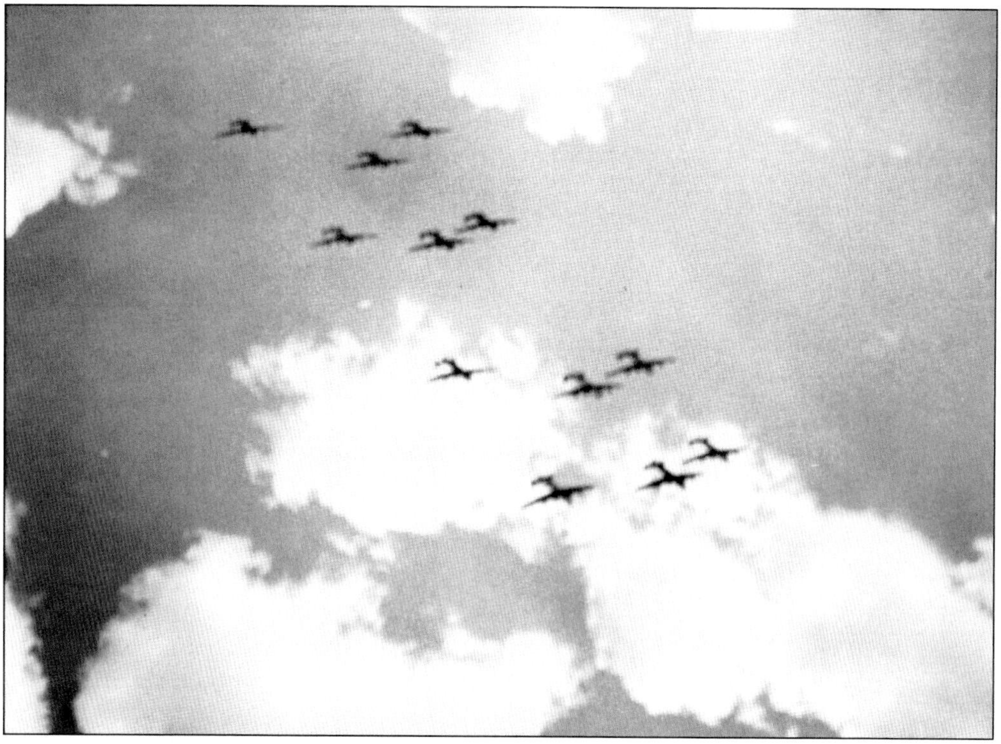

Twelve B-24s fly in formation to wow the crowd at the August 1945 open house to honor the 38th anniversary of the Army Air Force. Even though it was 100-plus degrees, a throng of 10,000 people attended. Demonstrations, award presentations, and displays entertained the crowd. Upon the conclusion and to impress everyone, 12 of Liberal's Liberators flew in formation over the field.

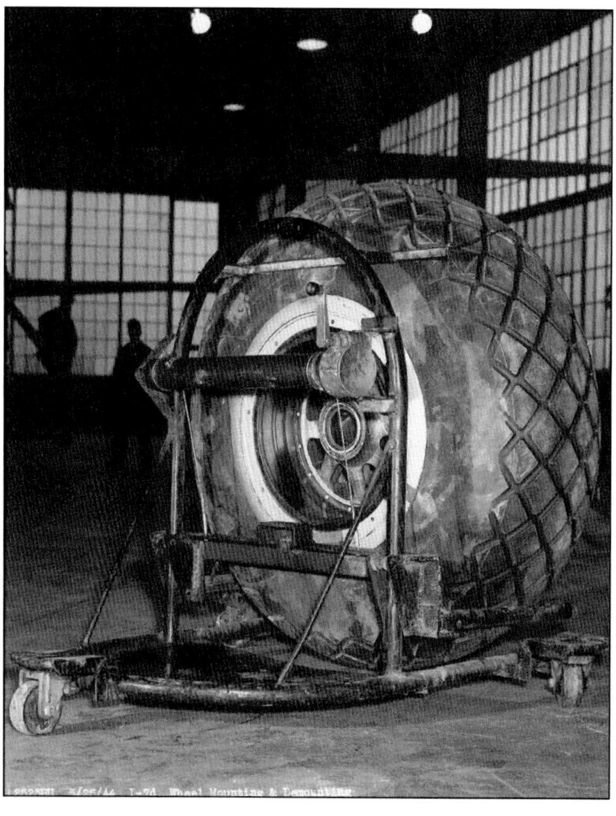

The giant tires on the B-24 had to withstand brutal take-offs and hard landings. An empty B-24 weighed 38,000 pounds, so consequently, tires would be ruined. The tires were big, but this mounting/demounting apparatus could be wheeled out and jacked into place, and the new tire could be easily installed.

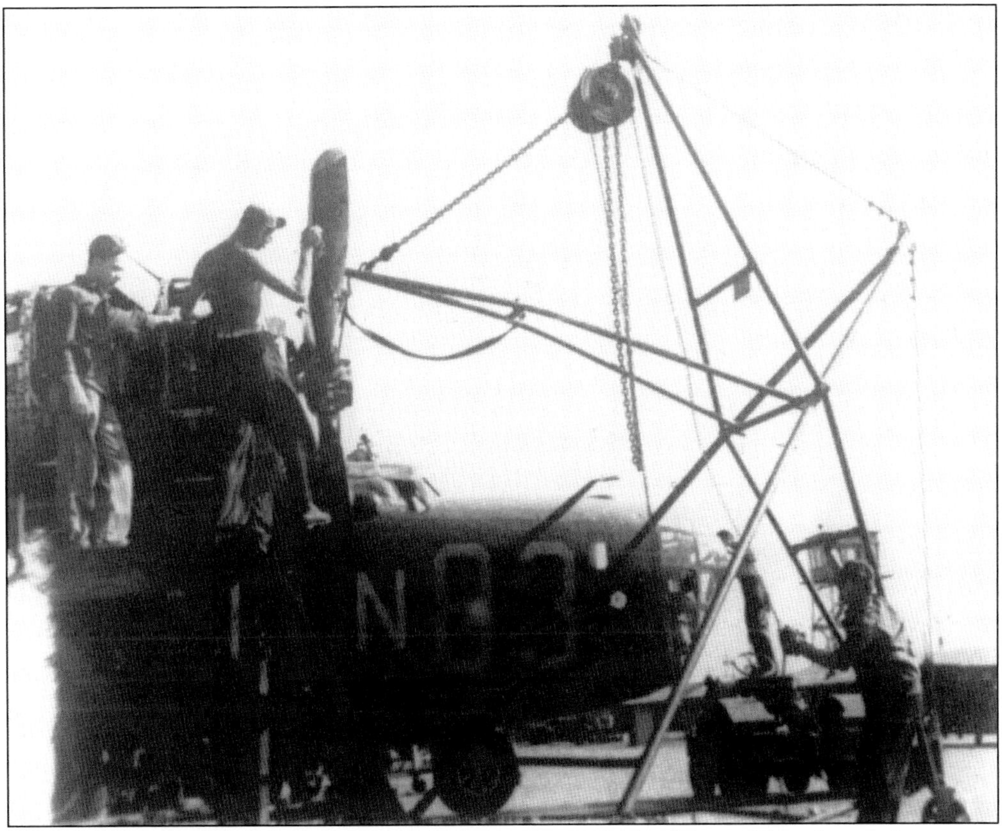

The Pratt & Whitney turbocharged engines, nicknamed the "Twin Wasps," were kept on a rigorous maintenance schedule, with inspections after every flight and work done after 25, 50, 70, and 100 flight hours. Replacing a tired engine on the wing of a heavy bomber took ground crews and mechanics hours. Crews sometimes worked throughout the evening to prepare for the next day's training schedule.

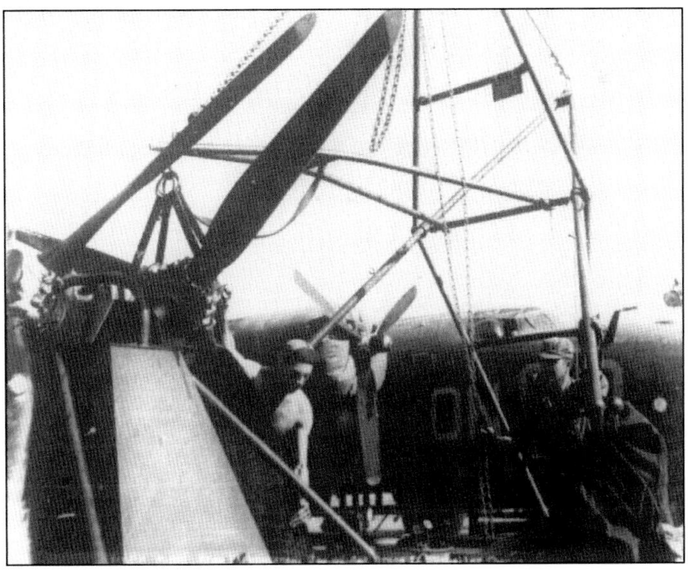

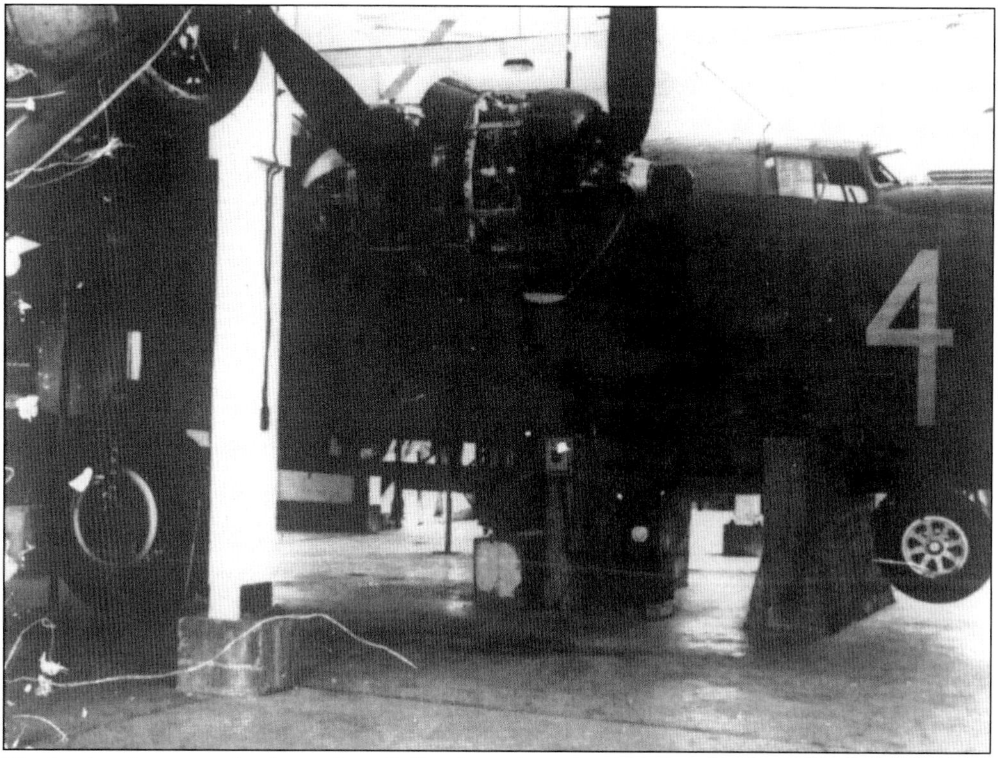

The big bombers were built to take off, fly a long distance, drop bombs, fly back, and land safely back home. Unfortunately, the base B-24s were subjected to numerous landings and take-offs, hard maneuvering, multiple instructors, and first-time pilots, causing the normal tough birds to experience lots of maintenance time.

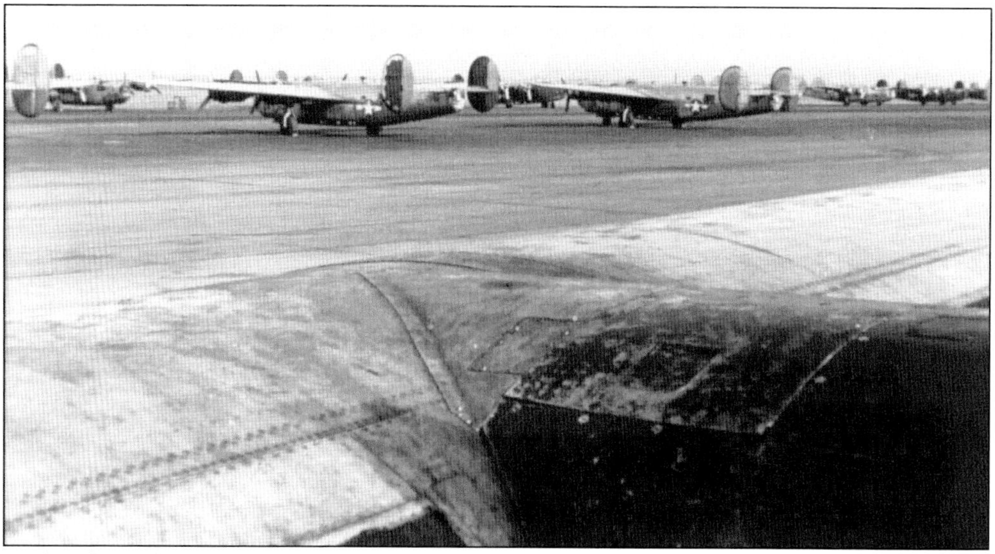

With only five hangars, most of the aircraft were parked outside on the expansive flight line. A parking apron of 276,318 square yards of concrete could accommodate dozens of B-24s. The planes were serviced after flying and returned to specific places so that instructors and crew members could find a plane easily and rapidly.

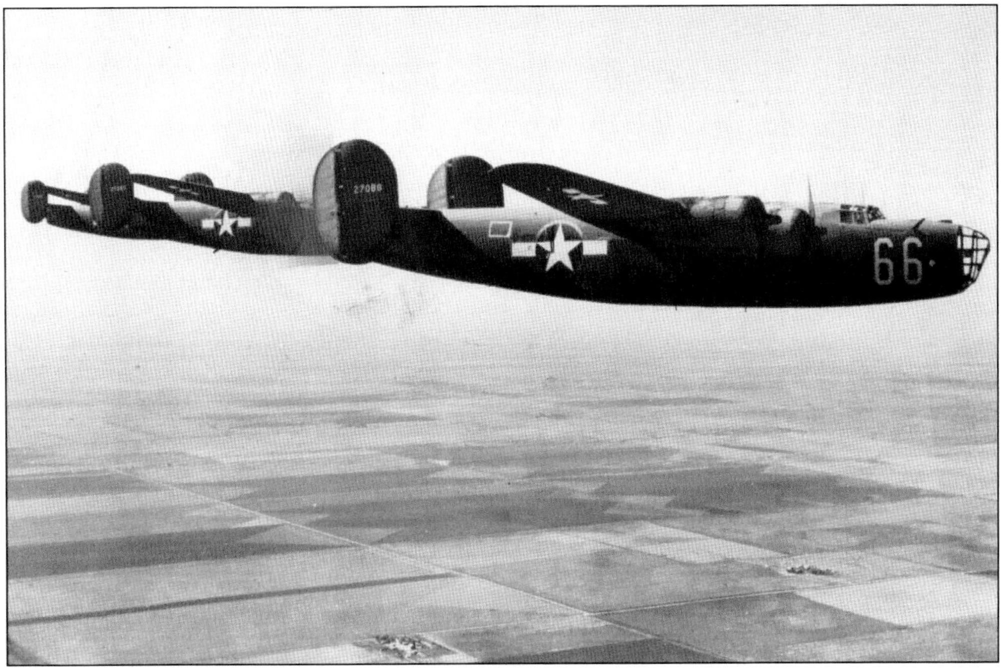

In perfect alignment, these three Liberators fly along the echelon, looking like a super plane. The photograph was taken over the countryside near Liberal. (Courtesy of Lidia Gray.)

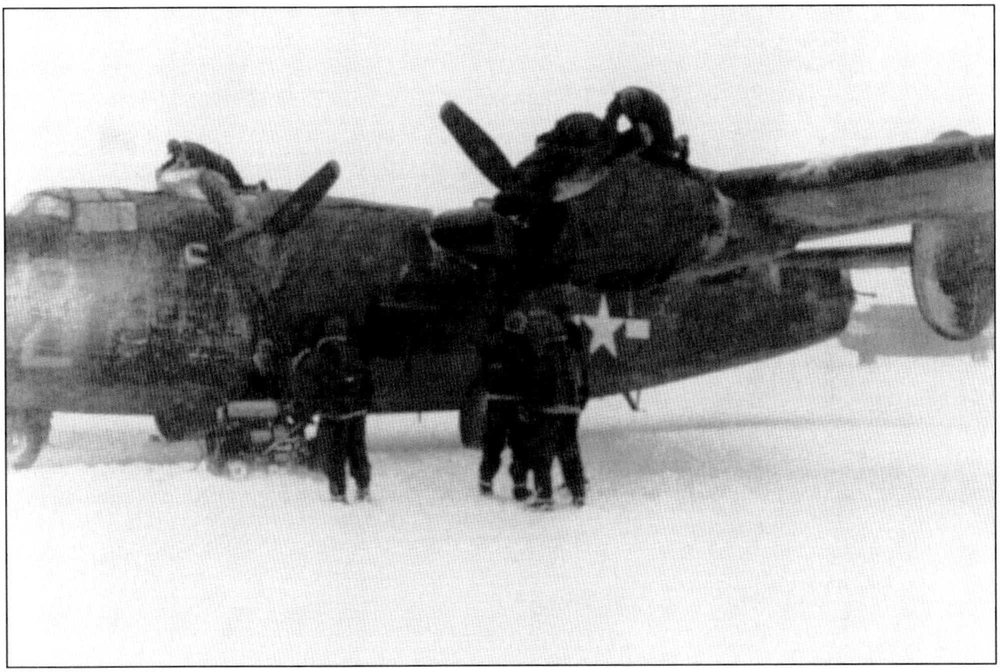

Nonflying members of a group often referred to as "ground pounders" or "paddlefeet" were the unsung heroes of any base. It took an enormous amount of training to perform their jobs, often in terrible weather for long hours. There was no need for training air crews without the ground crews to keep things running. Despite their different jobs, there was no rivalry or lack of respect between ground crews and flight crew members.

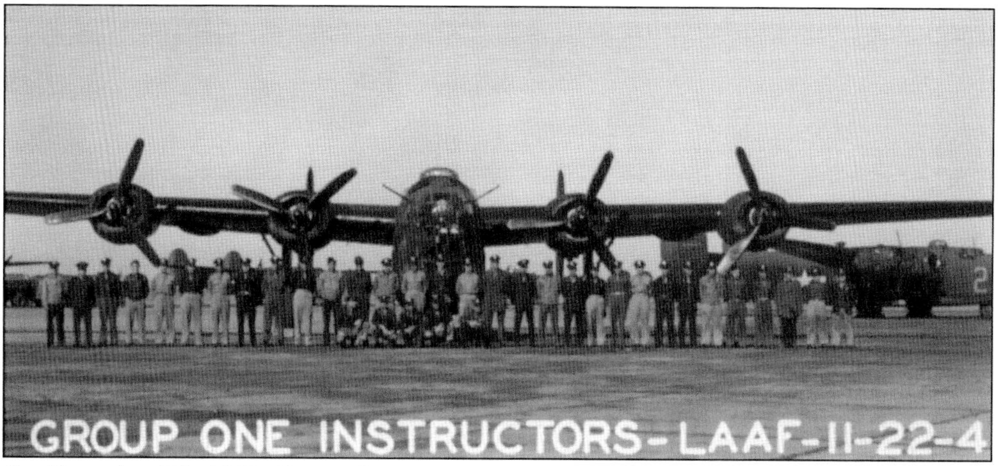

On November 22, 1943, Group One instructors pose in front of a B-24. These men had a difficult and tiring job to train the next set of newly transitioned pilots. There were four groups of instructors at the LAAF. The first group included Maj. Niels C. Christiansen Jr., operations officer; 1st Lt. Richard C. Gardner, flight commander; and 1st Lt. James H. McDaniel, squadron operations officer.

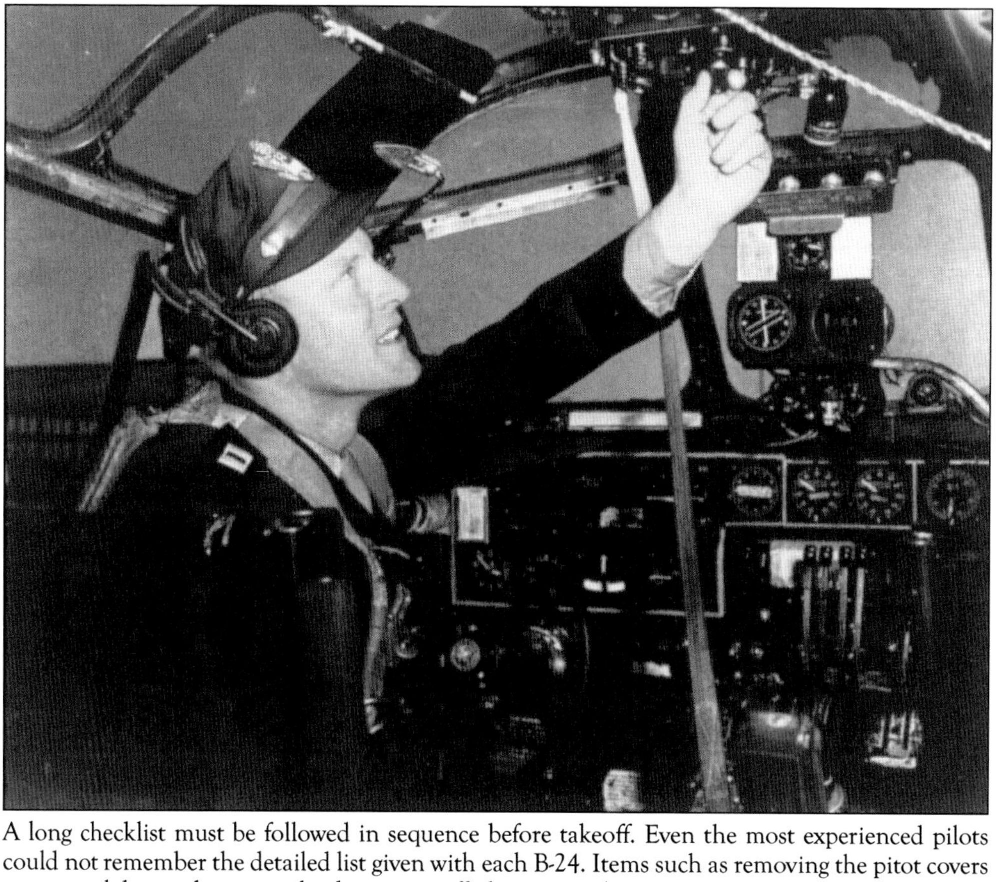

A long checklist must be followed in sequence before takeoff. Even the most experienced pilots could not remember the detailed list given with each B-24. Items such as removing the pitot covers are normal, but making sure the deicers are off, the intercoolers are open, and the cowl flaps open, in that order, had to be followed precisely.

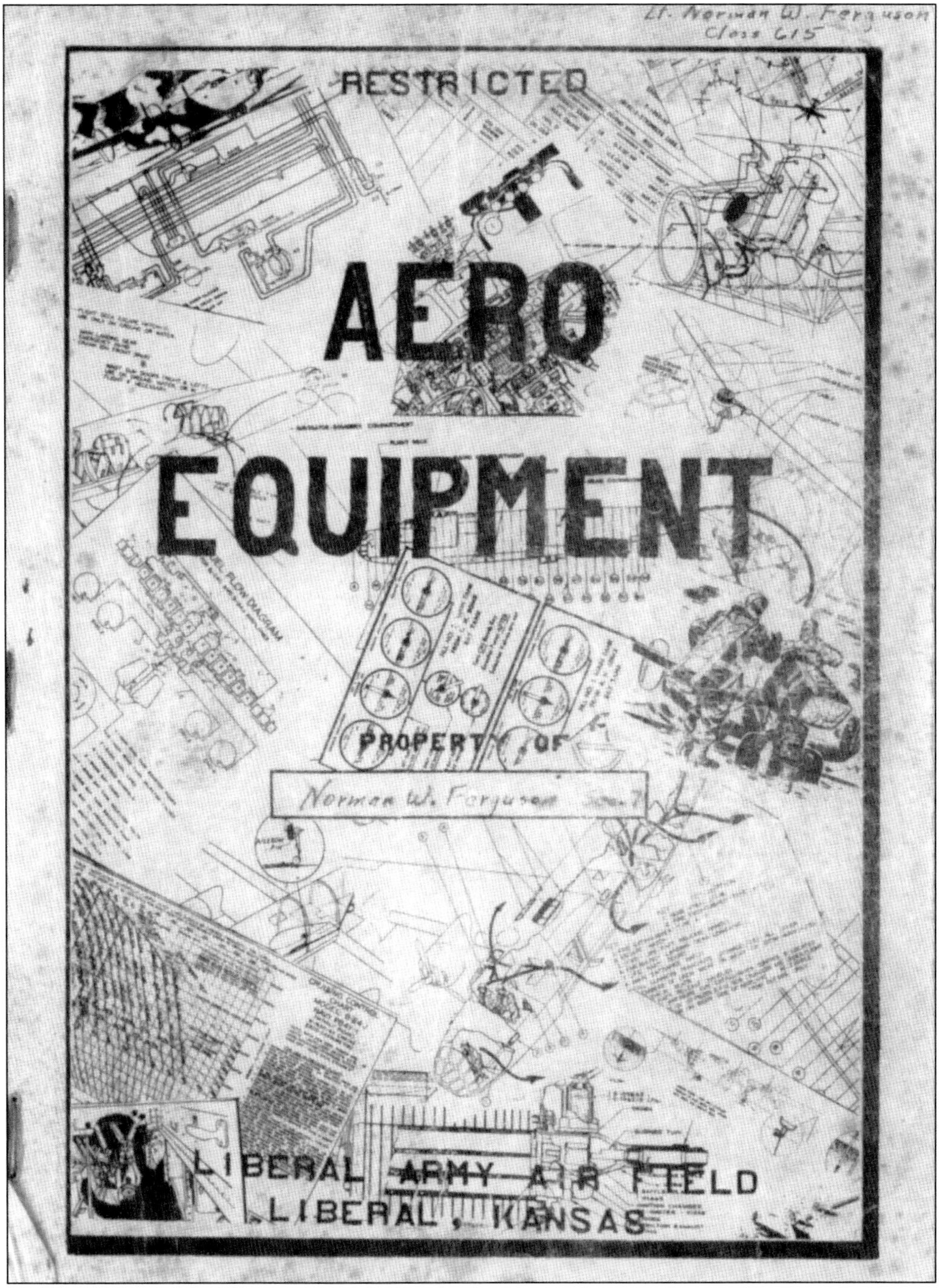

Commanders need to know all aspects of their Liberators. All student pilots were handed out Restricted Training Manuals such as this one studied by 2nd Lt. Norman W. Ferguson. An example of a test question was "The inverts are located where?" Second Lieutenant Ferguson answered correctly.

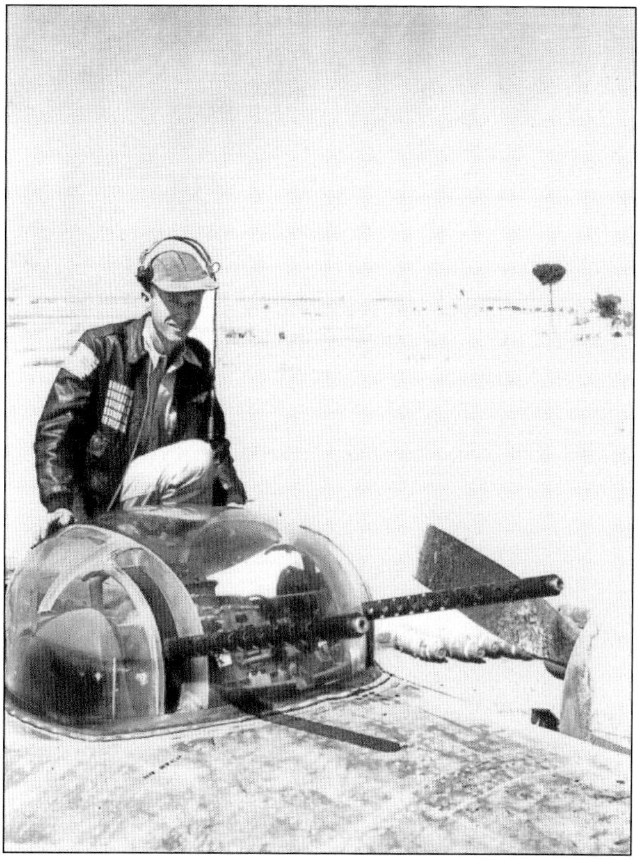

This image shows a serviceman sitting atop a B-24 turret, which was nicknamed the "High Hat." The Plexiglas dome with a replaceable centerpiece was a sighting window to aid in accuracy when shooting the twin .50 caliber guns. The dome, two stories up, gave him a 360-degree view. The bombs on the ground wait to be loaded. (Courtesy of Connie Bowman)

Inside a B-24, a waist gunner is lining up his 65-pound .50 caliber machine gun. Another gunner would be stationed directly behind him, both covering the right and left sides of the plane. With open doors, the waist gunner position was extremely cold, as was the nose gunner on a B-24. Protection from frostbite and noise was essential. (Courtesy of Connie Bowman.)

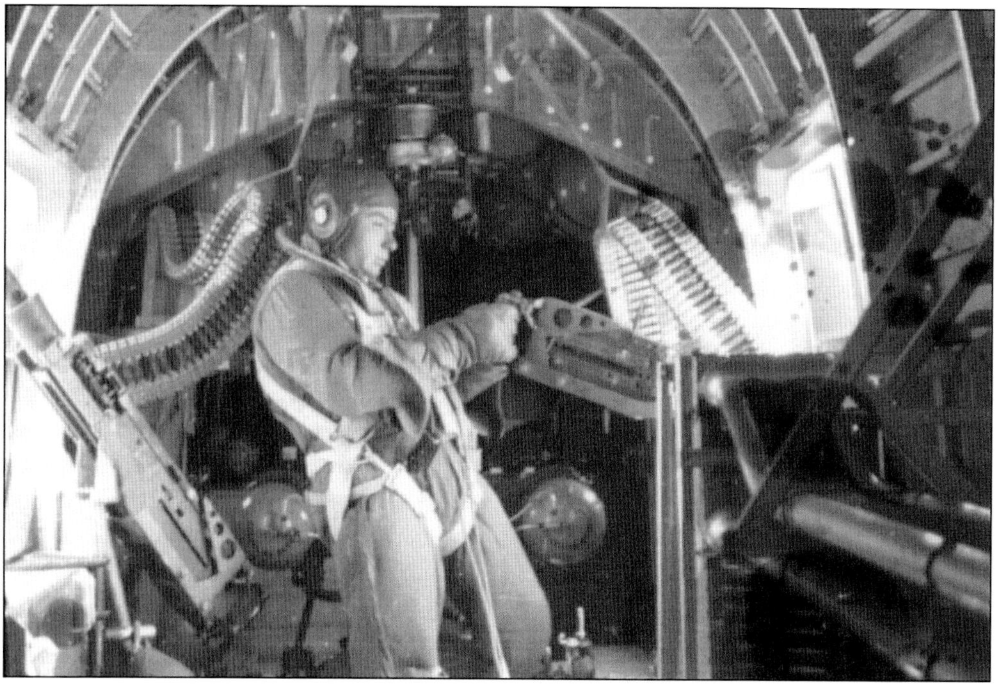

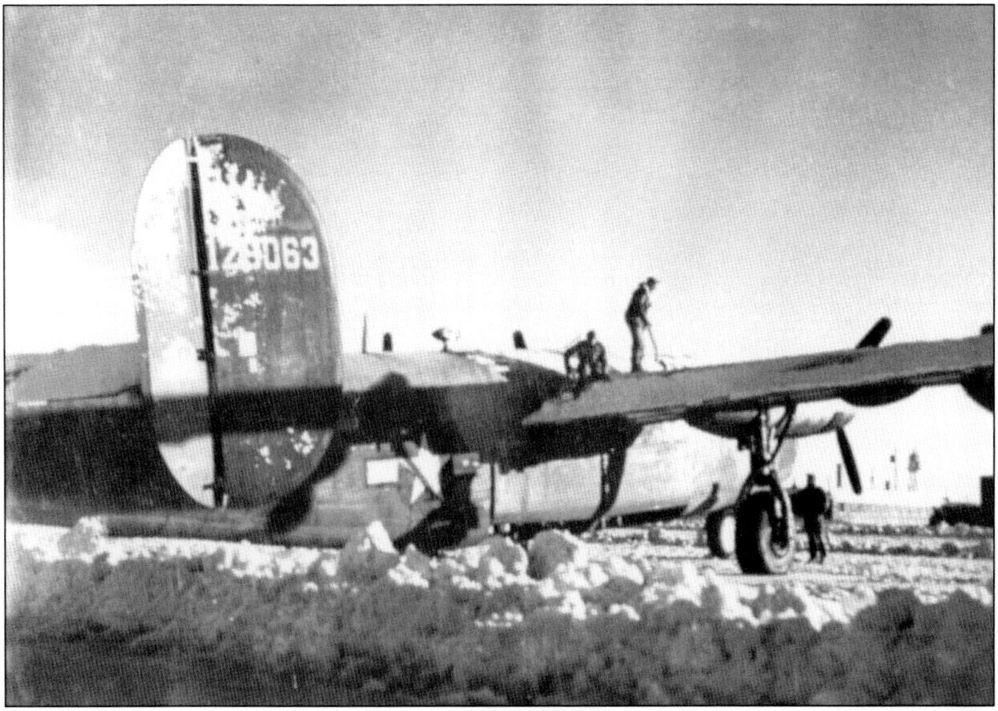

Snow and wind played havoc with the personnel and equipment during the harsh winters of 1943 and 1944. Flight engineer Oriole Rome recorded eight feet of snow on the runways, making it impossible for the big planes to fly, leading to wrecks and the destruction of equipment.

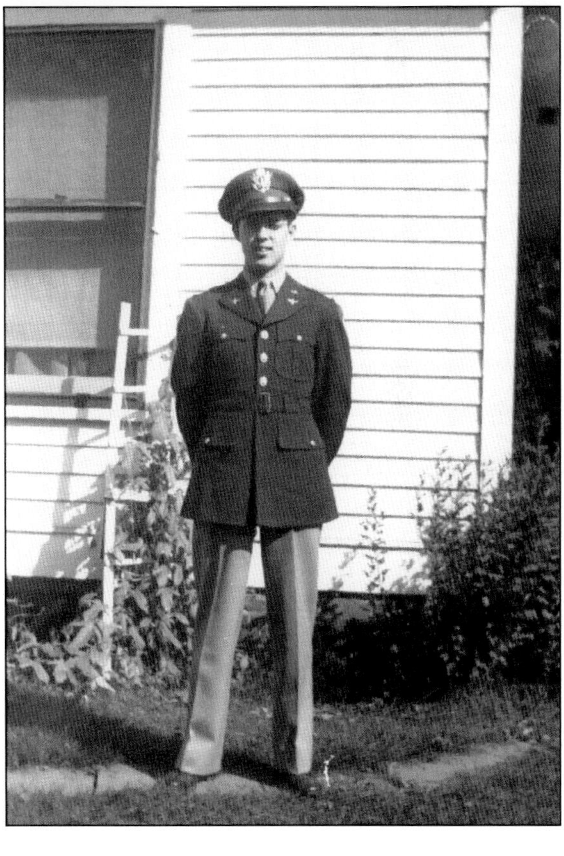

Born in Iowa, Eugene W. Slaymaker enlisted in the Army Air Force on June 17, 1942. First going to radio school, then basic and technical schools, 2nd Lieutenant Slaymaker transitioned to Liberal, becoming a ground school instructor. He married a local girl and remained in Liberal.

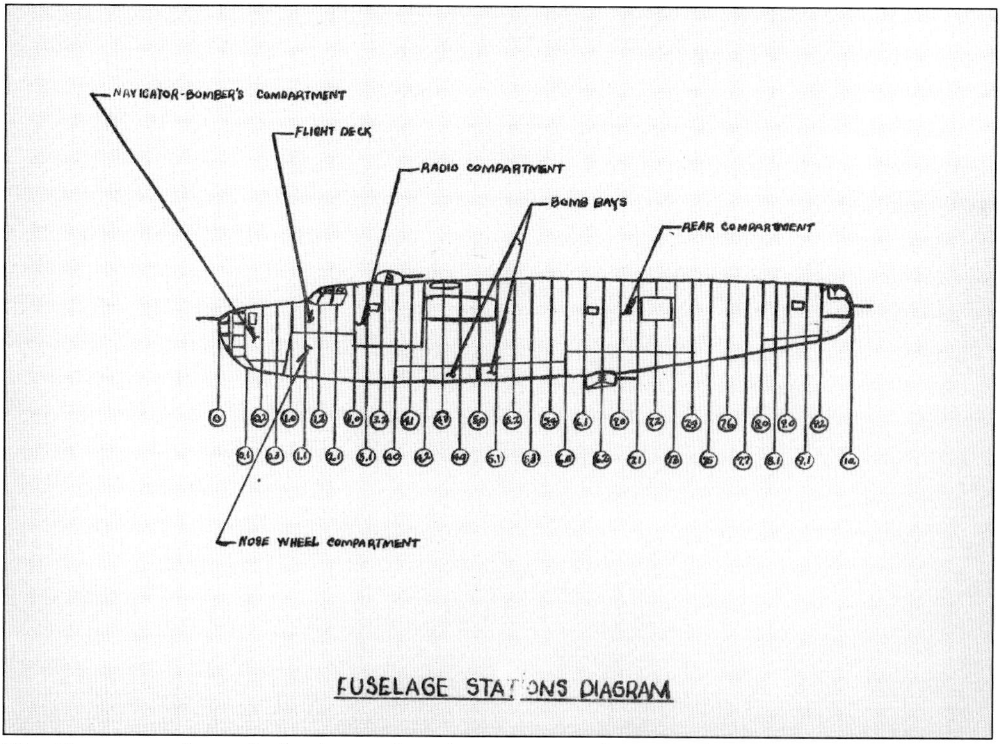

The Davis wing design had a lower drag than previous designs, which allowed higher speeds. Wings were also thicker, which allowed more fuel, giving the B-24 the ability to fly long distances as diagramed here. These diagrams were taken from a pilot's training manual.

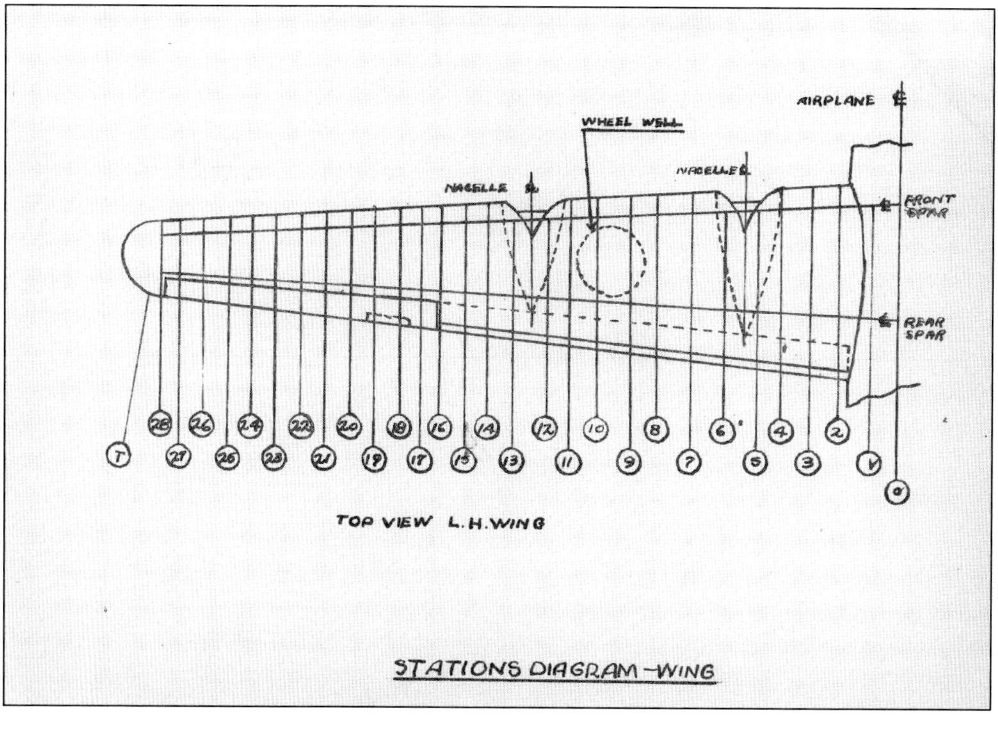

Standing under the 63rd (2 Engine) Flying Training Detachment sign are four friends. From left to right are Sgt. John M. Frey, S.Sgt. Elton Yates Dizmang, S.Sgt. Joseph Goyne, and S.Sgt. William E. Porton. Sadly, Staff Sergeant Dizmang was killed on Thanksgiving Day 1944 when two B-24s crashed head-on just north of the airfield. The 63rd was known as a primary flying school that taught flying concepts. Overseeing the unit was 1st Lt. Clare W. Reggin. This photograph was taken in 1943.

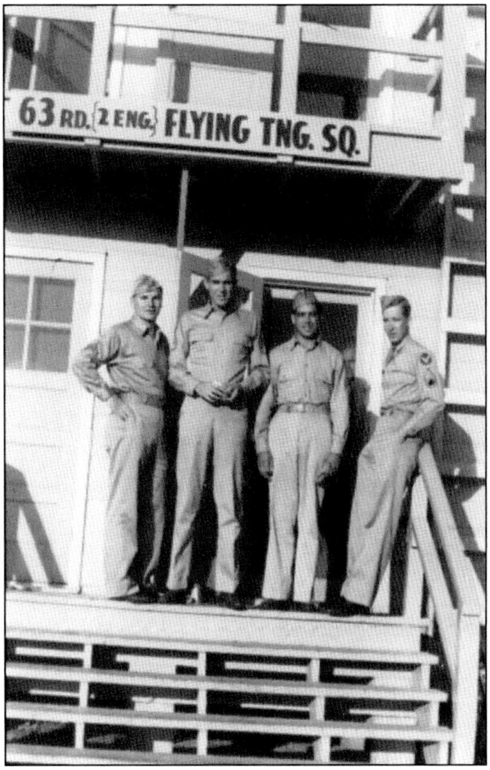

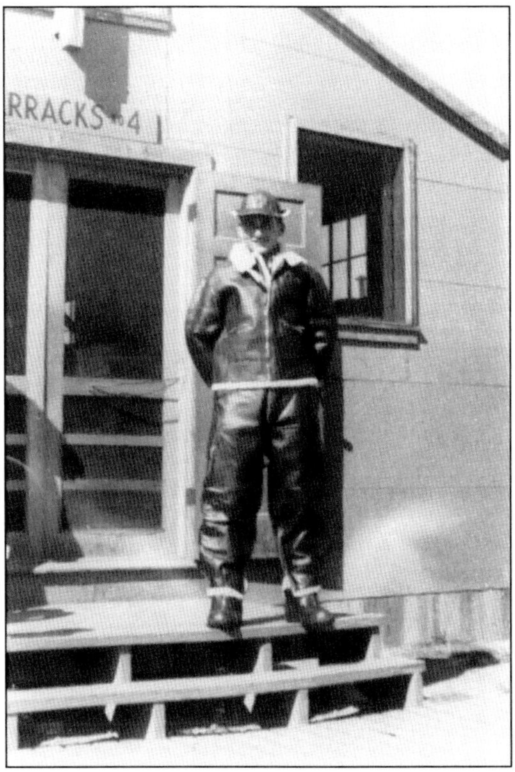

Just trying to stay warm in a non-pressurized aircraft like the B-24 at high altitude was a battle of its own. Sporting a B-2 hat, a B-3 jacket, and A-3 pants, all made of heavy leather shearling, this airman is ready for high-altitude training. Completing his ensemble are A-6 boots. Vast improvements were made as the war continued with lighter suits, boots, and gloves that all could be electrically heated.

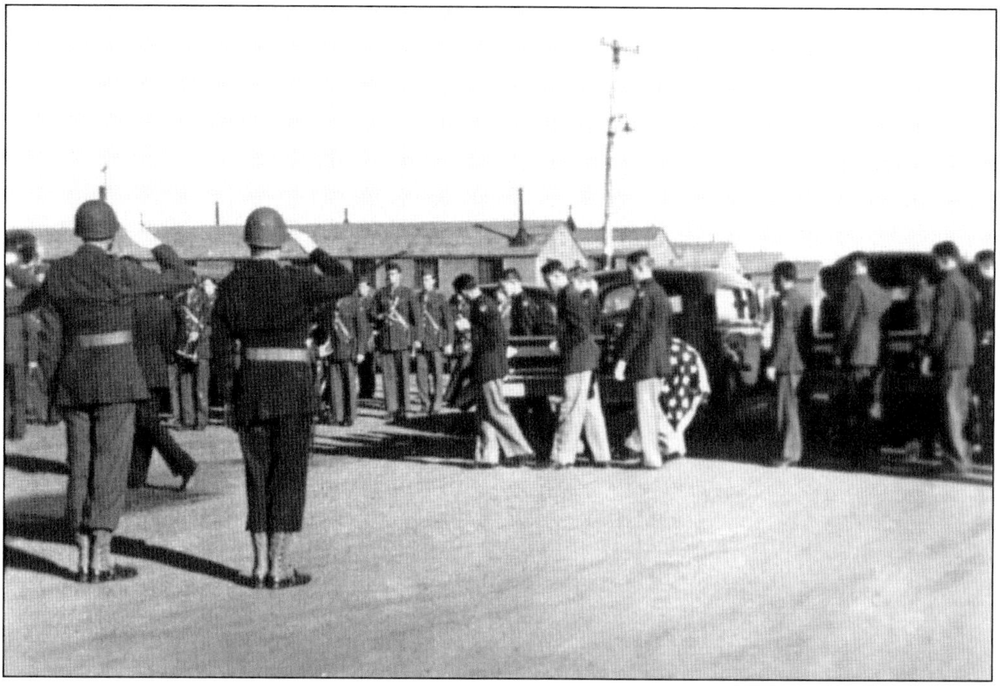

Regretfully, the base saw several occasions when a funeral was held at the LAAF chapel. A military funeral is a burial rite given for any soldier, sailor, marine, or airman who dies in service of his country. A military funeral may feature guards of honor, firing a volley of shots and usually concludes with the playing of "Taps." An American flag would be prominently draped over the casket and carefully folded by military personnel and ceremoniously presented to a surviving family member.

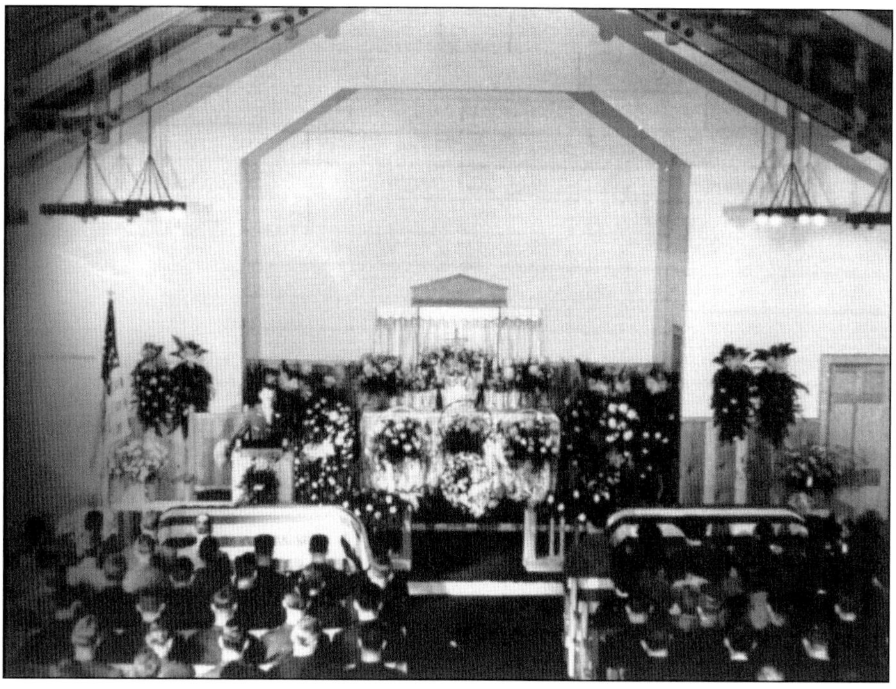

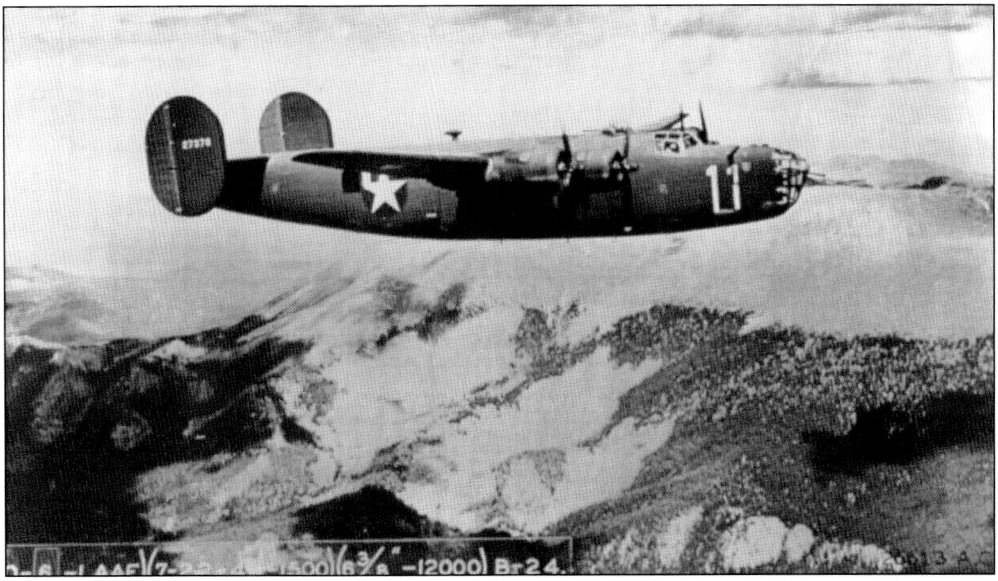

Training flights covered a great amount of area. This image was taken over the Rocky Mountains, which probably took the B-24 less than an hour to reach from Liberal. This plane was a B-24D manufactured by Consolidated. The B-24A, B-24D, the B24-E, the XB-24F, the B-24G, the B-24H, the B-24J, the XB-24K, the B-24L, the B-24M, and the B-24N went through 1,820 engineering changes while in production.

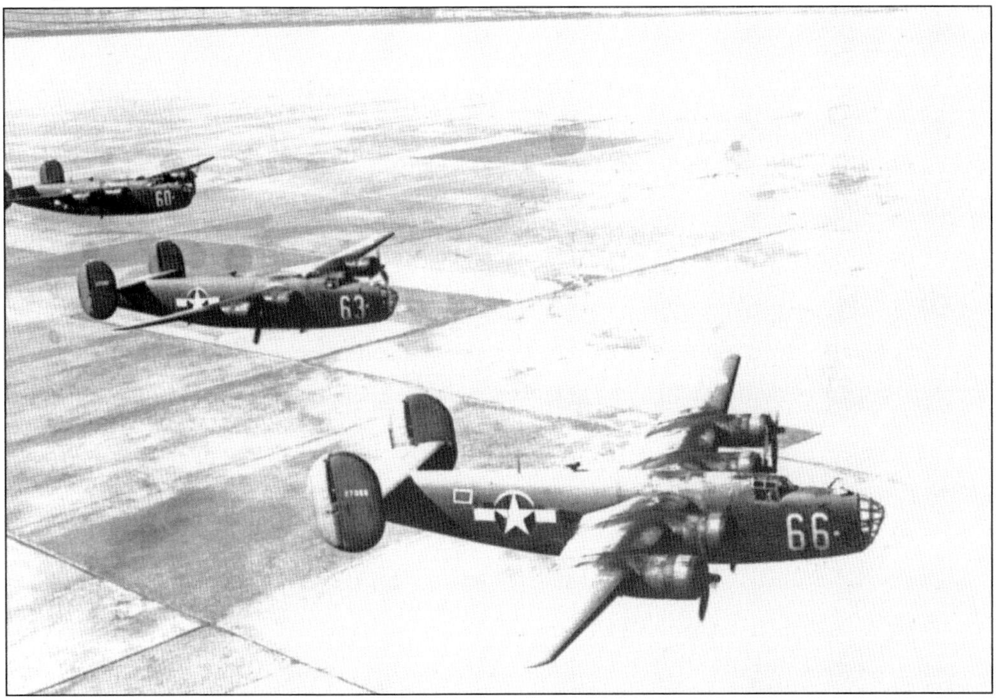

Three B-24s from LAAF fly in formation over an unpopulated area. The staggered formation, also known as the "combat box," was used as a defensive purpose to maximize the effectiveness of the bomber's guns. This formation was almost exclusively used in the European theater for combat missions during World War II.

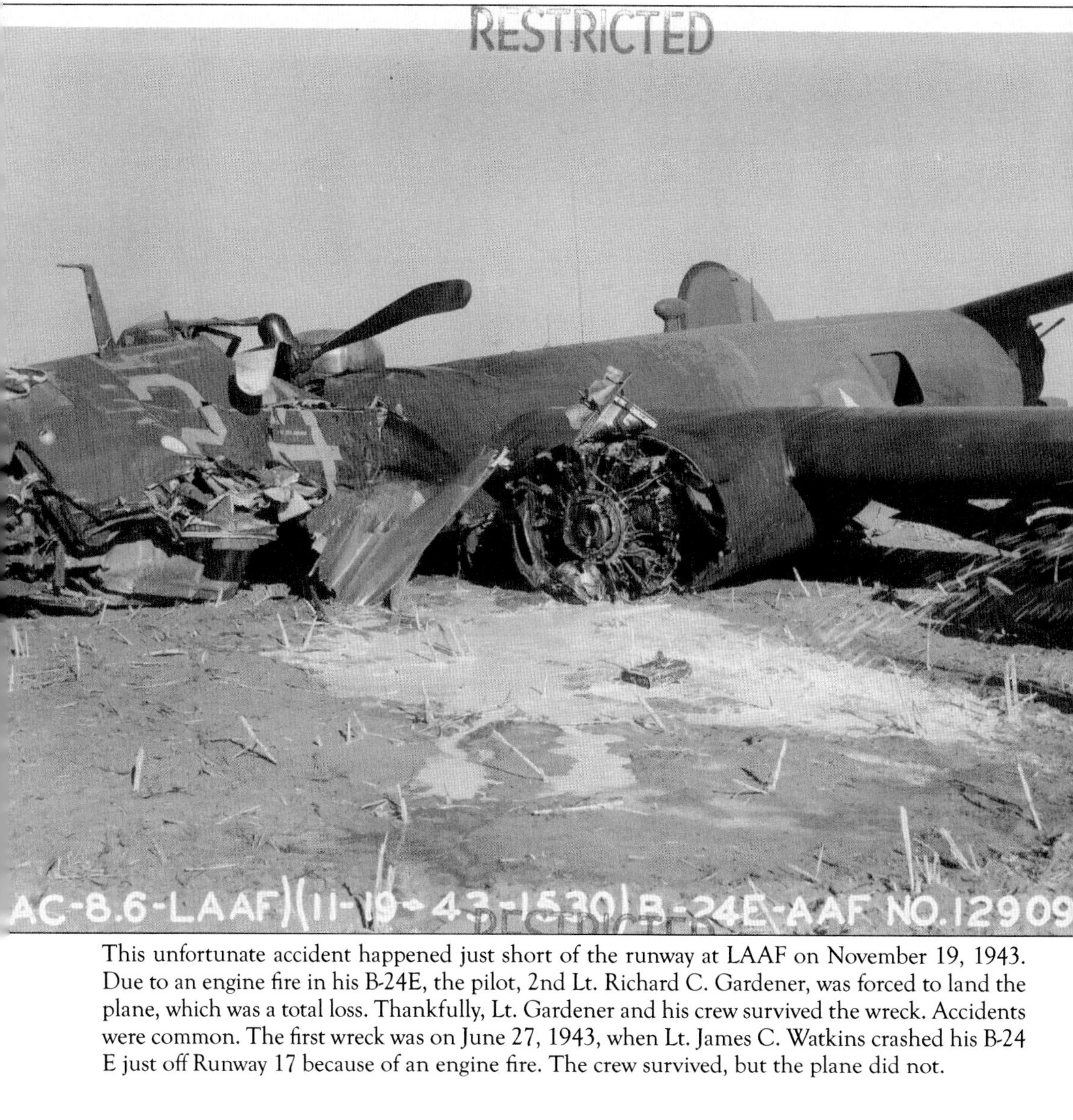

This unfortunate accident happened just short of the runway at LAAF on November 19, 1943. Due to an engine fire in his B-24E, the pilot, 2nd Lt. Richard C. Gardener, was forced to land the plane, which was a total loss. Thankfully, Lt. Gardener and his crew survived the wreck. Accidents were common. The first wreck was on June 27, 1943, when Lt. James C. Watkins crashed his B-24 E just off Runway 17 because of an engine fire. The crew survived, but the plane did not.

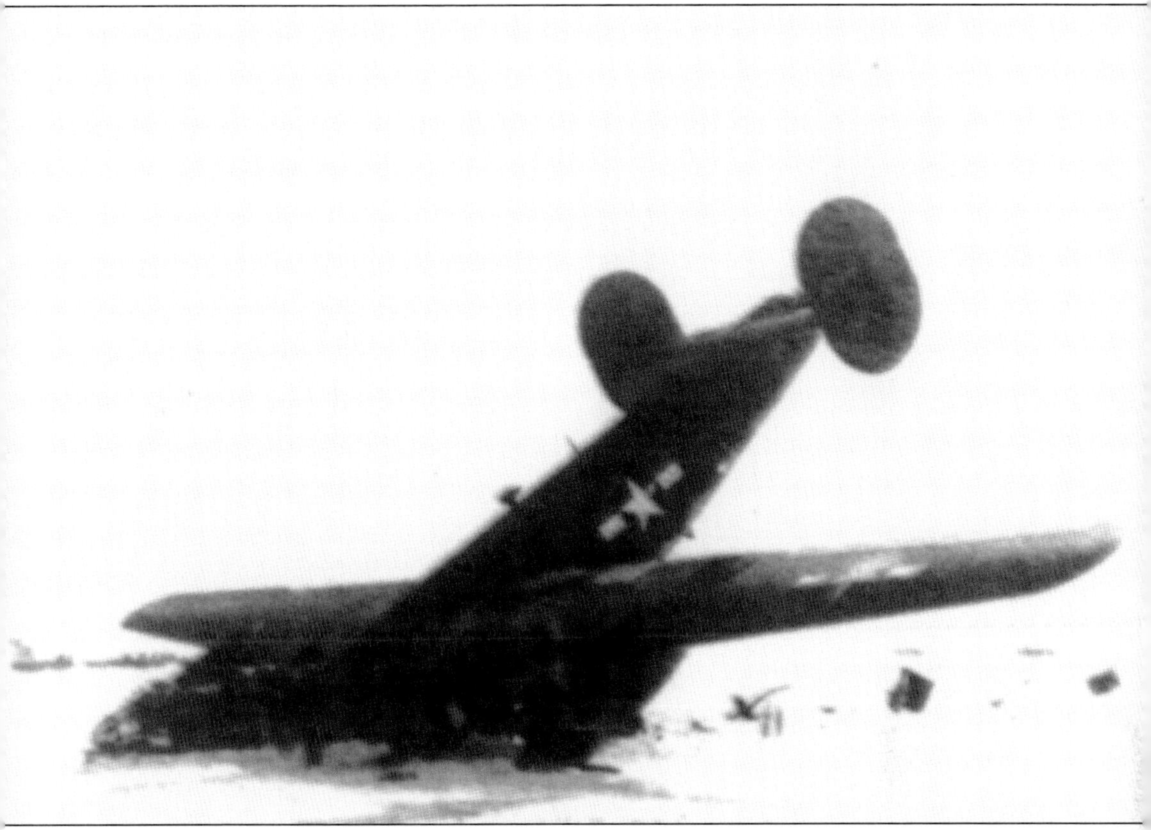

This B-24 crashed nose-down in the snow. It is unknown what caused this mishap but the weather conditions in the winters of 1943 and 1944 were very harsh. To be ready to fly in all conditions, crews were ordered to fly in the worst of conditions by Colonel Bump. An area at the edge of the base soon had a collection of wrecked planes. The planes supplied workers with everything from windshields to engine parts. There were 111 recorded crashes from the LAAF.

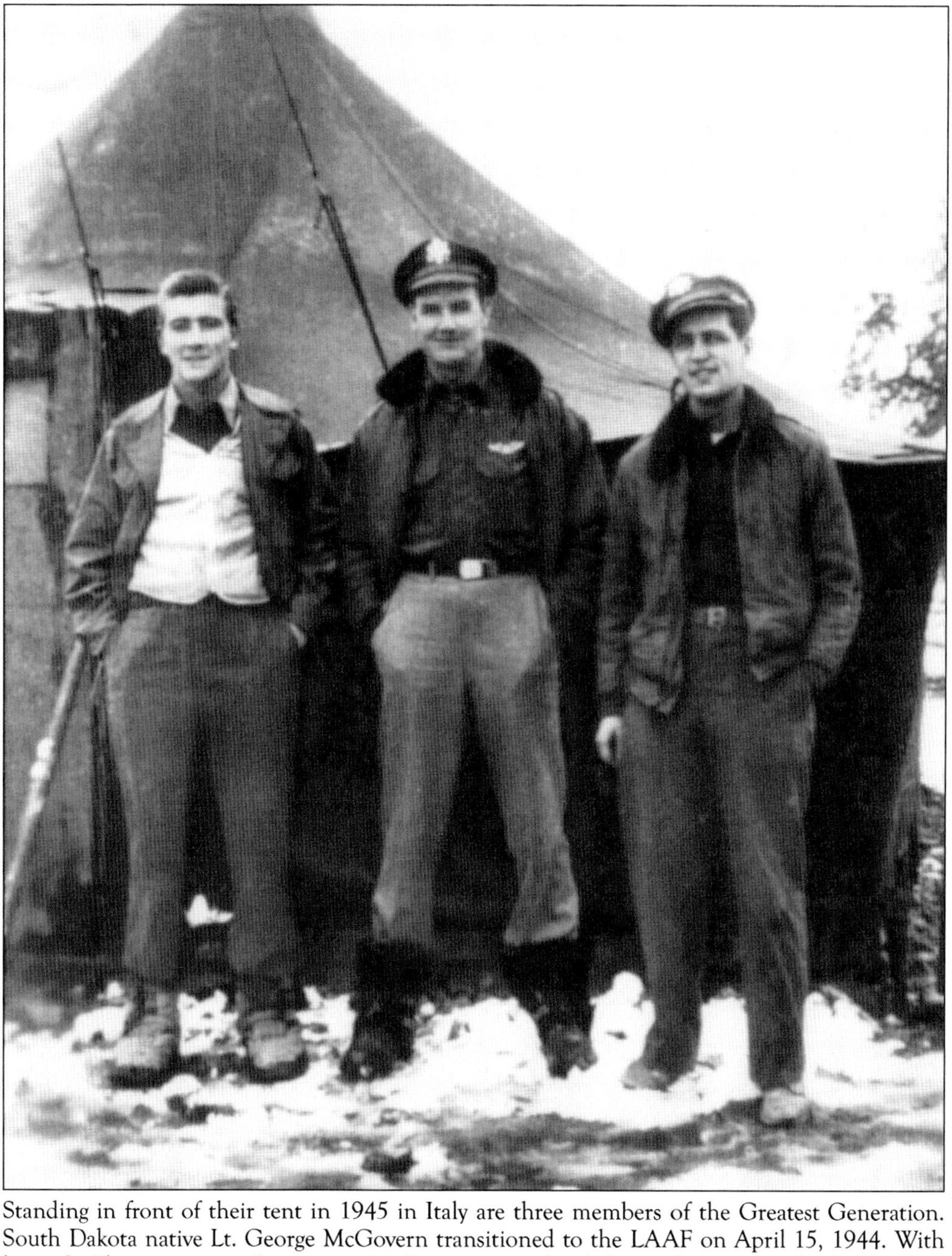

Standing in front of their tent in 1945 in Italy are three members of the Greatest Generation. South Dakota native Lt. George McGovern transitioned to the LAAF on April 15, 1944. With his wife, Eleanor, in tow, Lieutenant McGovern immediately began learning to fly the big four-engine planes. Unlike some, he found the B-24s reassuring. On his first day of training, Lieutenant McGovern was surprised to see the same man who encouraged him to fly in 1940 was his instructor, Norman Ray. Lieutenant McGovern flew 35 missions over Europe, earning the Distinguished Flying Cross. After serving in the US House of Representatives and Senate, McGovern ran for president in 1972, losing to Richard Nixon. Pictured here are Lt. Bill Rounds, co-pilot; Lieutenant McGovern; and Sam Adams, navigator/bombardier. (Courtesy of George McGovern collection, Dakota Wesleyan University Archives, Mitchell, South Dakota.)

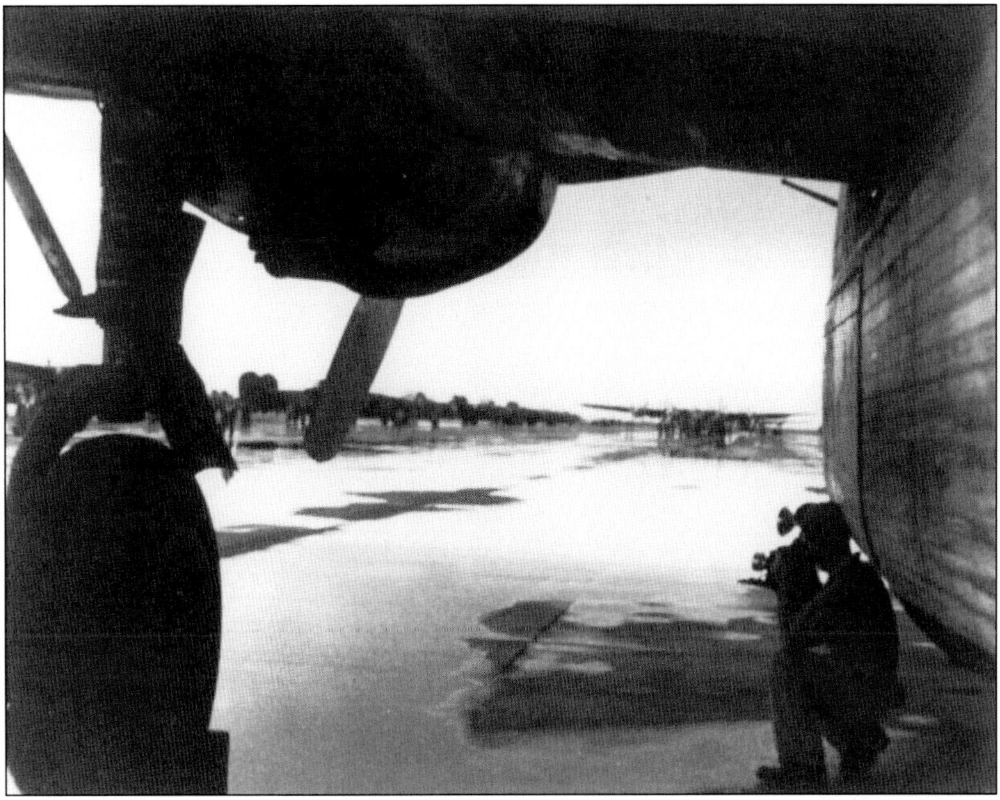

Taking shelter from an evening rainstorm under the wing of a B-24, a base photographer readies to capture a group of B-24s taxing down the tarmac. The base photographer recorded visual information for the Army Air Corps' record keeping. This image shows the photographer unknowingly being photographed.

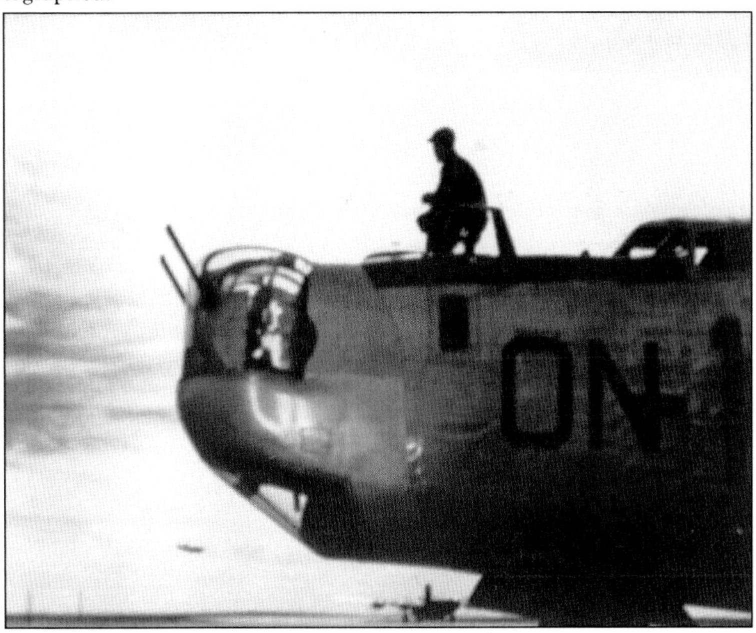

The silhouette of a lone serviceman sitting atop a B-24 nose as it taxied in on the tarmac is thought-provoking. Another B-24 follows it in, and another is about to land on an unusually calm day in southwest Kansas. The field was constantly moving men and planes.

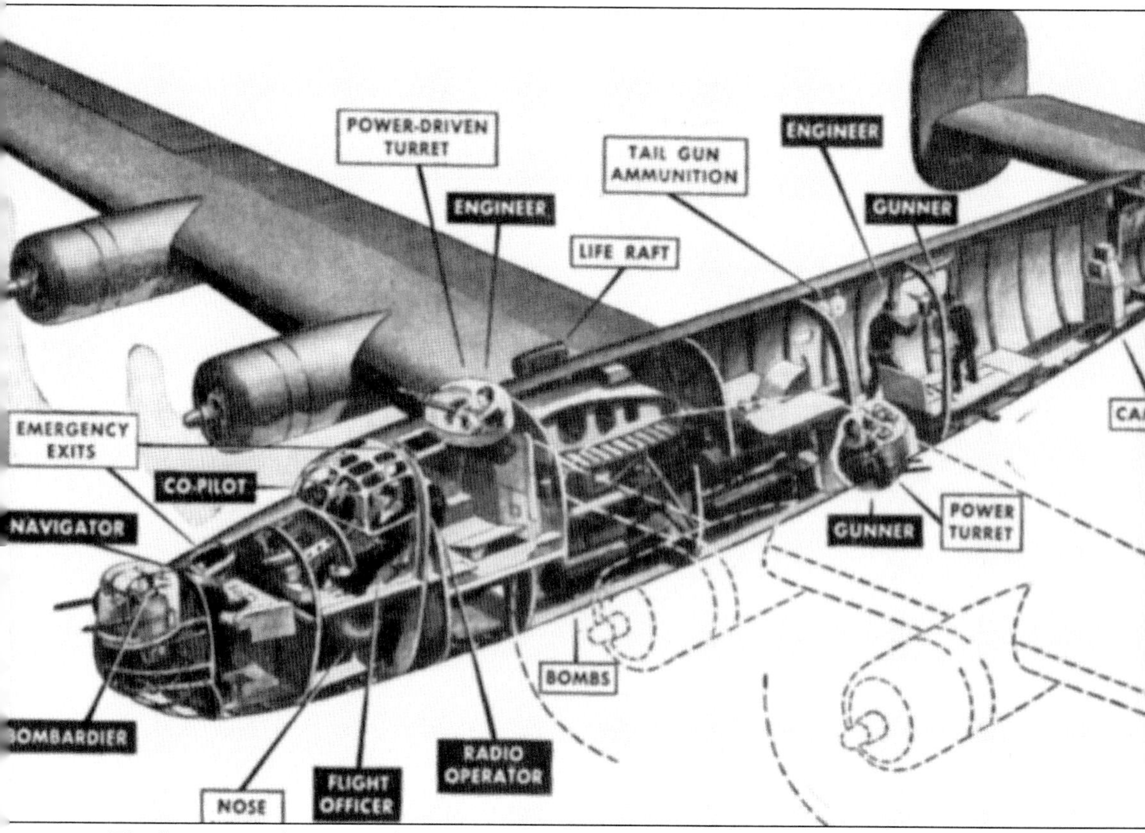

The four-engine, long-range bomber could travel 3,000 miles without refueling. Its airspeed could reach 300 miles per hour and could carry more than 10 tons of explosives. It was called many names but officially was named the Liberator. The bomber was considered the workhorse by many who flew it during World War II. Over 18,000 Liberators of different models and improvements were built. Consolidated Vultee Aircraft Corporation had 12 factories across America producing 100 planes every hour at the height of the war. The real beauty of the B-24 is the flight crewmembers, who occupied every position inside.

Four

LIFE ON BASE

The airfield became busy with over 4,000 people, including military and civilian personnel who worked and trained on the base. Life was hectic with personnel arriving, new buildings being constructed, planes coming in, and people getting to know each other. The two theaters played popular movies, and with admission being 15¢, they were well attended. The chapel ministered to all faiths and beliefs and was open 24 hours a day for all personnel. The three commissaries were busy keeping shelves stocked. Showers, latrines, and barracks for both enlisted men and officers were of the mobilization types, which went up quickly along with dining halls, a 142-bed hospital, the commissaries, theaters, and a chapel. The training facilities included three school buildings and four Link training facilities. Also constructed were five hangars, massive gasoline storage facilities, and a spur off the main Rock Island Railroad that supplied the airfield. Those tracks can still be driven over today. The base quickly doubled the population of Liberal. The airfield was a city on its own, with services offered from A to Z.

The base always included the Liberal townspeople in celebrations, and in turn, the base personnel were always welcome to town events. Everything from dances to dinners, to holiday celebrations to funerals, were attended by all. The USO and the Red Cross were popular venues in Liberal and on base. The local economy received a boost from the additional construction workers and base personnel who patronized local businesses.

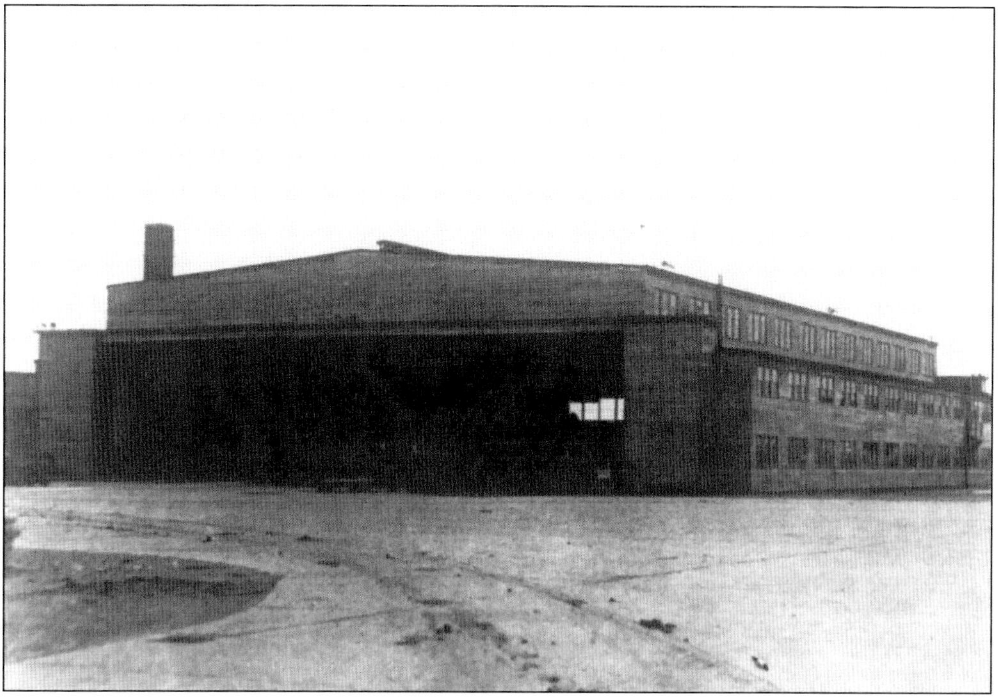

This hangar was one of three wooden hangars built. The aircraft inside the hangar are smaller than the B-24; they could be trainers, including the AT-6, the AT-7, the AT-11, the BT-13, or the B-25. Maintaining the planes provided practical training for the enlisted ground crew.

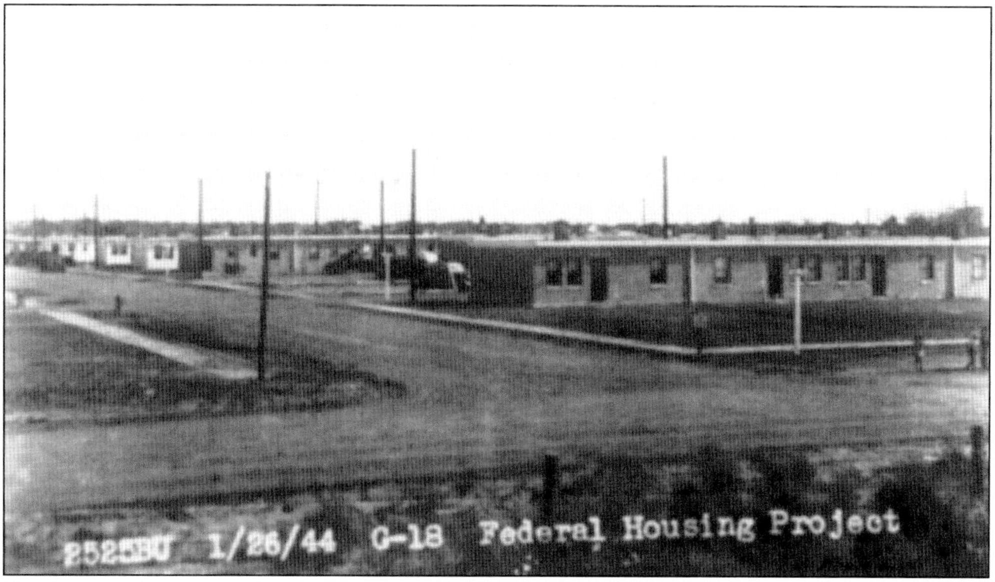

Bluebonnet Courts were born of necessity. With an additional 5,000 workers and base personnel, construction on the courts began in 1943, finishing in late December 1943. Bluebonnet had 120 family units, renting for $30–$40 per month. They were of cinder block construction with natural gas heat and built-in refrigeration units. After the airfield was deactivated, the courts were occupied for years by Liberal townsfolk. It was demolished in 1979 and is now a beautiful park named Bluebonnet Park.

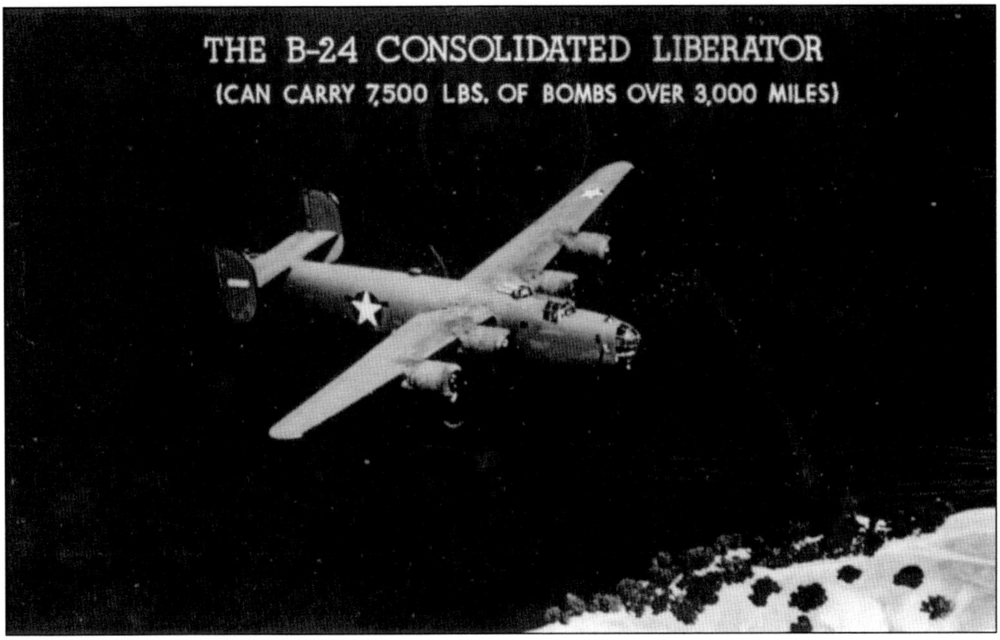

Postcards from loved ones were a welcome thing for the folks back home. Lt. William Skuskis from Brooklyn let his parents know he was now flying a "super boxcar." Postage was free to all servicemen during the war.

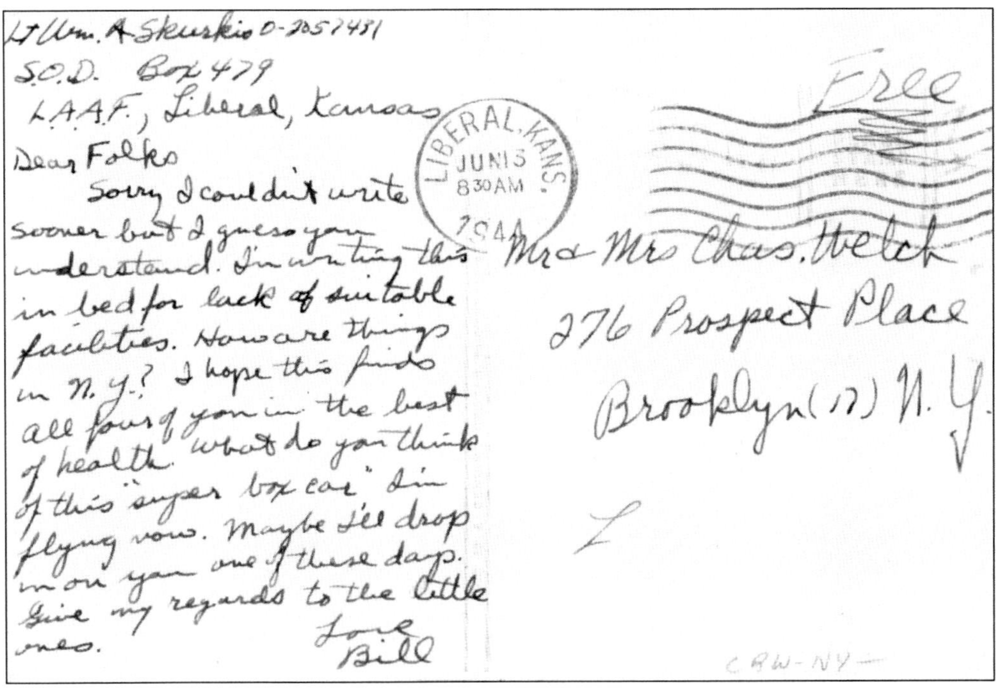

Lt Wm. A Skuskis O-2057481
S.O.D. Box 479
L.A.A.F., Liberal, Kansas

Dear Folks

Sorry I couldn't write sooner but I guess you understand. I'm writing this in bed for lack of suitable facilities. How are things in N.Y.? I hope this finds all four of you in the best of health. What do you think of this "super box car" I'm flying now. Maybe I'll drop in on you one of these days. Give my regards to the little ones.

Love
Bill

LIBERAL, KANS. JUN 15 8 30 AM 1944

Free

Mr & Mrs Chas. Welch
276 Prospect Place
Brooklyn (17) N.Y.

CRW-NY

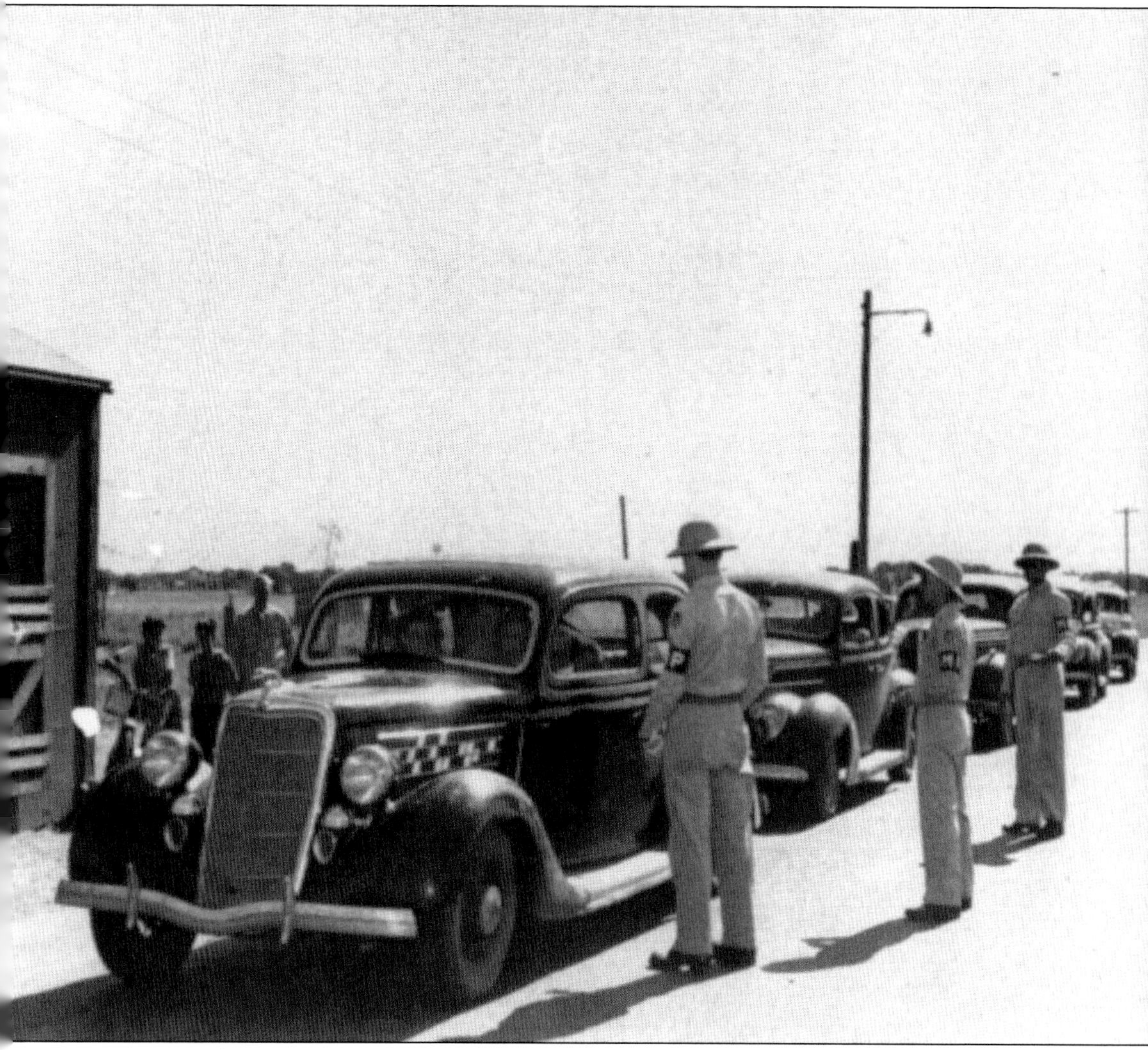

Security is high when there is a war going on. Anyone heading to the airfield through the South Gate was checked and scrutinized by base military police. The two children in the front auto do not seem to realize the seriousness of the situation.

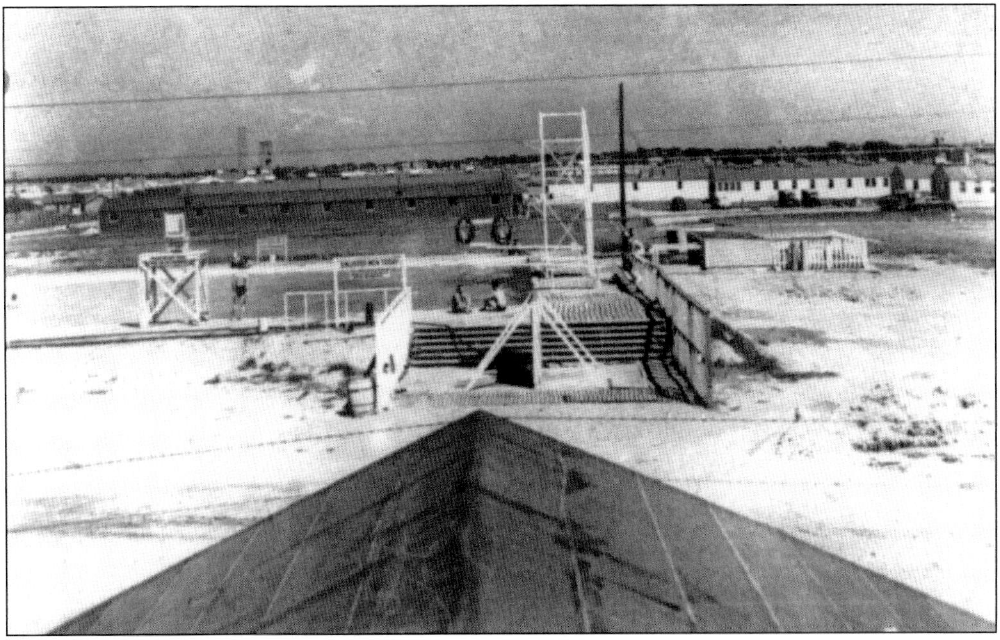

Dug by the airmen themselves, the base swimming pool offered a bit of reprieve from the hot summers. Enlisted men and officers alike enjoyed the cool water. A sign was posted indicating who could use the pool that day. The pool was located north of the ground school buildings and was also used to train men on surviving in the sea.

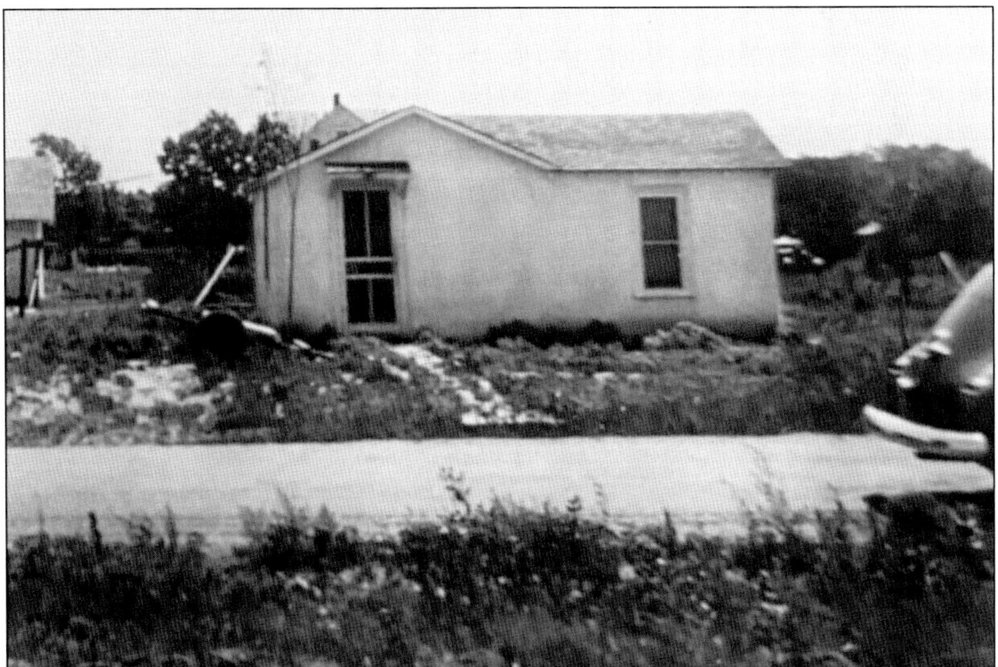

Looking like a garden shed, this little building is typical of a house that was rented off-base by an airman. The living room, dining, kitchen, bedroom, and bath were all in a convenient 140 square feet.

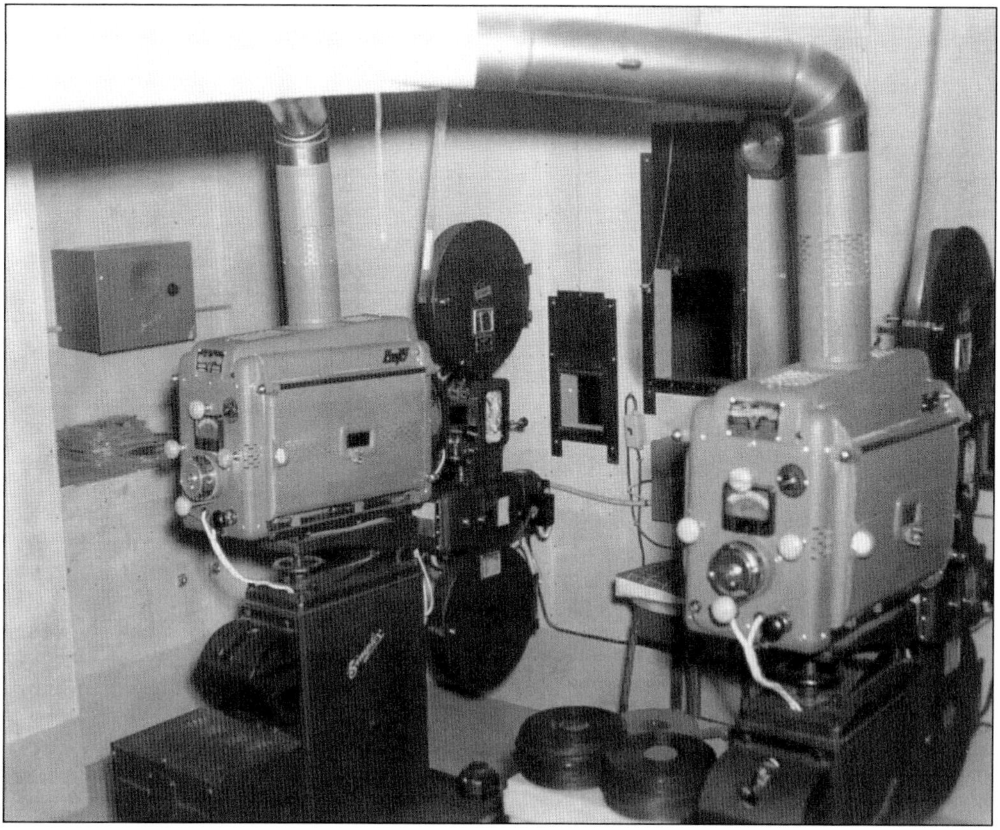

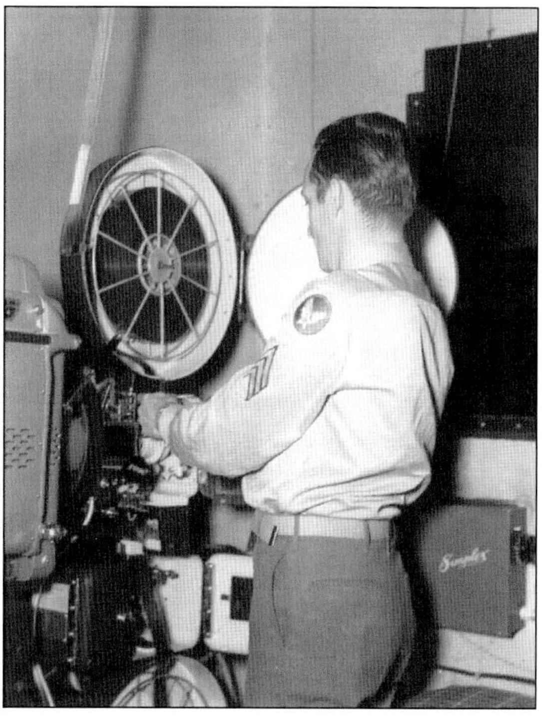

The base theater was equipped with the latest projectors. These 35 mm reel-to-reel carbon arc projectors were a difficult job for the projectionist to run. Two projectors were used because reels had to be changed every 18 to 20 minutes and rewound before loading another reel. Hollywood, like other industries, encountered many wartime problems. The government cut the amount of available film stock by 25 percent. It did not stop the servicemen or citizens from going to the movies. The war boosted movie attendance to near-record levels.

Jerry Colonna, pictured here, entertained many troops and was often Bob Hope's favorite sidekick. Colonna started his career as a trombonist and played in several orchestras. He is better known for his deadpan screech and comedy. Colonna took part in several of Bob Hope's early USO tours during the 1940s.

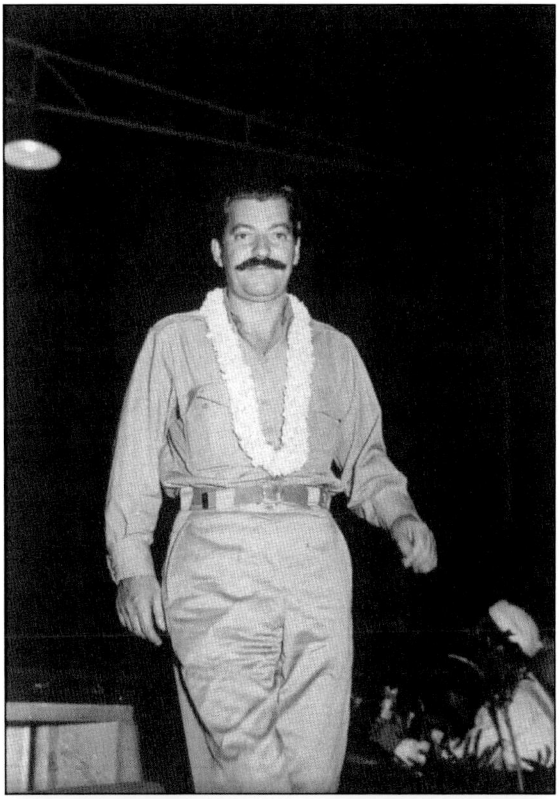

It was popular to poke fun at Adolph Hitler in comedy skits. Spike Jones and His City Slickers or Flanagan and Allen might have inspired this comedy routine put on by base soldiers. An essential part of maintaining morale was keeping troops entertained. Special Services also worked to ensure the GIs could produce their own entertainment. GIs staged and starred in "Soldier Shows," a wide range of variety shows, plays, and musical performances using scripts and songs distributed by Special Services.

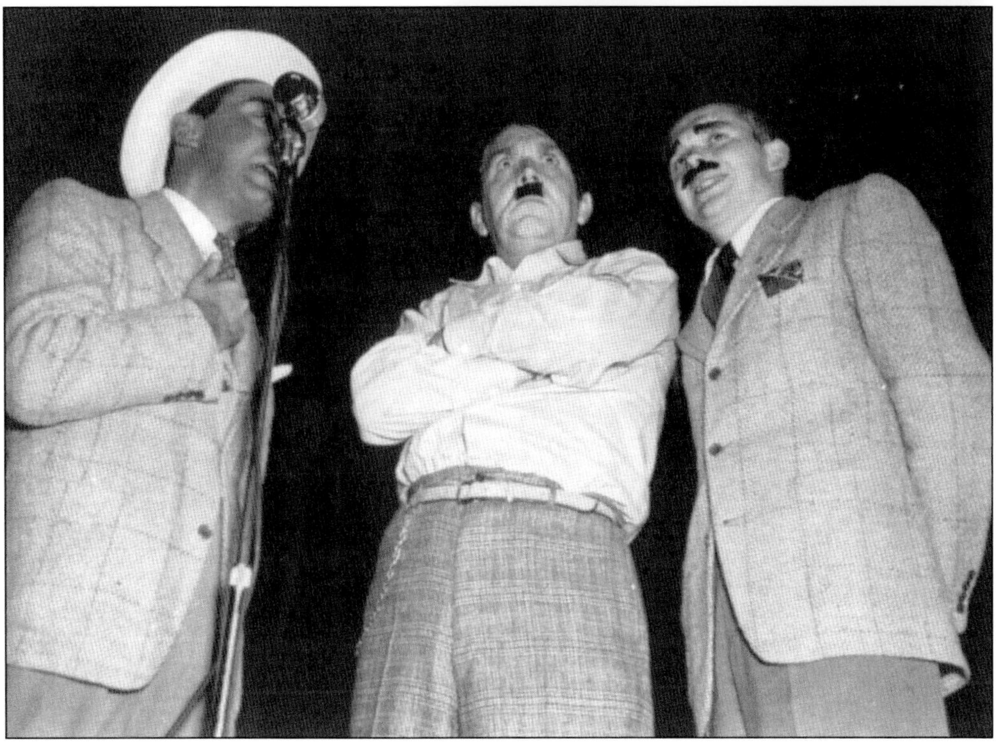

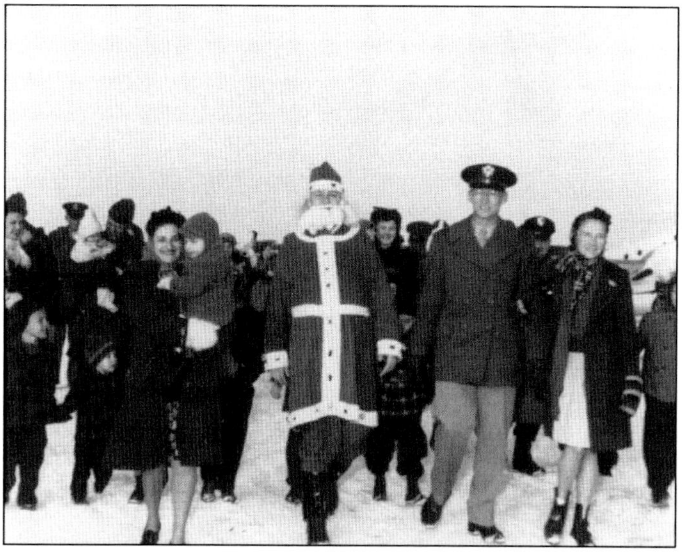

Is this a Christmas party or a walk to the North Pole? Base personnel, ladies, children, and of course, Santa are walking and smiling. Excitement was had even with boots, coats, and hats on with snow on the ground. Traditional Christmases looked a lot different to the families and soldiers during the war.

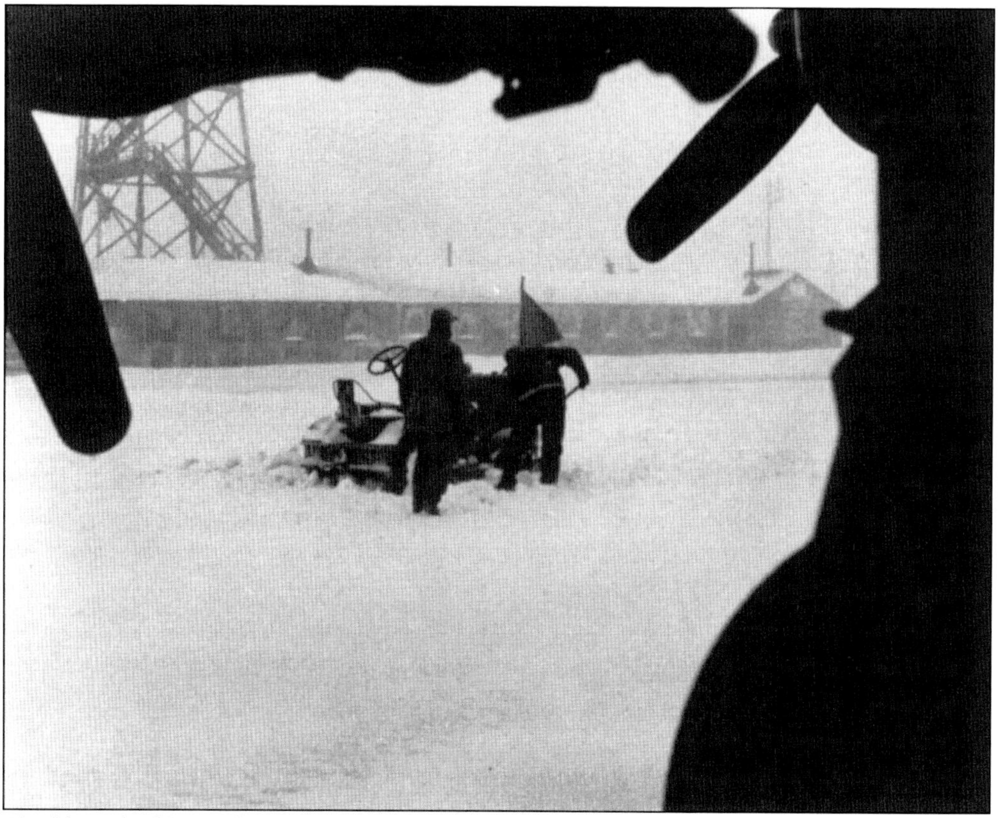

The blizzard of December 1943 was significant enough to shut the base down and have planes reassigned to other bases until conditions improved. Servicemen pictured here try valiantly to remove snow from the stuck vehicle. It was one of the worst winters, with snow drifts 10 feet high. It was so cold that S.Sgt. Oriole Richard Rome wrote that he wore two sets of wool pants, two wool shirts, a GI sweater, a lambskin fur jacket, an earmuff hat, gloves, and heavy-lined flight boots just to go to the mess hall.

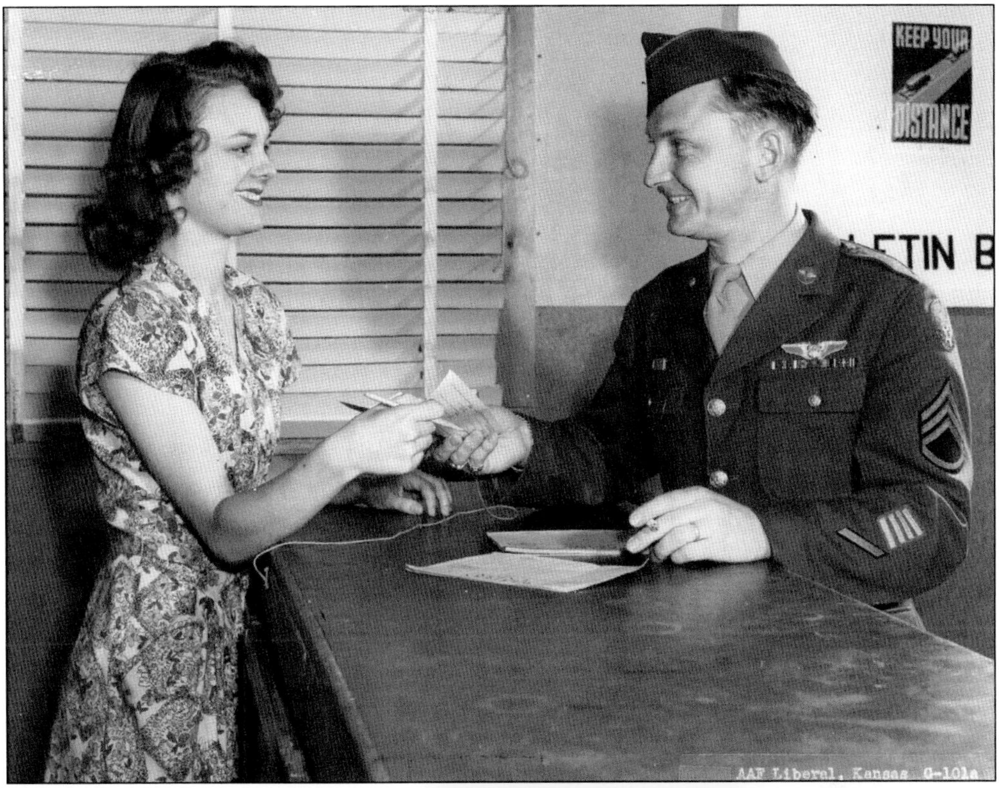

S.Sgt. Granville "Chick" Meseke came to Liberal from California. With a big smile and sharp appearance, Chick made a great model for LAAF life. After his training in Liberal, Chick joined his B-24 crew of "Little Lady," completing 25 missions. On the crew's last mission bombing Ploesti, the plane was damaged so badly, they could not hold altitude and crashed just into Turkey. Somehow, all crew members survived the crash landing. Chick and his fellow crew members were awarded the Distinguished Flying Cross and Air Medal.

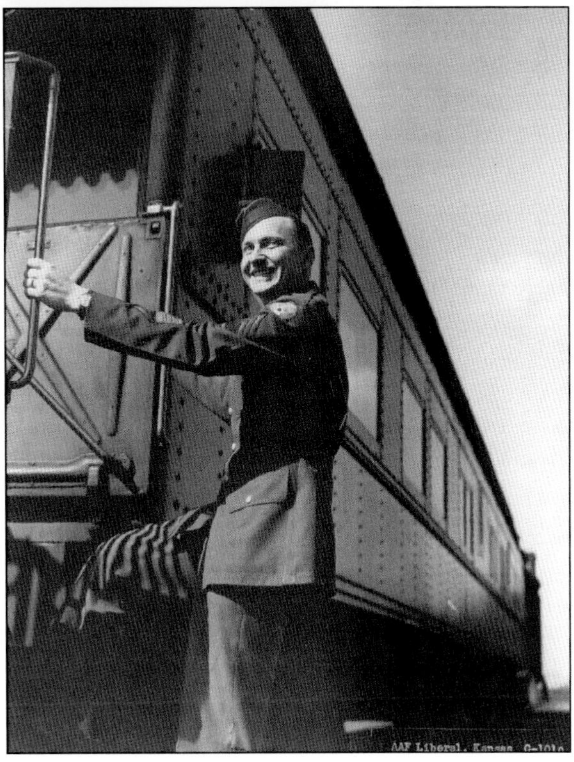

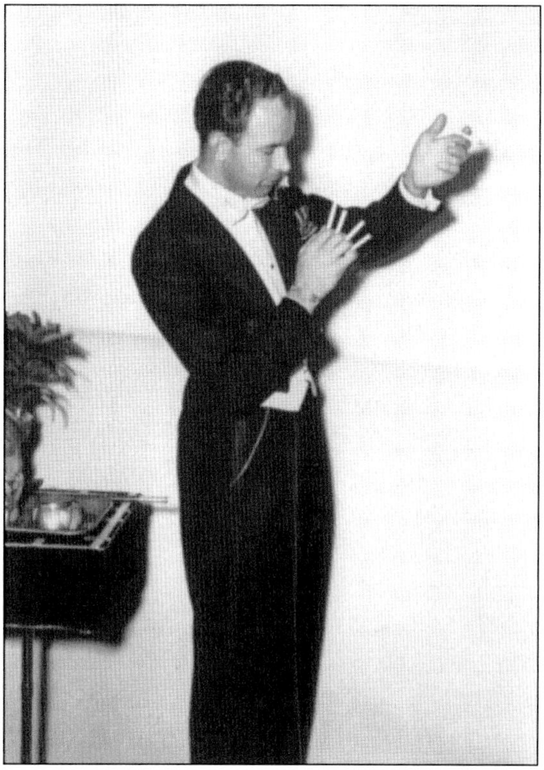

In 1944, Armed Services Edition published 100,000 pocket-sized copies of a popular book of magic so soldiers could entertain themselves. Entertainers from all over the country traveled in troupes or singularly, from base to base, with some putting on magic shows, like this magician.

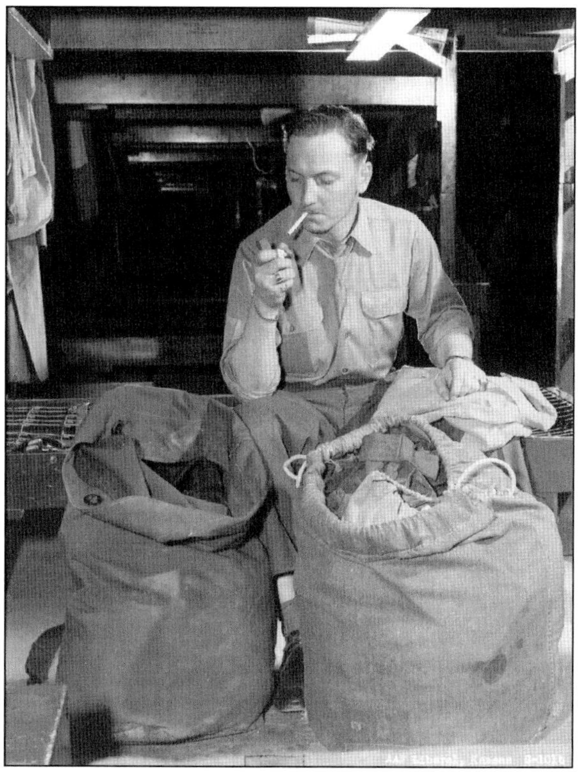

Is he headed out or transitioning in? Whichever it is, this airman seems to be contemplating what the future will bring. When men transitioned out of LAAF to their next base, it was to join their B-24 crew.

Taking a turn on the dance floor are the airfield's commander, Colonel Bump, and local beauty Jean Randall. Taken at a USO dance, they both seem to be having a great time. (Courtesy of the Jean Randall family.)

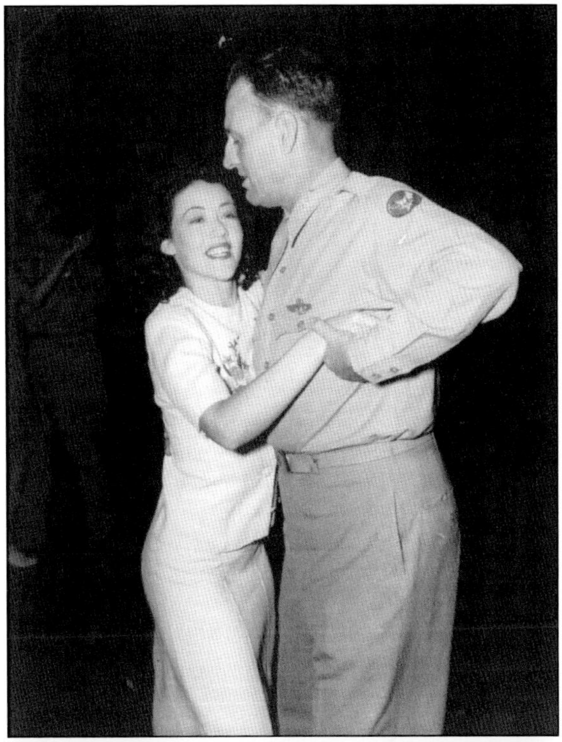

Colonel Bump seems delighted in cutting a cake decorated with the Army Air Forces insignia while a staff member looks on. Reflections in the mirror show several uniformed officers helping cheer on the event. A notation on the back of the photograph says, "Cake was excellent Jack." The cake was decorated by local bakery owner Jack Randall.

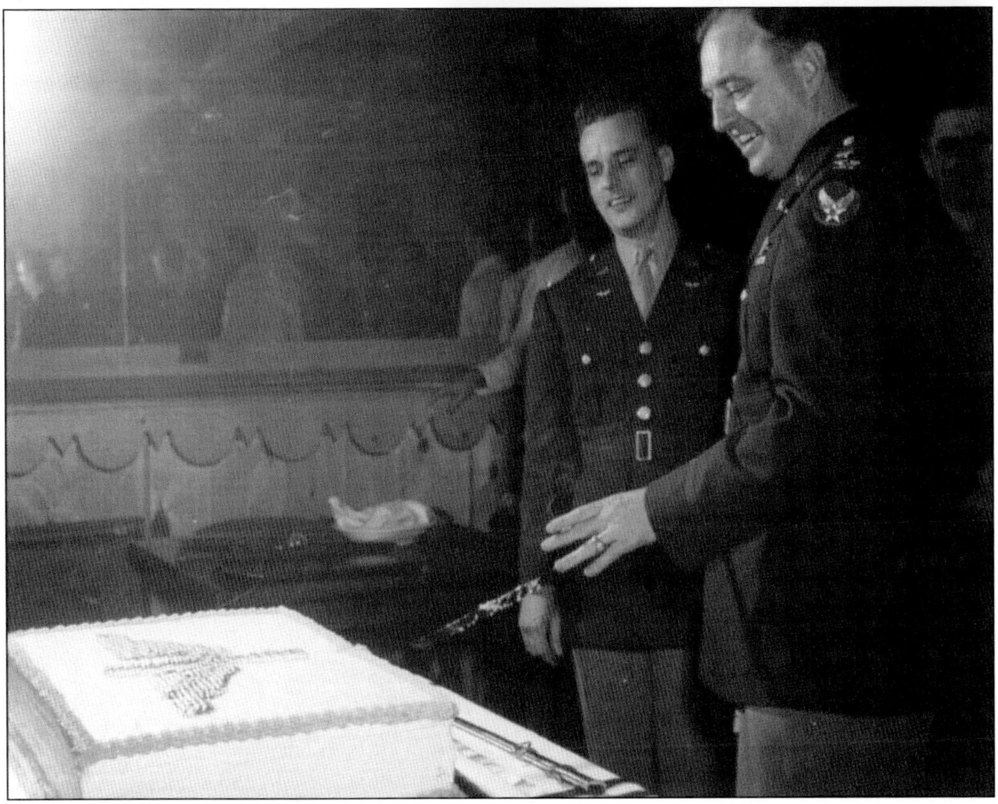

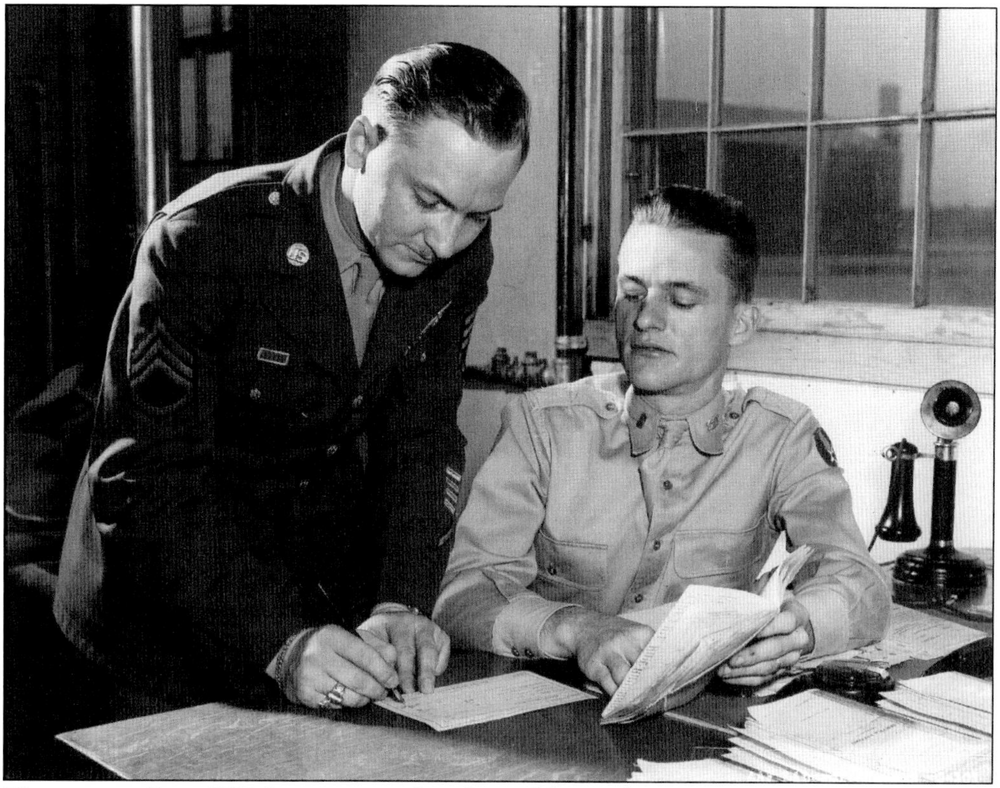

The warrant officers (WOs) comprise a relatively small but vital group of technicians and specialists who manage the requisitions, receipts, storage, retrograde, and distribution of supplies. They provided technical guidance to supported units/activities to maintain adequate stockage levels for everyone on base. Seated is WO H.C. McSwain; the sergeant is unknown.

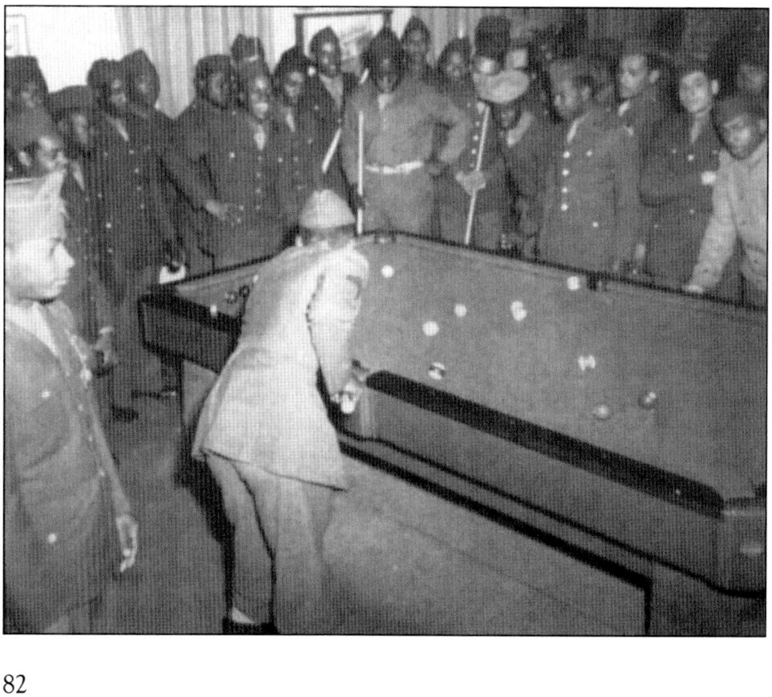

A little rest, relaxation, and a friendly game of pool do a lot to make the thoughts of war go away. The LAAF also carried on programs that featured basketball and baseball teams. In 1944, the baseball team, the Liberator Loops, won third place in the Kansas Semi-Pro Tournament in Wichita, Kansas.

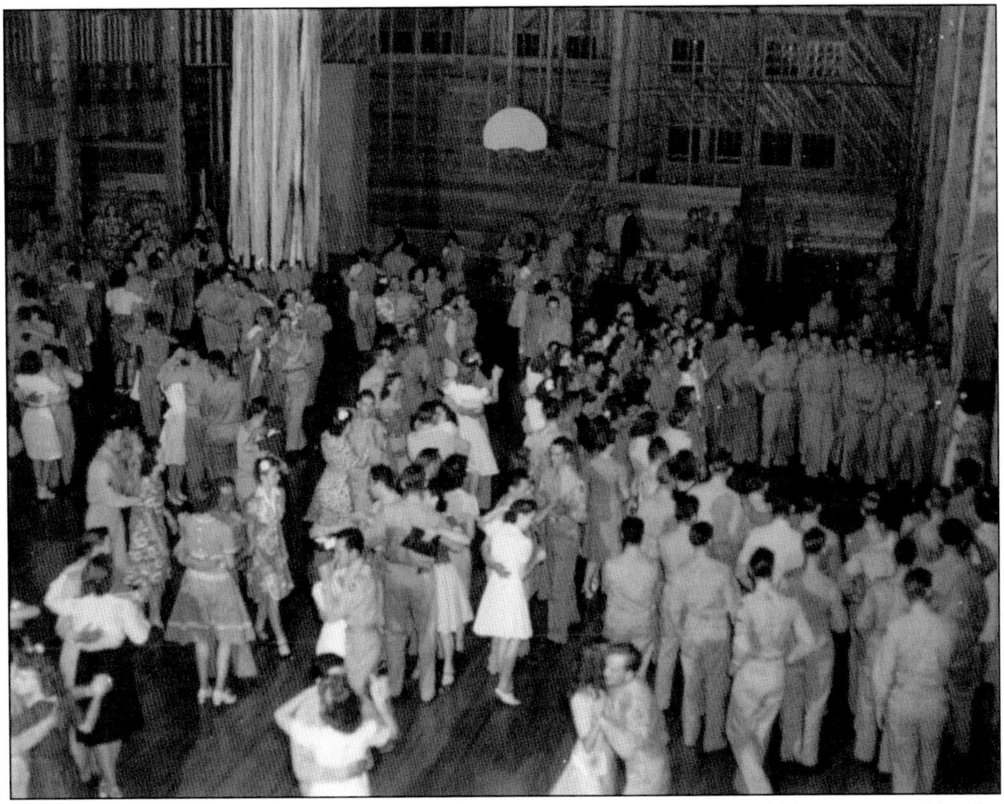

This dance is being held in the spacious gymnasium on base, which could be sponsored by the USO or the Red Cross. The band, part of the LAAF, played songs by popular artists of the day, such as Glenn Miller, Tommy Dorsey, and the Johnny Long Orchestras. In the photograph above, young ladies known as junior hostesses in the USO are dancing with soldiers. It was common for soldiers to stand waiting for their turn to dance. Young ladies in the USO were bussed in from all regions and were required to wear a dress. They were also told to never turn down a serviceman for a dance.

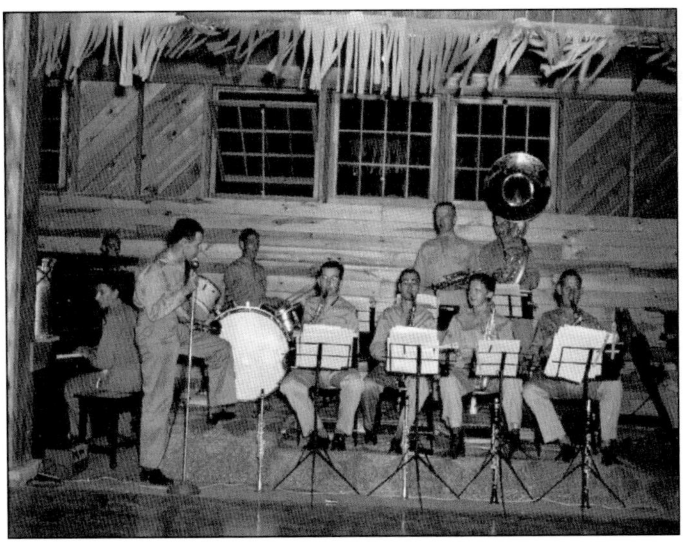

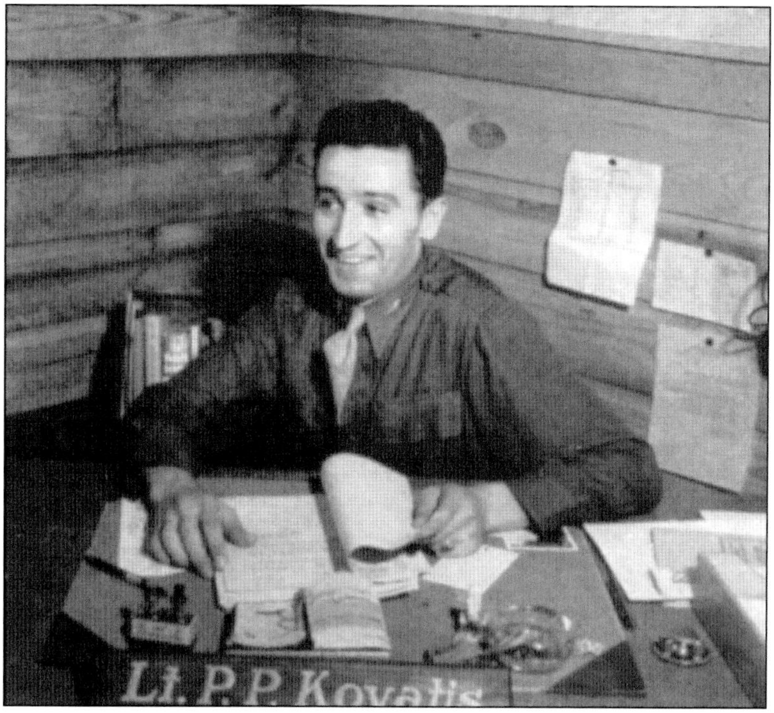

Second Lt. Pericles P. Kovatis was born March 6, 1917, in New Hampshire. Working as a grocer in Brockton, Massachusetts, Pericles enlisted in the military on September 10, 1941. While serving at LAAF, he became the adjutant to the commanding officer. He remained in the military and retired as a lieutenant colonel.

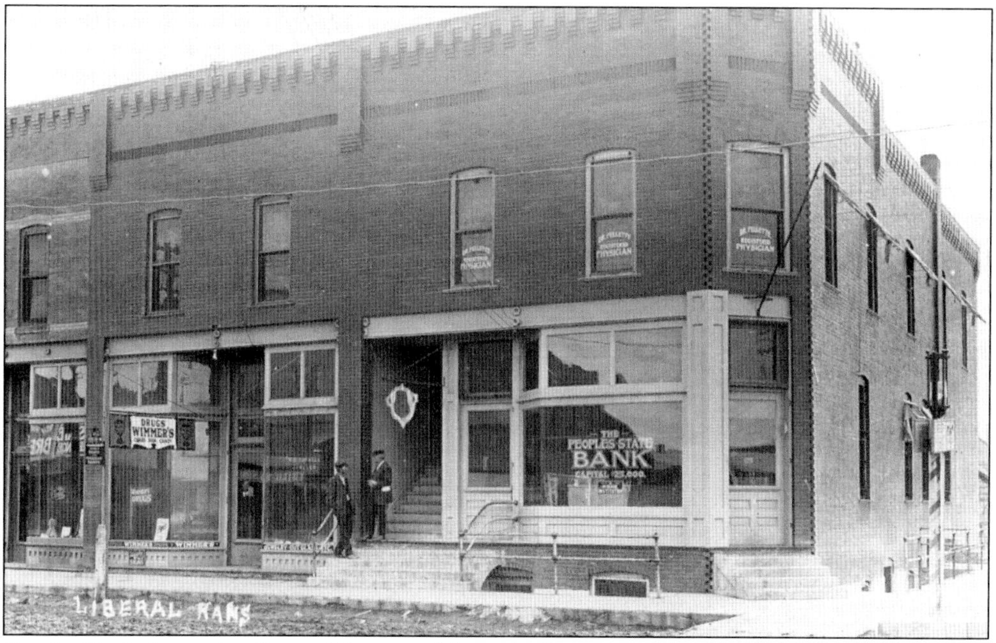

Peoples Bank, located at Second Street and Lincoln Street, was the official bank for the airfield. Payroll would come into the post office and then be deposited at the bank. Payroll was then drawn out and given to payroll officers, who were escorted by nine jeeps and heavily armed guards for the trip back to the base. The payroll was then taken to the finance office and placed in a concrete vault before distribution to personnel. (Courtesy of Lidia Gray.)

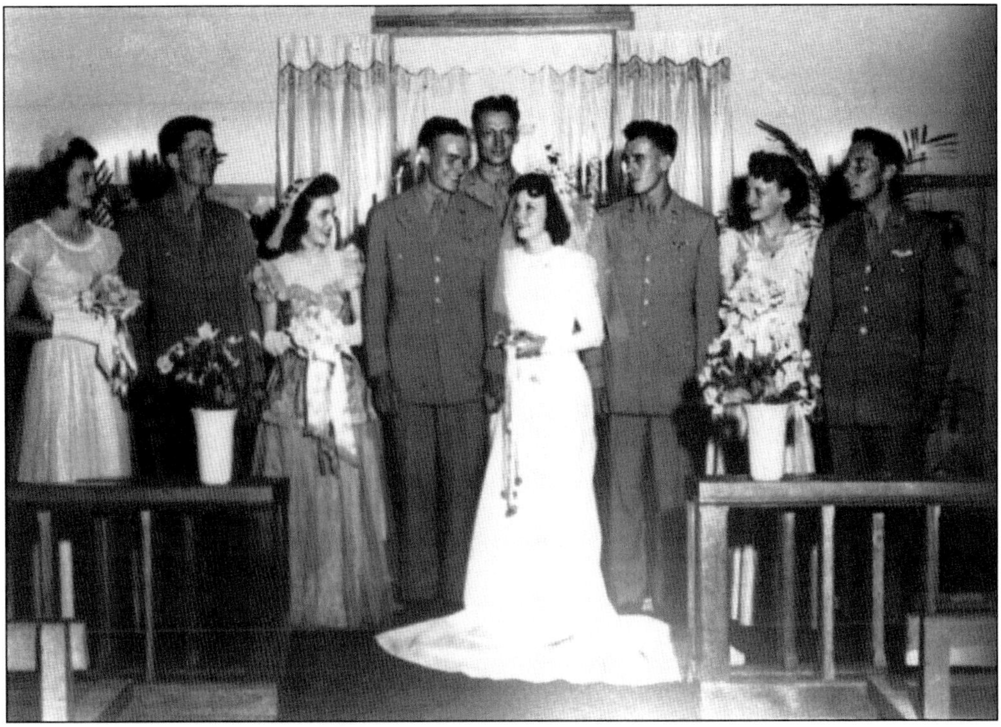

With so many dashing men in uniform and pretty local girls, romance and marriage were inevitable. Rex A. Harmon, base chaplain, performed the ceremonies. The count of marriage licenses at the Seward County Courthouse increased at least three-fold while the airfield was active.

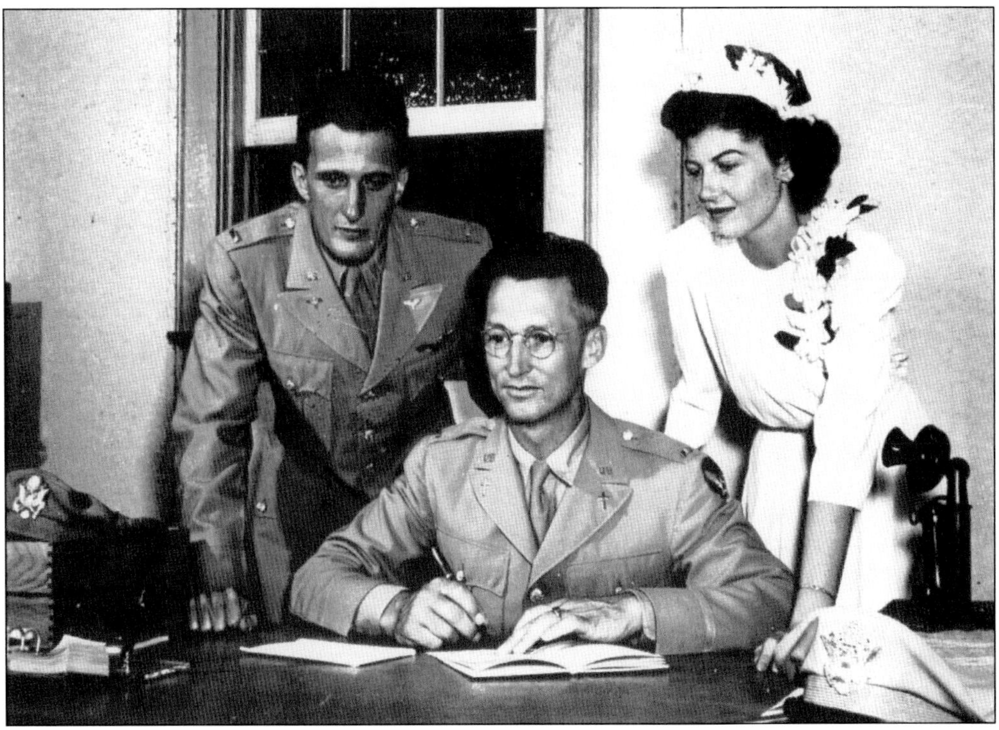

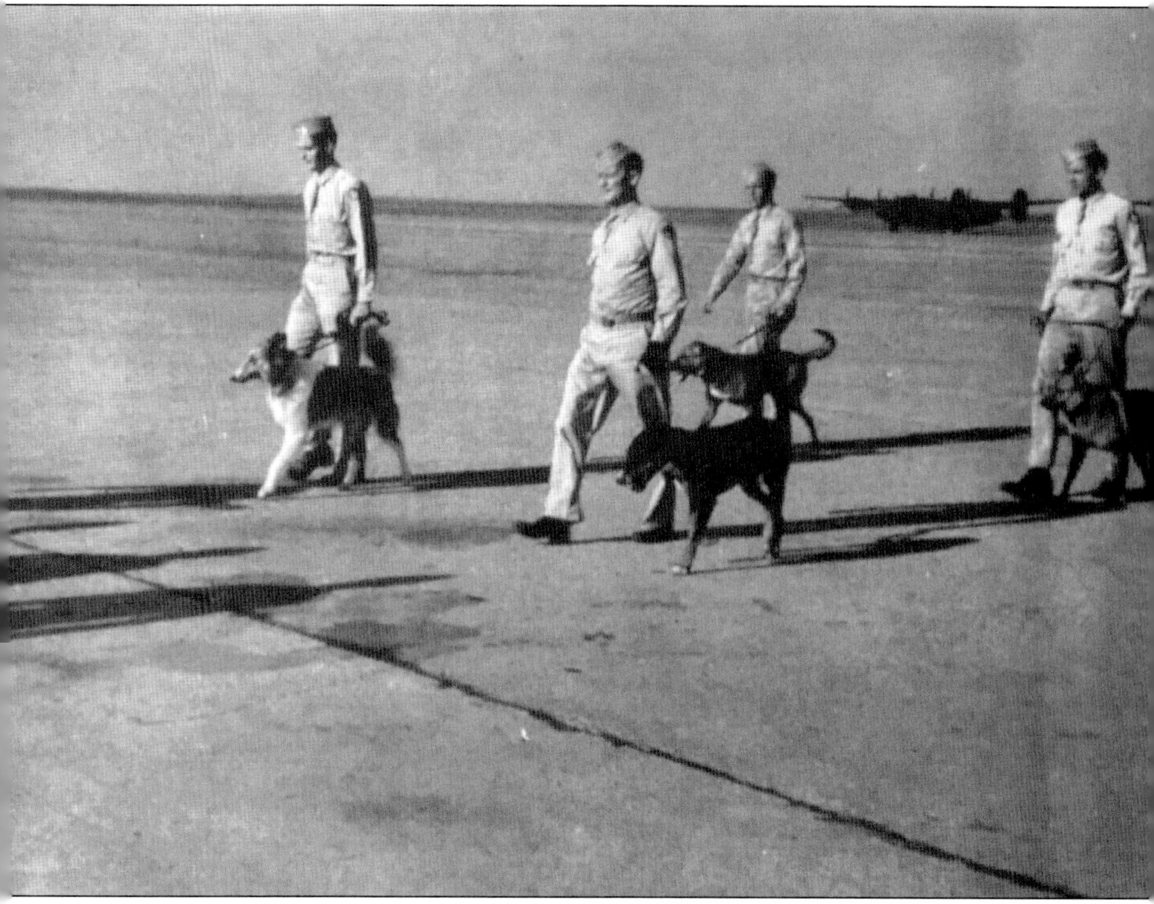

In 1941, the US Army possessed only a small number of sled dogs. A group of civilians after Pearl Harbor came together in the belief that dogs could serve the Army and a variety of other functions. A coalition was formed, Dogs for Defense, Inc. (DFD). This organization encouraged dog owners across the country to donate their dogs for training for sentry dogs. Civilian training was inconsistent, so in July 1942, Secretary of War Henry Stinson had training in the procuring of dogs to war department responsibility. Acceptable breeds were reduced to seven: the German shepherd, Doberman, Belgian sheepdog, collie, Siberian husky, malamute, and Eskimo dogs. Both dogs and handlers provided an invaluable contribution to the American war effort.

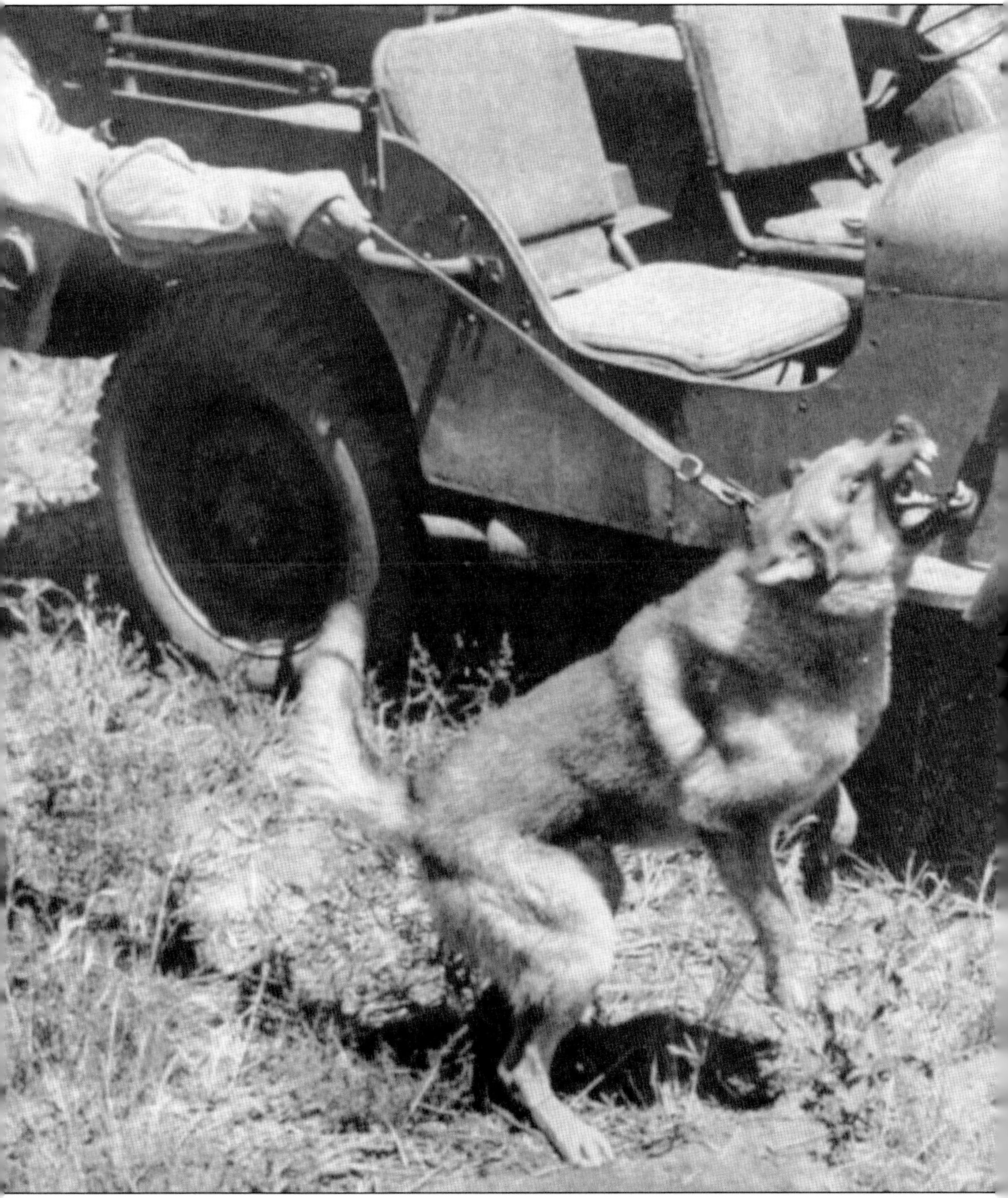

The German shepherd descends from the Belgian shepherd. Its historical role was as a hunting dog. It is also commonly kept as a companion dog, or used as an assistance dog, detection dog, guard dog, guide dog, police dog, or search and rescue dog. It has a long history of being used by military forces. In this photograph, it is safe to assume the dog's handler has trained the dog as a guard dog. During World War II, approximately 75 percent of dogs used during combat were the Doberman pinscher, with 25 percent being German shepherds.

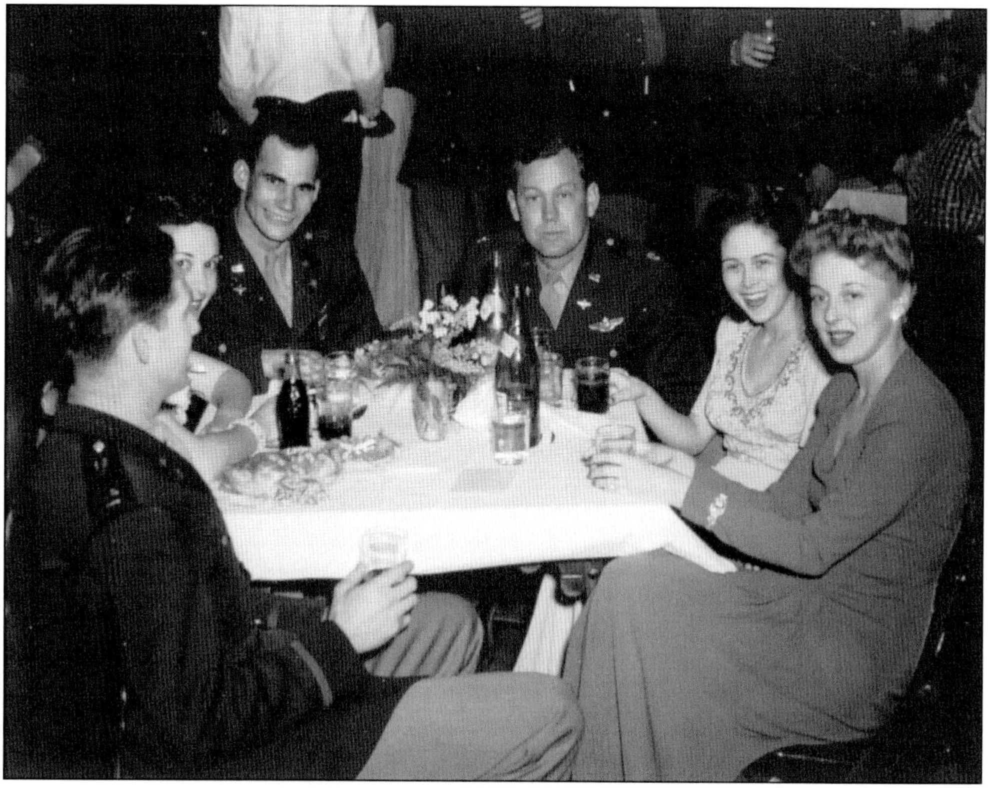

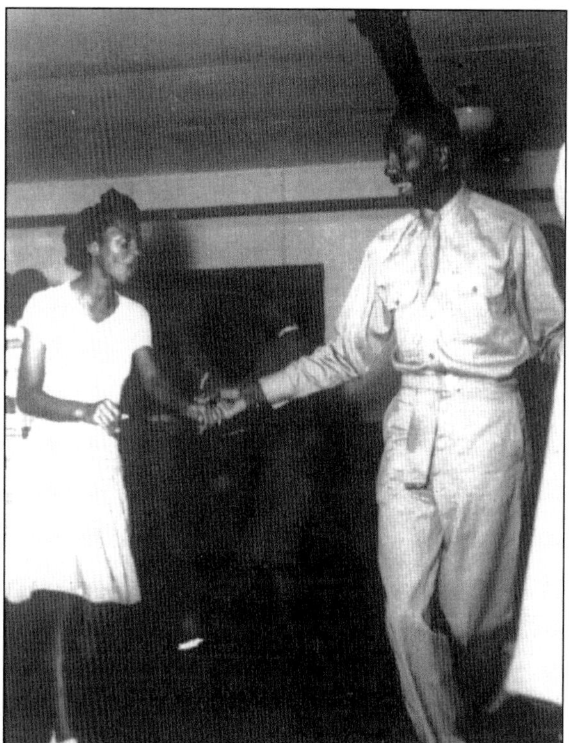

Attending a dinner party at LAAF are, from left to right, Officer Floyd Wikstrom, Hazel Plotner, Capt. Chet Plotner, Lt. Col. James C. Watkins, Mary Edwards, and Cecilia Wikstrom.

The USO was a great place to unwind and have a little fun. The military did not desegregate until 1948, so Liberal had two USOs, both managed by Envoy and Luvenia Carroll with the assistance of Mabel Travis. One USO was located at 307 North Kansas Avenue, and the other was at 8 East Fourth Street. The door count for both locations was 673,000 people who had attended a dance, watched a movie, had dinner, played pool, or just relaxed.

All decked out and ready for the dance at the LAAF, Benjamin "Blinky" Tuttle, originally from Philadelphia, poses for a photograph before he heads out to pick up his date. That evening, he escorted Arlee Wallace, who was from the area. (Courtesy of Karen Martin.)

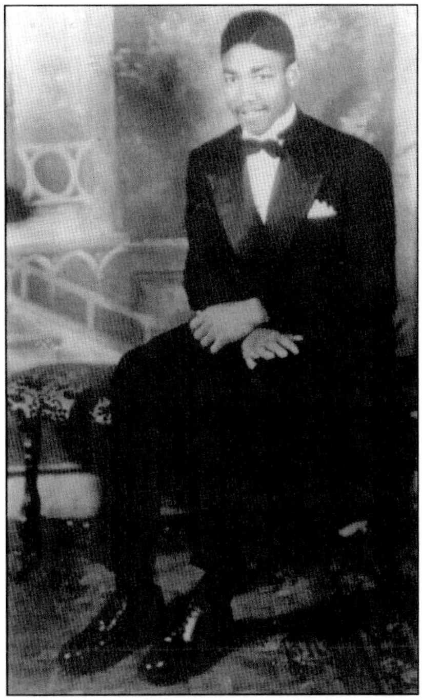

Inside the officer's club on base, this photograph shows servicemen seated around tables with one man reading the latest newspaper and others playing games or just relaxing. Tables and chairs are efficient but not necessarily made for comfort.

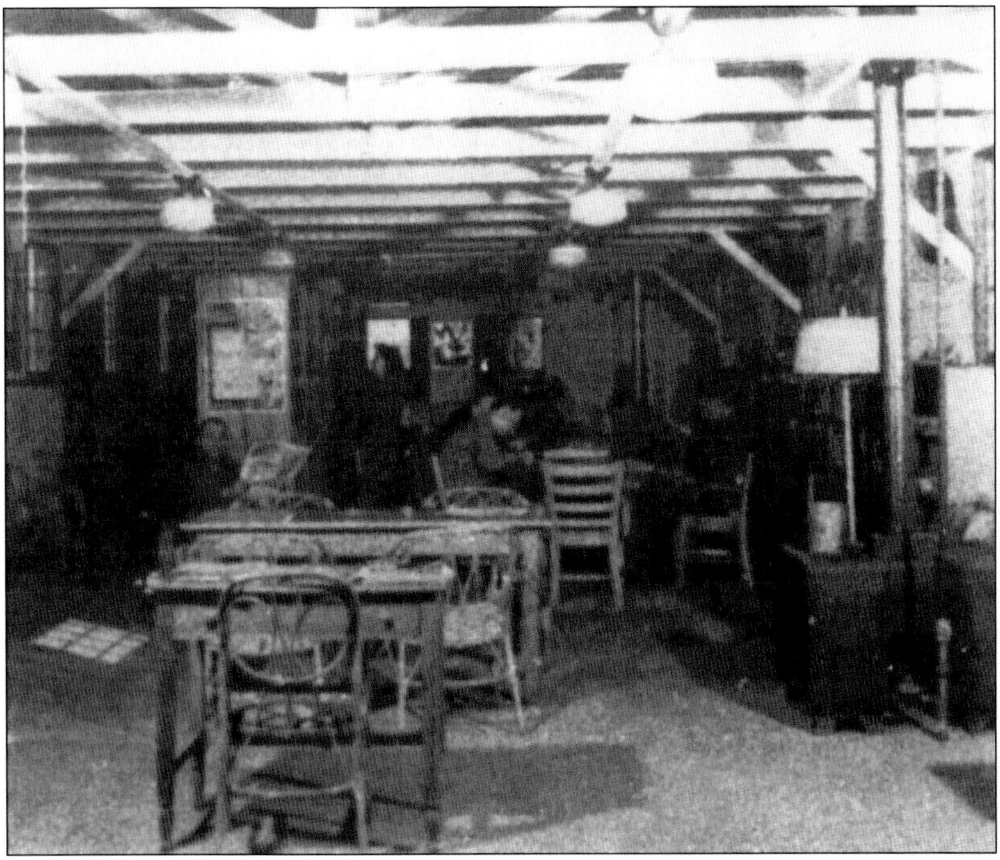

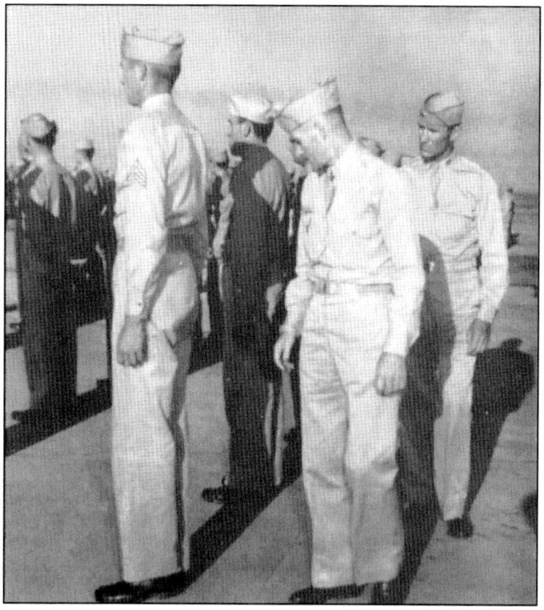

This image shows open ranks inspection of the summer service uniform. The inspector is a field grade officer supported by a captain, so likely this a squadron-level inspection. Military uniforms and appearance were strictly enforced from haircuts to shoes.

In the office, military men and civilian workers fill many positions. A great number of women from Liberal found jobs on base in clerical work. In many instances, they left their homes and families to earn extra income, especially if their sweethearts or husbands went off to war.

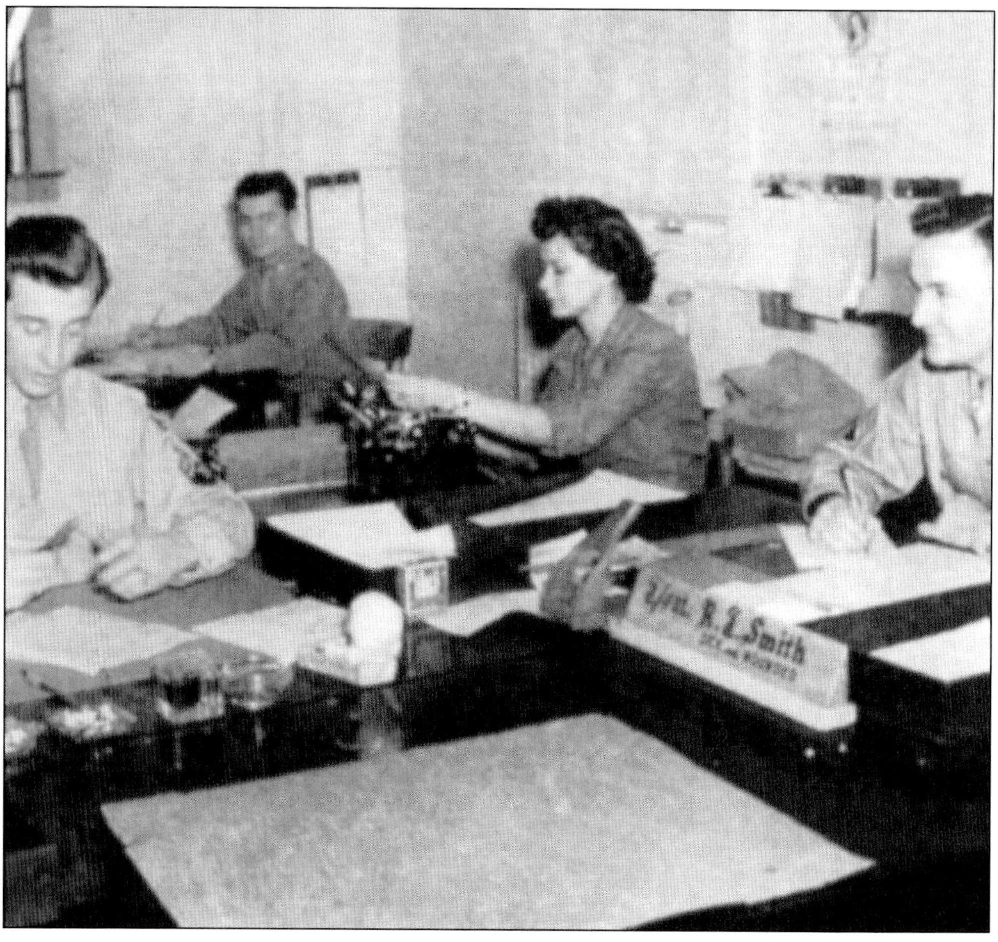

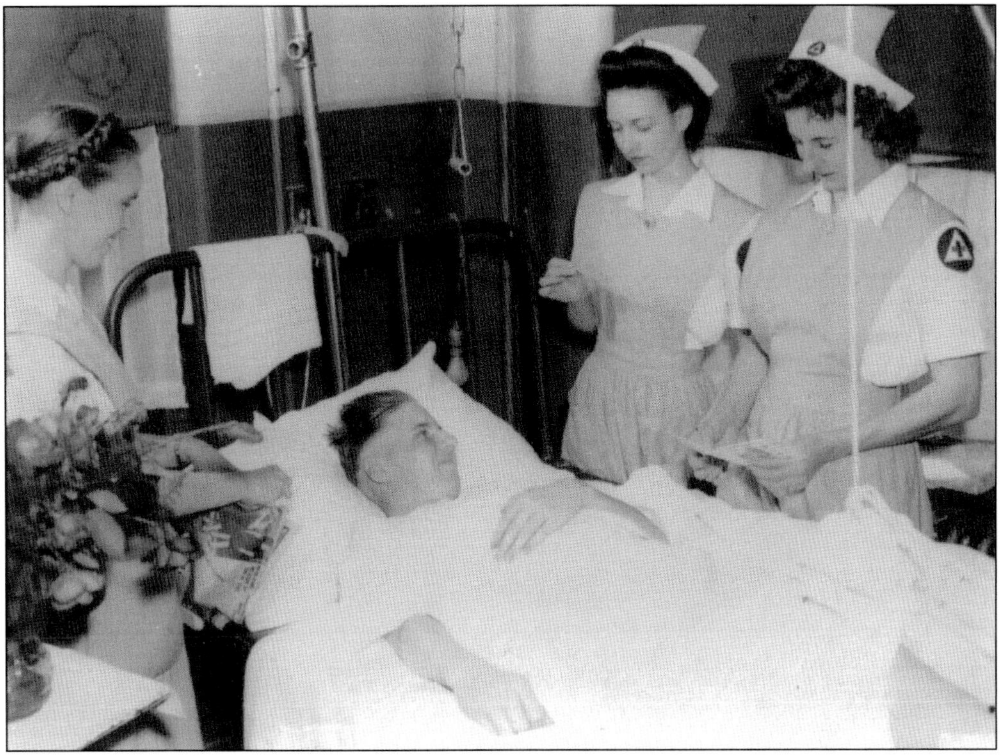

It is unknown the extent of this serviceman's injuries, but he is certainly receiving excellent attention from the Red Cross volunteers at the base hospital. The Red Cross had approximately 104,000 nurses involved in military service and 153,000 active-status nurses overall. The striped pinafore uniform worn by the ladies was made of a high-quality seersucker material that replaced the heavy, solid grey material of World War I. Like the military, uniforms were inspected for appearance, and hair was to be worn off the collar.

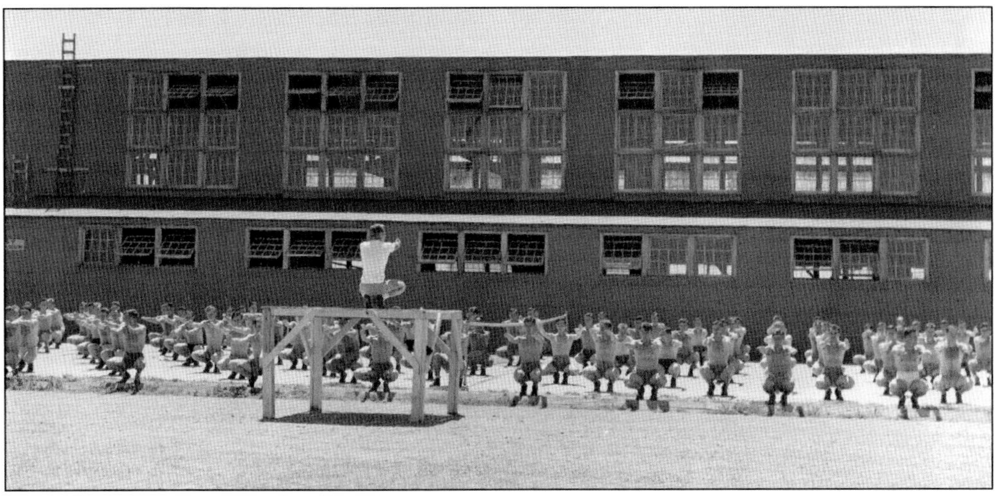

Already in good physical condition, B-24 commanders had to be in excellent shape to handle the unwieldy, heavy bombers. This image shows an impressive number of airmen undergoing rigorous squats under the critical eye of their instructor. The building behind the men is the airfield's gymnasium.

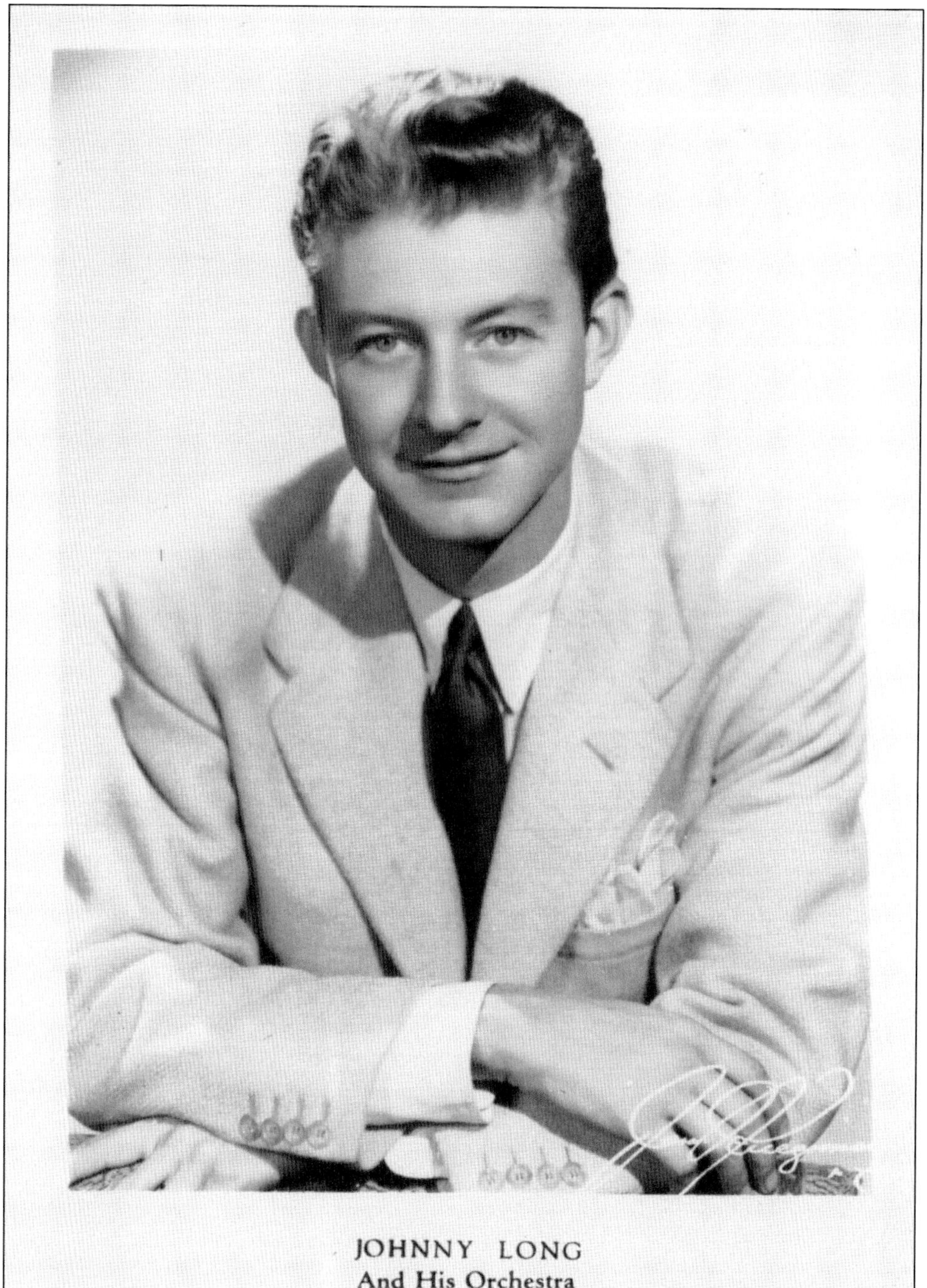

Johnny Long was known as "the Man Long on Music." He began playing the violin at six years old but was bitten by a pig on his left hand, so Johnny taught himself to play with his right hand. As a freshman at Duke University, Johnny and his friends formed an orchestra that adopted the swing/big band style. The orchestra often accompanied Ella Fitzgerald and had a smash hit, "In a Shanty in Old Shanty Town." Johnny and his musicians came to Liberal in June 1945 as part of the Coca-Cola Victory Parade of Spotlight Bands. The orchestra played for the base personnel and townspeople, broadcasting nationwide out of one of the B-24 hangars.

At this dance, the band leader and musicians were wearing Hawaiian leis around their necks. Notice the young couple dancing and sharing a kiss. It also features Hawaiian girls performing the hula in traditional costumes. Perhaps it is part of a USO show, also known as Camp Shows. It is estimated there were over 3,000 clubs and camp shows with over 7,000 performers, mostly civilians. Ninety-eight percent of the entertainers were unknown. They were amateur singers, dancers, and performers who wanted to contribute their talents to the war effort.

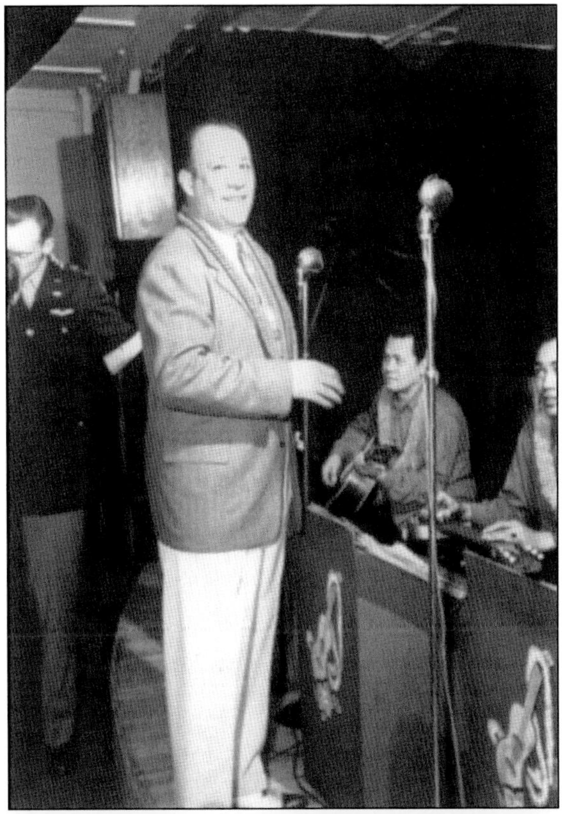

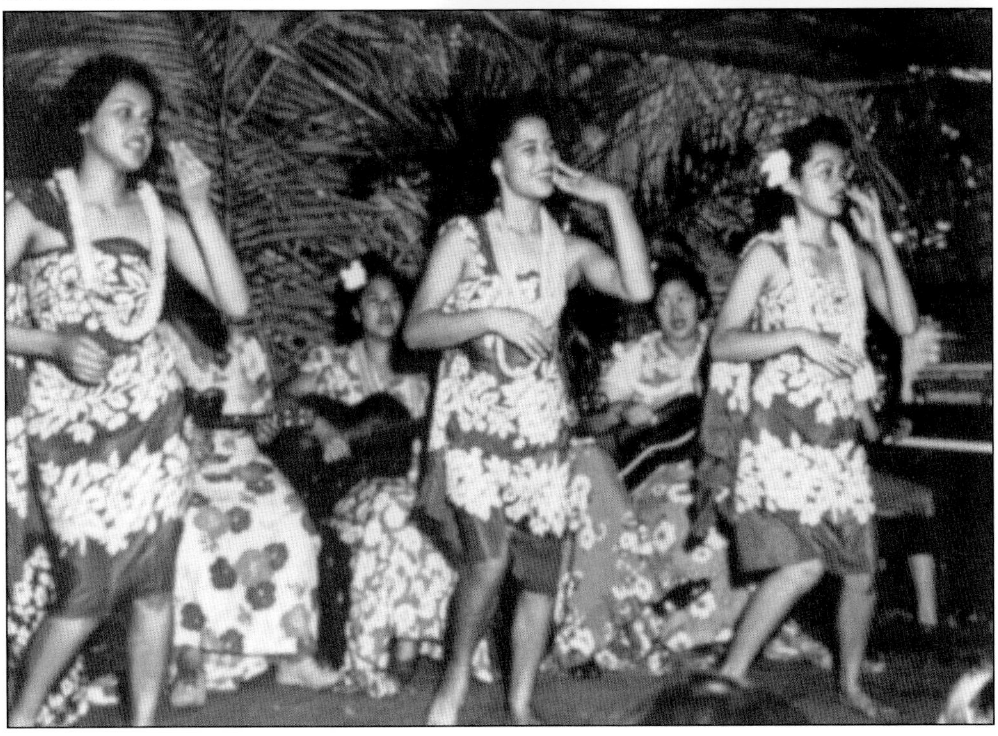

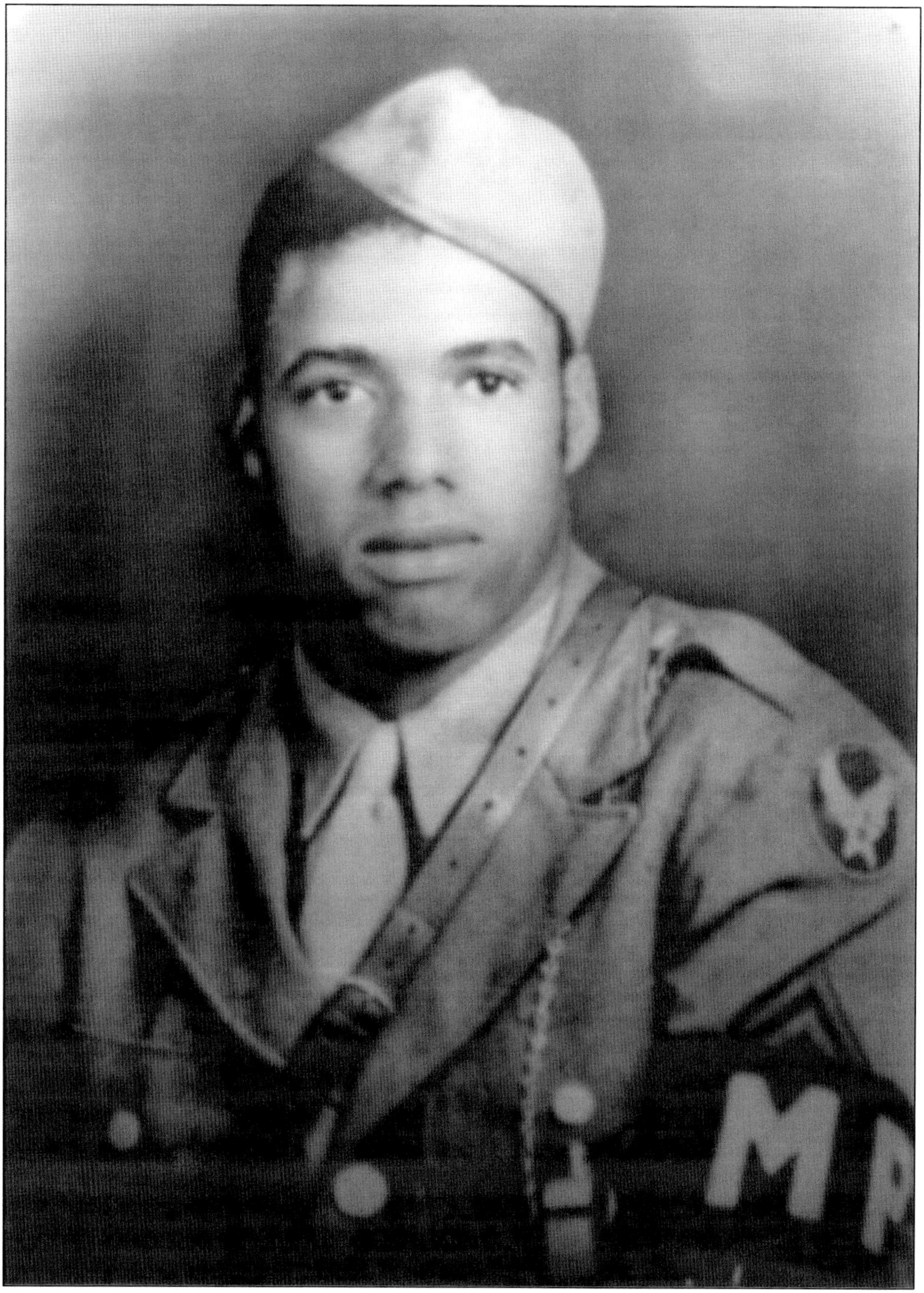

Herby Frazier was born in 1916 in Woodville, Texas, and was a farmer. He enlisted in the US Army on July 29, 1942, and was stationed at the LAAF, arriving with the first personnel. Sergeant Frazier became an MP and guarded the base until deactivation in 1945. Sergeant Frazier married a local girl, Susie Jennings, and made Liberal his home for the rest of his life. (Courtesy of Karen Martin.)

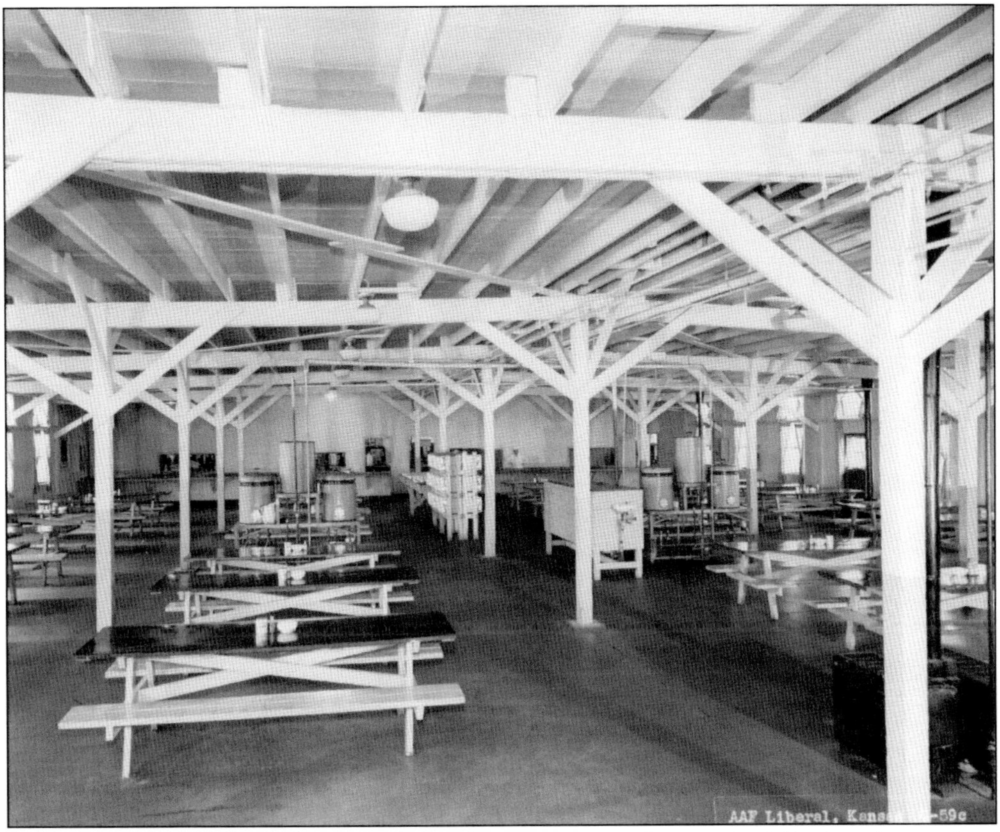

Just as important as the base commanders and instructors was the mess hall. Feeding thousands of people a day was a monumental task since breakfast began at 5:00 a.m. and continued with lunch and dinner. Lockers full of whole beeves and massive amounts of chickens supplied the always busy kitchen. First Lt. Eugene "Buck" Schnierle, with the assistance of 2nd Lt. Mary J. Caswell and their 100-plus helpers, kept the mess hall going and the base well-fed.

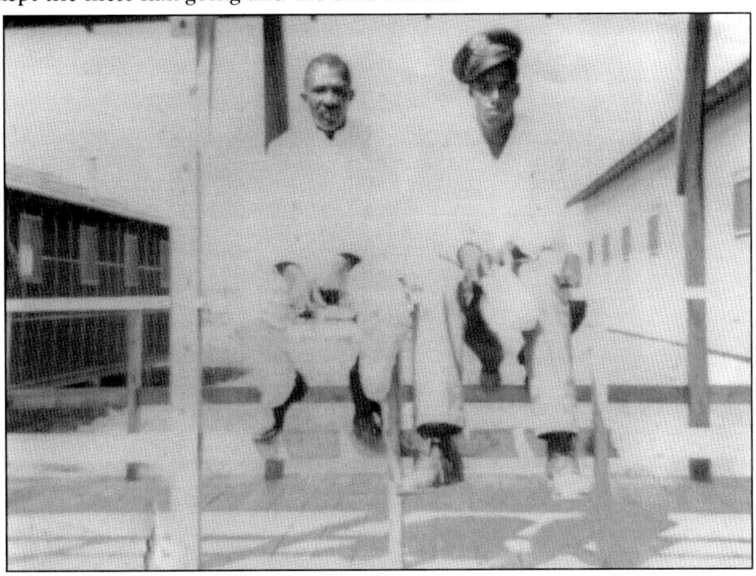

Captured in this photograph are Herby Frazier (right) and his friend taking a few minutes break outside the mess hall. Moments of relaxation were rare on the LAAF. Herby assisted in the enforcement of military laws and regulations. He performed patrol work in town, supervising work of 12 men. (Courtesy of Karen Martin.)

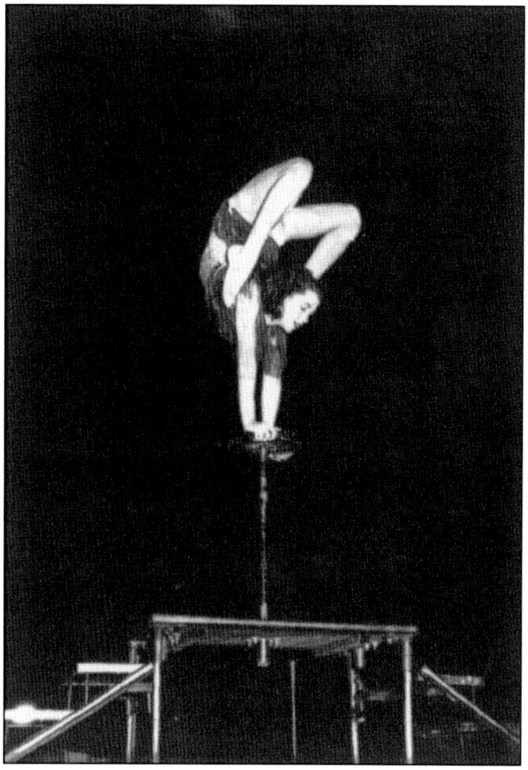

The leadership of the airfield was determined to keep up morale. The on-base theater, two USOs, and on-base swimming pool helped, but nothing cheered the men and women like live entertainment. This image of local Jean Randall shows homegrown talent can be impressive. Jean was a professionally trained dancer and did not mind giving her time to help the field's personnel forget their intense duties.

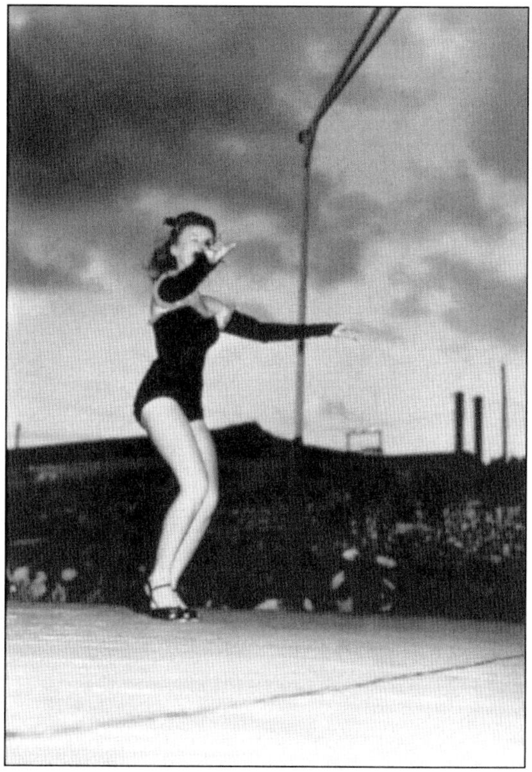

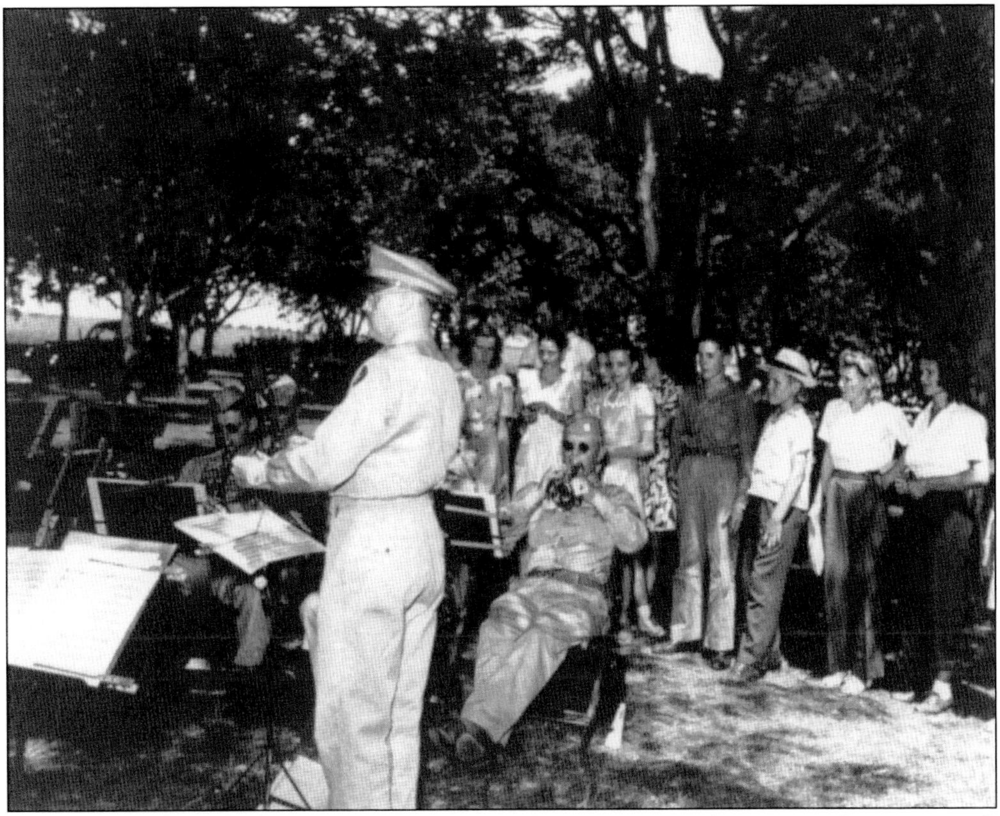

Local Liberal citizens stop to enjoy the base band led by 1st Lt. Richard A. Ferris. The concert took place in Liberal's main park, Light Park. In all likelihood, they are playing popular music of the time or a rousing John Phillip Sousa march.

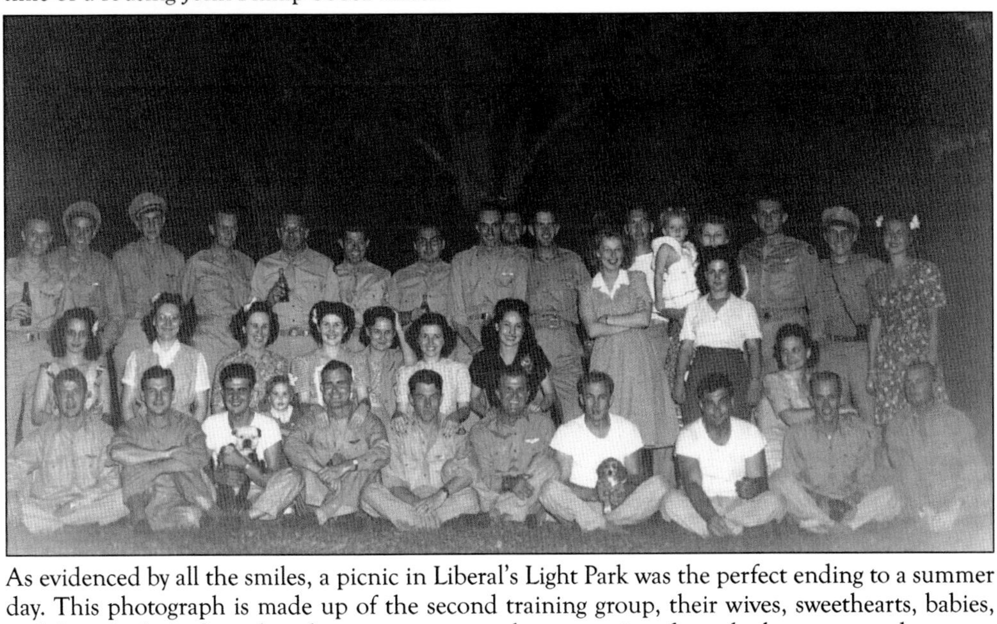

As evidenced by all the smiles, a picnic in Liberal's Light Park was the perfect ending to a summer day. This photograph is made up of the second training group, their wives, sweethearts, babies, and dogs. Light Park, with its large trees, was a welcome reprieve from the hot summer days.

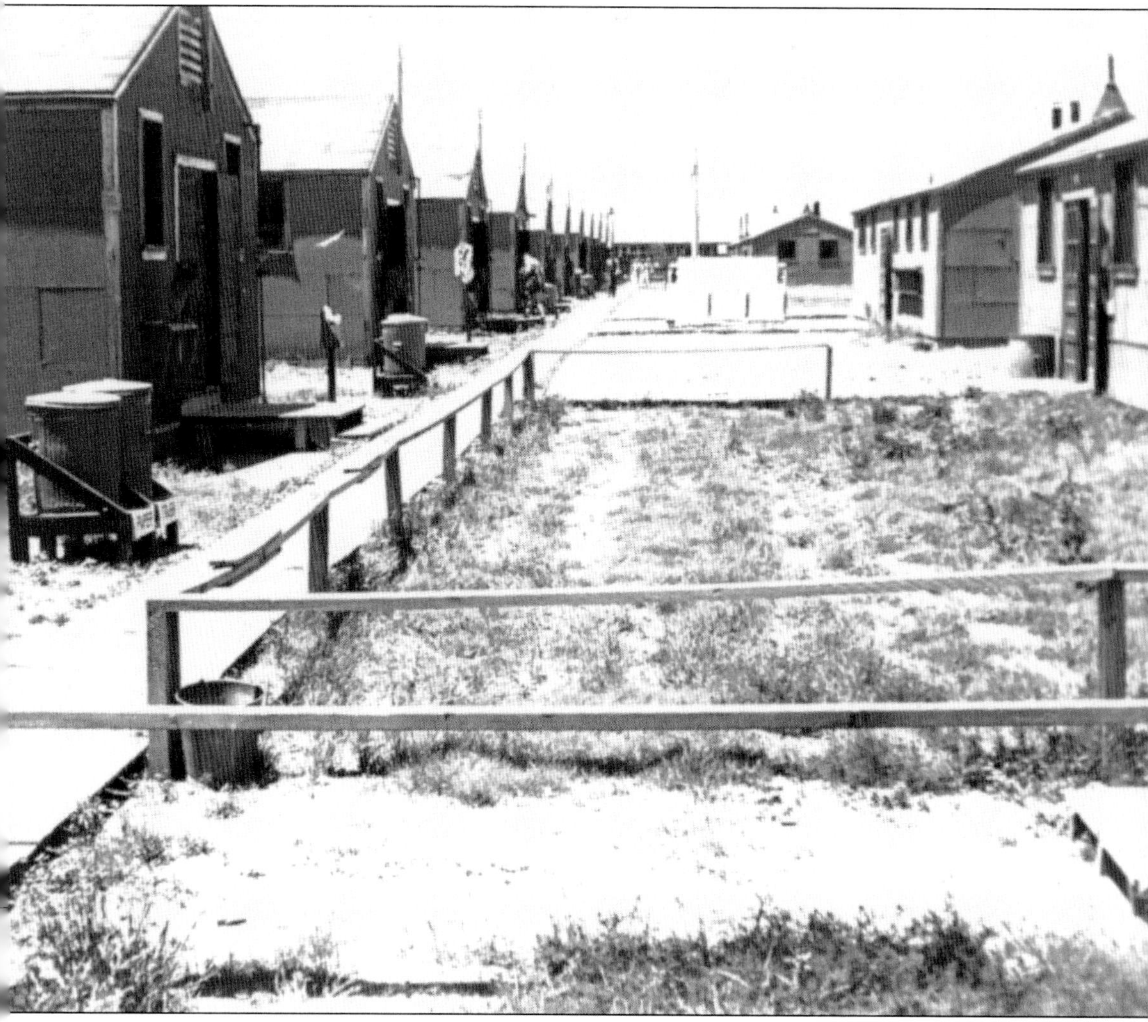

Living standards in the country had risen. Not having indoor plumbing or electricity was a thing of the past. The 700 series plans were built that could be adjusted, were simple, and did not need skilled workers to assemble. Most barracks used locally sourced materials, had electricity and radiant heat, and best of all, could be constructed in a matter of hours. In this image, the barracks are on the left, and the latrines are on the right.

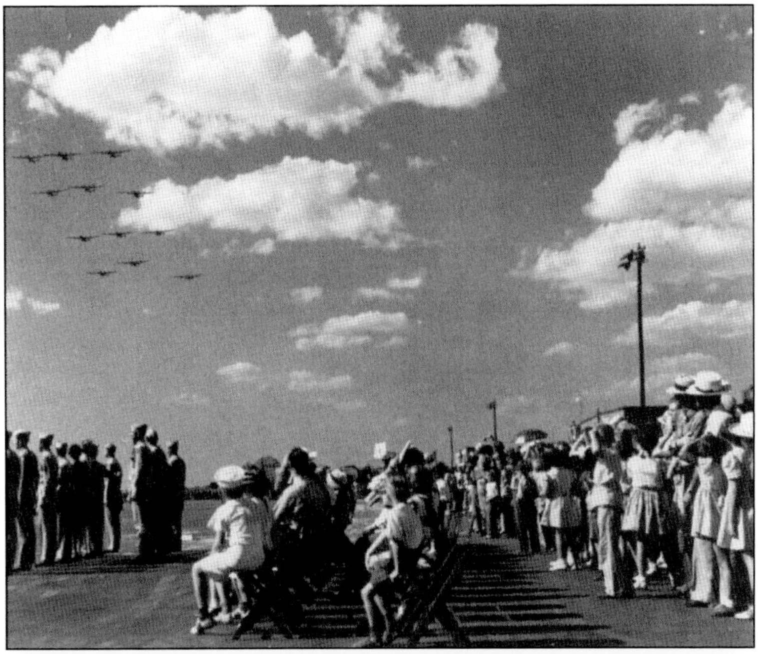

The Army Air Force celebrated its 38th anniversary on August 7, 1945. Tens of thousands attended to see the B-29 Fortress, demonstrations, and 12 B-24s flying in formation. Awards were also given. Billy Toadvine posthumously was awarded an Air Medal. Lt. Holbert D. Arnold, Lt. John A. White, and T.Sgt. Albert H. Davison were all given the Distinguished Flying Cross.

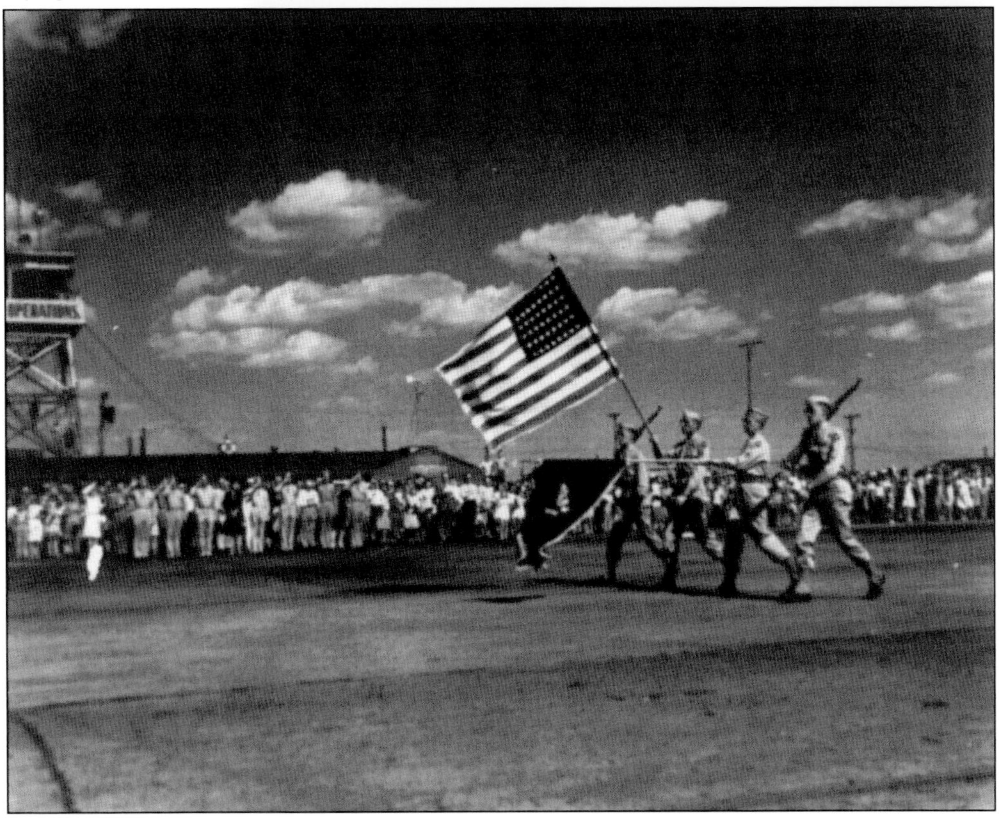

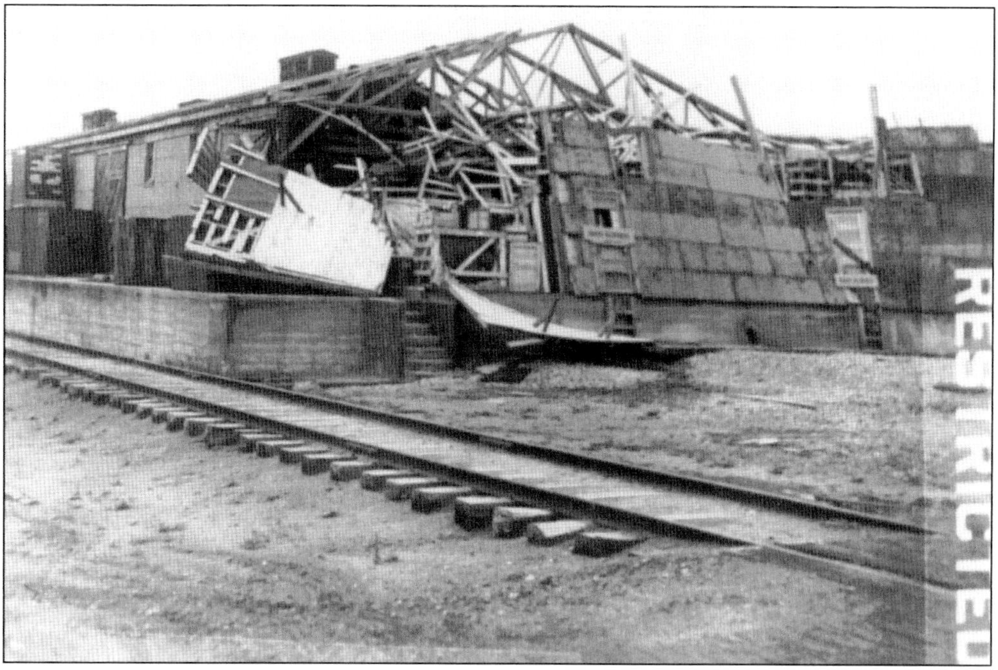

Kansas weather can be unpredictable in any season. Coming from the southeast on the evening of April 9, 1944, the southern portion of the airbase was hit hard by an unexpected tornado. Another earlier tornado took almost the same exact path of destruction.

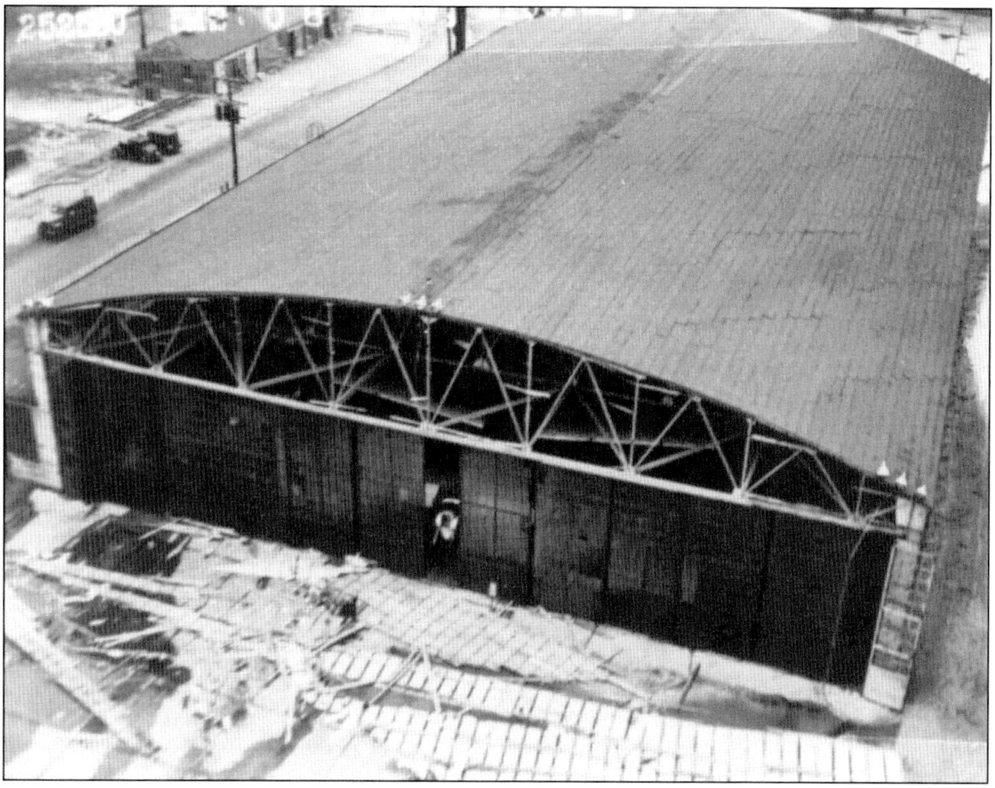

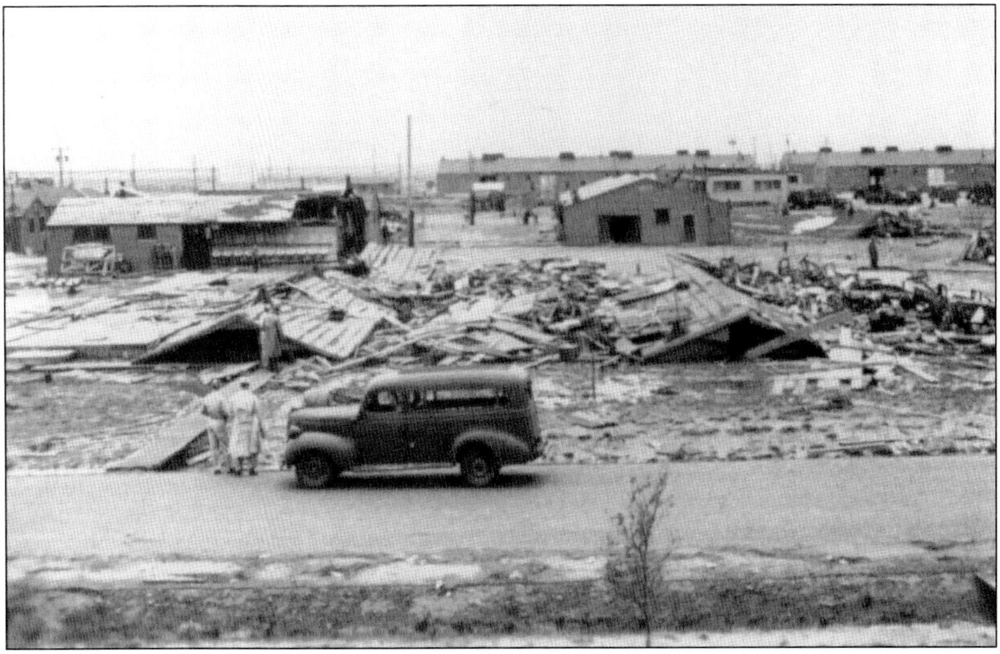

Damage was done to four barracks, three quartermaster warehouses, the post engineer's office, the electrical distribution system, and general roof damage to many buildings. Damages were estimated to be $113,700. Mercifully, no one was injured.

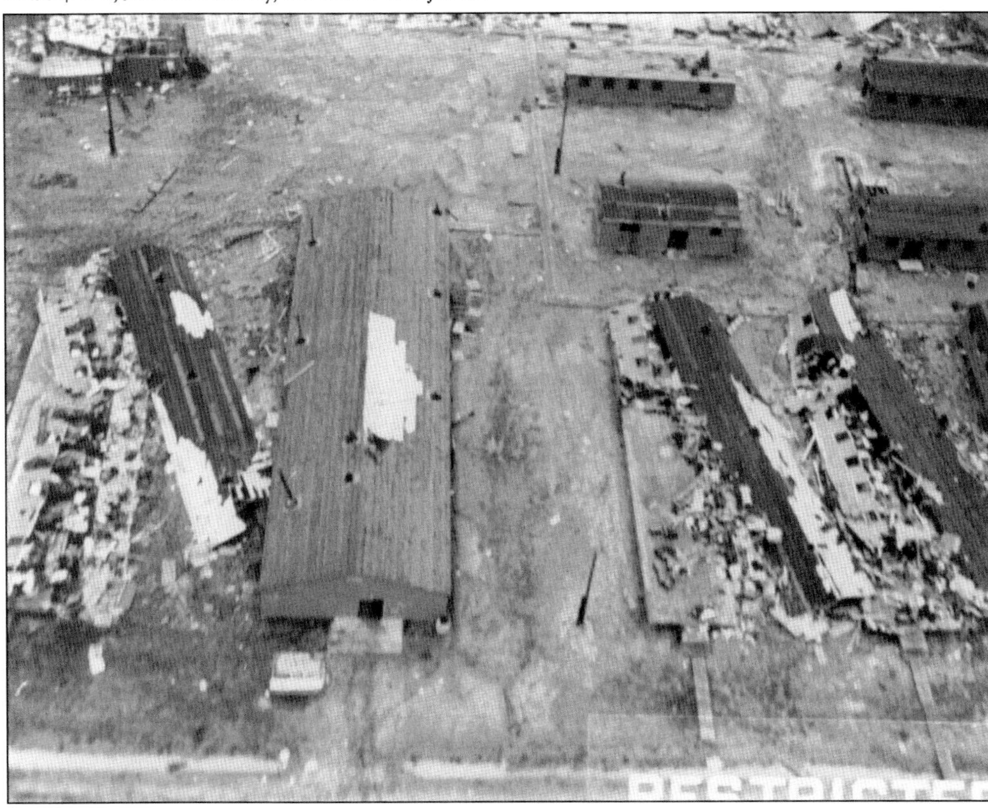

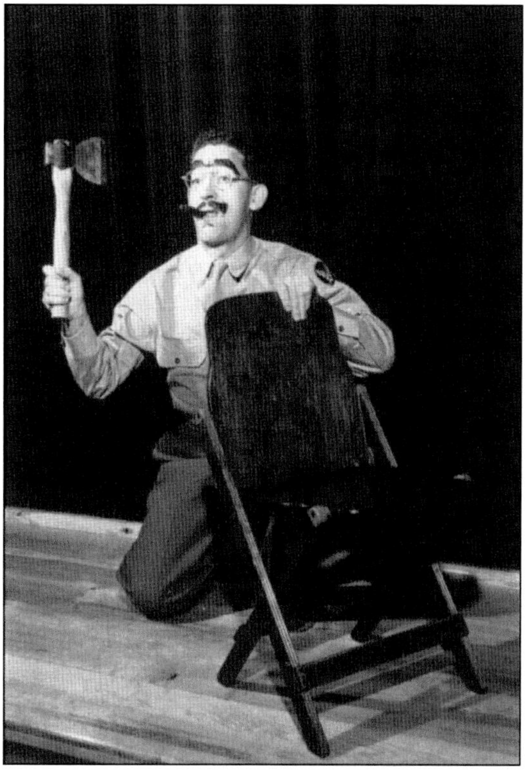

An entertainer/soldier is imitating a popular comedian of the 1940s, Groucho Marx. He is wearing Marx's famous eyeglasses, nose, mustache, and cigar.

A hot, dry, windy day in August 1945 did not deter the thousands of civilians who came to the airfield to celebrate the 38th anniversary of the Army Air Forces. The all-day program began with a memorial service at the post chapel, followed by demonstrations. Line taxis were provided to help people get from place to place on the massive airfield. A picnic at Light Park serenaded by the 744th LAAF band, an appearance by a B-29 Superfortress, and a flying formation of B-24 Liberators concluded the day.

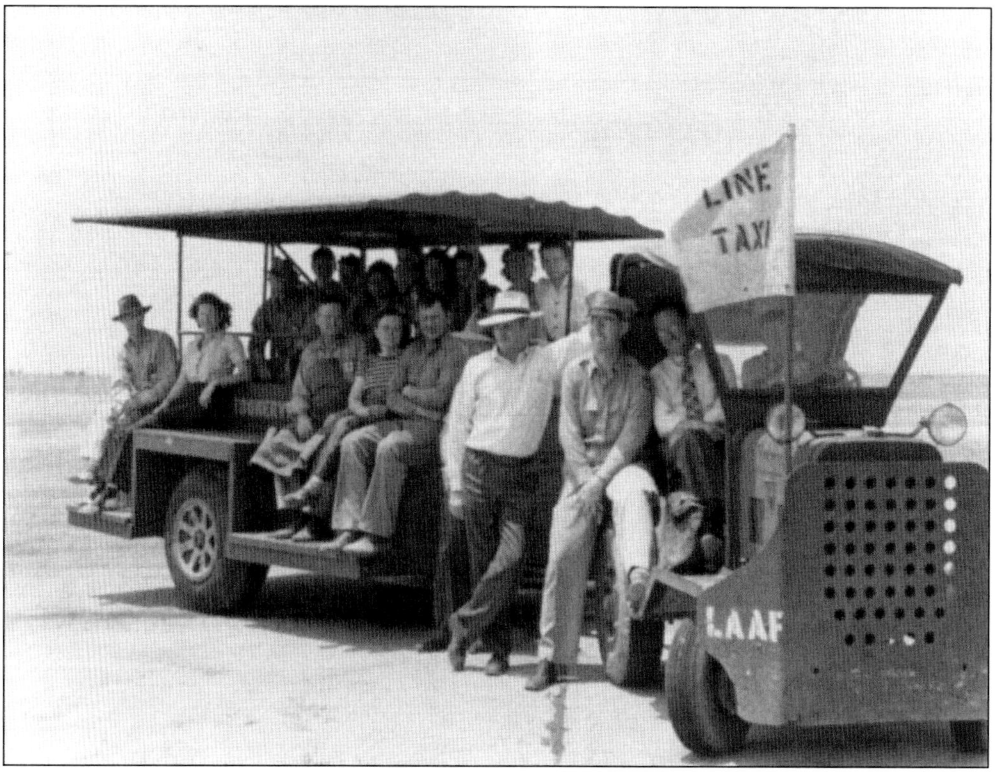

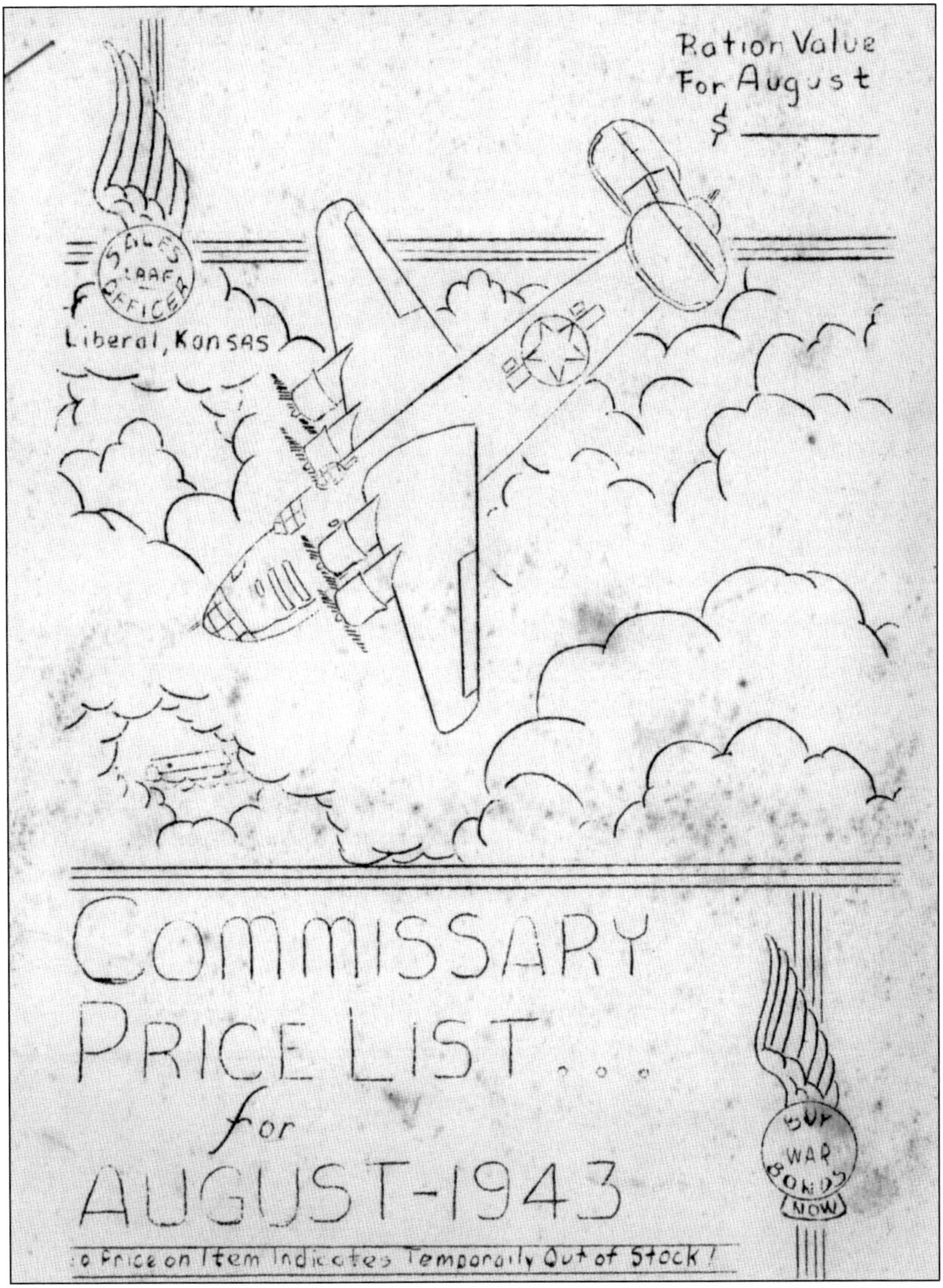

Hand-drawn and dated August 1943 is the cover of the commissary price list. Usually distributed at the commissary, the price lists indicate items for sale and those temporarily out of stock. The cover reminds soldiers to buy war bonds. The unknown artist depicts a B-24 going through the clouds.

ARTICLE	UNIT	COST
APPLES		
*#10 (R)	can	.48
Evap., boxed	lb.	.19
APPLE BUTTER, 28 oz.	jar	.13
APPLESAUCE		
#2	can	.08
#10	can	.41
APRICOTS		
#2½	can	.19
Evap., 25# box	lb.	.24
ASPARAGUS		
Stalk, #2	can	.23
Cut, #10	can	1.06
BACON		
Slab-smoked, 8/12 (R)	lb.	.24
Sliced, 1# ctn.	lb.	
BEANS		
Dry, Lima	lb.	.07
Dry, Pinto	lb.	.06
Dry, Red Kidney	lb.	.06
Dry, White (R)	lb.	.05
Lima, #2	can	.10
Lima, #10	can	.49
String, #2	can	.09
String, #10 (R)	can	.48
BEETS		
#2½	can	.08
#10	can	.33
BOUILLON CUBES	cube	.08
BUTTER, Issue (R)	lb.	.42
CATSUP, Tomato, 14 oz.	bot.	.12
CEREALS		
All Bran, 10 oz.	pkg.	.10
Bran Flakes, 8 oz.	pkg.	.08
Corn Flakes, 11 oz.	pkg.	.07
Cream of Wheat, 28 oz.	pkg.	.19
Grapenuts, 12 oz.	pkg.	.13
Grapenuts Flakes, 7 oz.	pkg.	.08
Krumbles, 9 oz.	pkg.	.09
Pep Whole Wheat Flakes 8 oz.	pkg.	.08
Rice Krispies, 5½ oz.	pkg.	.10
Rolled Oats, 20 oz. (R)	pkg.	.07
Rolled Oats, 48 oz.	pkg.	.15
Shredded Wheat, 12 oz.	pkg.	.09

ARTICLE	UNIT	COST
CHEESE		
Philadelphia Cream 8 oz.	pkg.	
Velveeta, 8 oz.	pkg.	
CHERRIES, Sweet, #2½	can	.21
CIGARETTES		
Camels, 20's.	ctn.	1.20
Chesterfields, 20's	ctn.	1.20
Lucky Strikes, 20's	ctn.	1.20
Old Golds, 20's	ctn.	1.20
Raleighs, 20's	ctn.	1.20
COCOA, 5# (R)	can	.43
COFFEE		
Issue, 1# (R)	lb.	.17
Folgers, 1#	jar	.29
Hill Bros., 1#	jar	.30
Maxwell House, 1#	jar	.29
CORN		
Cream Style, #2	can	.10
Whole Grain, #2 (R)	can	.10
CORNMEAL		
Yellow, 24 oz.	pkg.	.07
10# sack	lb.	.04
CORNSTARCH, 1#	pkg.	.04
DRESSING, SALAD		
Issue, 1 gal.	jar	1.08
Mayonnaise, 1 gal.	jar	1.34
EGGS		
Issue, 30 doz. to case(R)	doz.	.44
Sales, 1 doz. to ctn.	doz.	
EXTRACT FLAVORING		
Lemon, Pure, 2 oz.	bot.	.17
Lemon, Imit., 8 oz.	bot.	.11
Vanilla, Imit., 2 oz.	bot.	.07
Vanilla, Imit., 8 oz. (R)	bot.	.07
FLOUR, hard, wheat (R)	lb.	.03
FRUIT COCKTAIL		
#2½	can	.21
#10	can	.72
GELATIN, DESSERT POWDER		
Lemon, 10#	co.	1.43
Strawberry, 10#	co.	1.54
Prepared with starch		
Chocolate, 10#	co.	.79

Page one of the commissary publication lists a variety of food items, including a lengthy list of cigarettes for sale. The prices appear very low, but a typical enlisted serviceman's pay was only $71.33 a month.

ARTICLE	UNIT	COST
SALT		
3# carton	ctn.	.03
10# bag	lb.	.01
100# sacks (R)	lb.	.01
SAUCE		
Cranberry, 2#	jar	.19
Red Hot, 2 oz.	bot.	.18
SAUERKRAUT, #10	can	.23
SHAVING CREAM, Barbosol, Barracks Special	tube	.08
SHRIMP Wet Pack, #1	can	.23
SIRUP		
Corn, Refined, #10 (R)	can	.39
Karo, Blue Label, 1½#	bot.	.12
SOAP, LAUNDRY		
Ivory, 10 oz.	cake	.09
P & G, 10 oz.	cake	.04
SOAP, POWDER OR FLAKES		
Dreft, 8 3/4 oz.	pkg.	.20
Lux, 12½ oz.	pkg.	
Oxydol, 24 oz.	pkg.	.20
Rinso, 24 oz.	pkg.	
SOAP, TOILET		
Ivory, Guest, 4 oz.	cake	.04
Lifebuoy, 4 oz.	cake	
Lux	cake	
SODA, BAKING, 1#	co.	.02
SPAGHETTI		
Bulk, 20 # box	lb.	.07
Quakers, 8 oz.	pkg.	.06
SPICES		
Allspice, ground, 4 oz.	co.	.11
Chili Powder, 4 oz.	co.	.07
Chili Powder, 1#	co.	.36
Cinnamon, ground, 4 oz.(R)	co.	.21
Cinnamon, ground, 8 oz.	co.	.41
Cloves, ground, 4 oz.	pkg.	.09
Cloves, whole, 4 oz.	co.	.08
Curry Powder, 4 oz.	co.	.08
Ginger, ground, 4 oz.	co.	.09
Mace, ground, 4 oz.	co.	.25
Mustard, ground, 4 oz.	co.	.04
Nutmeg, ground, 4 oz.	co.	.15
Pepper, black, 1# (R)	co.	.10
Poultry Seasoning, 4 oz.	can	.14
Sage, rubbed, 4 oz.	co.	.12
SPINACH		
#2	can	.08
#2½	can	.11
#10	can	.41
STARCH, Linit, 12 oz.	pkg.	.08

ARTICLE	UNIT	COST
SUGAR		
Brown, 1# carton	ctn.	.06
Granulated, bulk (R)	lb.	.05
Powdered, 1#	ctn.	.07
Tablets, 2# carton	ctn.	.16
TEA		
5# (R)	co.	1.96
Lipton's, 20 bags	pkg.	
TOBACCO, SMOKING		
Bugler, 3/4 oz.	pkg.	.03
Granger, R.C., 16 oz.	pkg.	.62
Prince Albert, 2 oz.	pkg.	.09
TOMATOES		
#2 (R)	can	.08
#2½	can	.11
TOMATO PUREE, #10	can	.39
TOOTH BRUSH, 50 tuft	ea.	
VINEGAR		
1 qt.	bot.	.11
1 gal. (R)	jar	.34
YEAST, Compressed	lb.	.11

1. No price on an item indicates that it is temporarily out of stock.

2. Items marked with an asterik are not on hand, prices taken from Kansas City QM Depot Price List and Seventh Service Command.

- 3 -

Pages one and two of the commissary lists show the costs and availability of items listed. Notice there was little prepackaging, and items were priced in bulk. Personnel were advised to bring their empty toothpaste or shaving tube to be surrendered before a new tube could be purchased.

VETERANS ADMINISTRATION

WASHINGTON 25, D. C.

OFFICE OF
THE ADMINISTRATOR OF
VETERANS AFFAIRS

DEAR FELLOW VETERAN:

I congratulate you upon completion of your service in the armed forces and for your part in bringing to a conclusion a two-front war which resulted in the unconditional surrender of the Axis Powers.

Having been appointed by the President as Administrator of Veterans Affairs, I want to state generally the provisions made by our Government for you and other veterans.

Among the benefits that you may be entitled to are compensation for disabilities, hospitalization, home, farm and business loan guarantee, readjustment allowances, insurance, rehabilitation and vocational training, educational courses, assistance in obtaining employment and provision for your dependents.

Eligibility for each one is dependent upon the facts in the individual case.

If you are interested in any of these provisions, you should write or contact the Veterans Administration office nearest your home. For your convenience, there is, on the reverse of this letter, a list of the Regional Offices with the address of each office.

I feel I should warn you the last deduction for your Government insurance premiums has been made from your service pay. This means from now on you must make these premium payments directly to the Collections division, Veterans Administration, Washington 25, D. C.

DON'T LET YOUR INSURANCE LAPSE! YOU
OWE THIS TO YOURSELF AND YOUR FAMILY.

I assure you that the Veterans Administration stands ready to serve you.

Sincerely yours,

Omar N. Bradley

OMAR N. BRADLEY,
General, U. S. Army,
Administrator.

This letter from Gen. Omar N. Bradley at the end of the war was sent to all veterans, congratulating them on their service. General Bradley had a distinguished career from 1915 to his death in 1981. One of his most famous quotes was, "In war, there is no second prize for the runner-up."

Five

Deactivation and Airfield Today

On September 7, 1945, the commanding officer received official orders for inactivation of the field on or before September 30, 1945. The B-24 was deemed obsolete, the war had ended, and there was a large surplus of new B-24s, with over 400 aircraft were in storage. Most of those planes were flown straight from the factories to the desert and eventually wound up on the scrap heap without ever seeing service. After the war ended, many airfields were declared surplus by the USAAF and were sold to local communities like Liberal. Two of the runways are maintained for general aviation and commercial airline service. The large airfield remains intact, with only a few sections removed to limit access. When flying over the airfield today, a pilot can still see the layout of the runways. Only a small number of structures remain intact. The original tetrahedron wind indicator was only recently removed. A collection of buildings with ruins shows the size and activity within the airfield. Mid-America Air Museum sits on the large parking apron where large bombers once stood. Excess buildings and equipment were sold or transferred to other bases. Some were torn down, and materials were auctioned off. The Liberal Municipal Airport and surrounding businesses today are likely not aware of the importance the area had on the City of Liberal and the war effort during the 1940s. Even though the look of the airfield has changed, the Mid-America Air Museum has been influential in keeping the history and traditions alive.

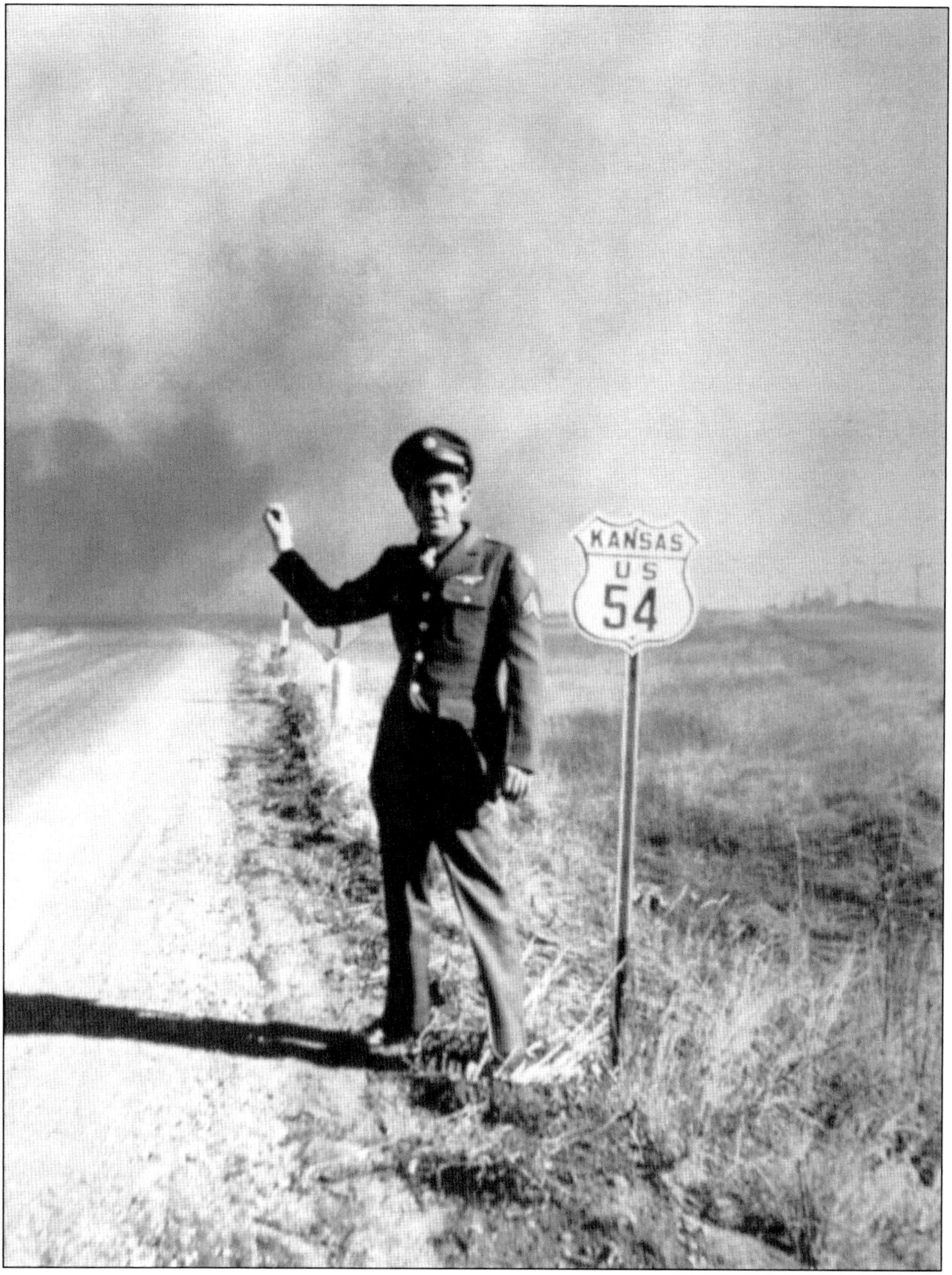

After victory in Europe and the surrender of Japan, B-24 training was over. On September 7, 1945, the commanding officer received orders for inactivation on or before September 30. Col. Ford V. Lauer placed the base on standby, and by October 1, the base was prepared to shut down. Whether airman Pete Pettris was headed out, on leave, or put on movement orders, he appears to be happy to be headed down US Highway 54.

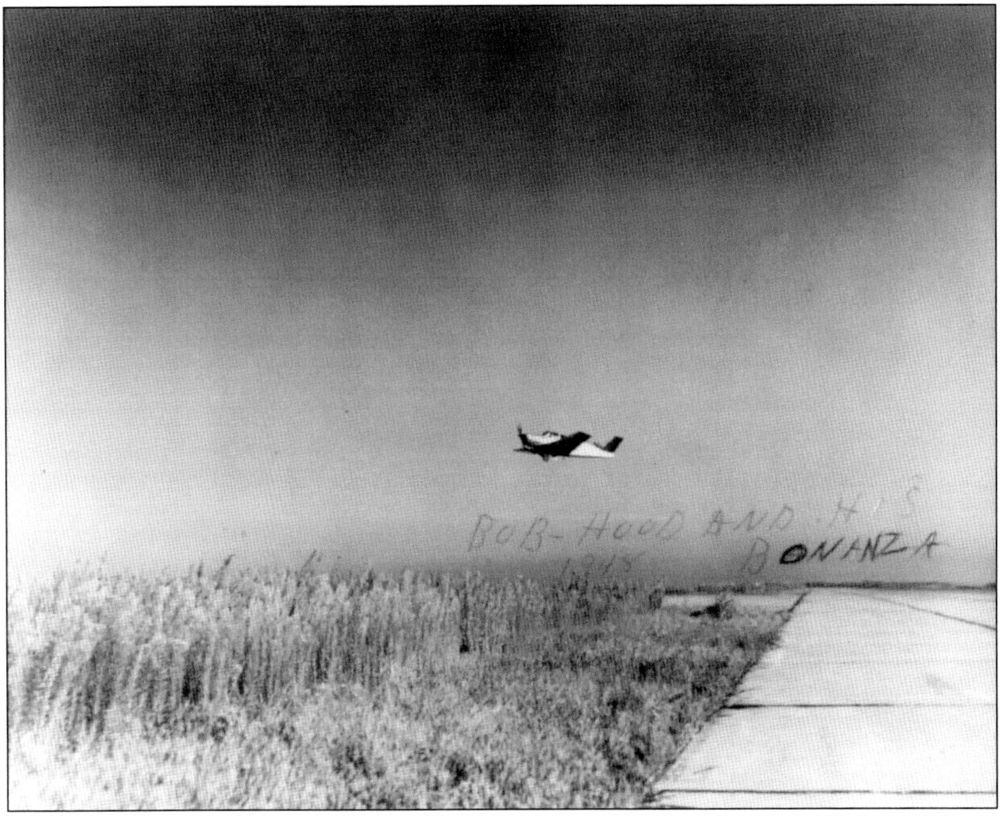

Local rancher and aviation enthusiast Bob Hood had just purchased this 1948 V-Tailed Beech Bonanza and was taking advantage of the long and wide runways the airbase had left. The airfield eventually became the Liberal Municipal Airport.

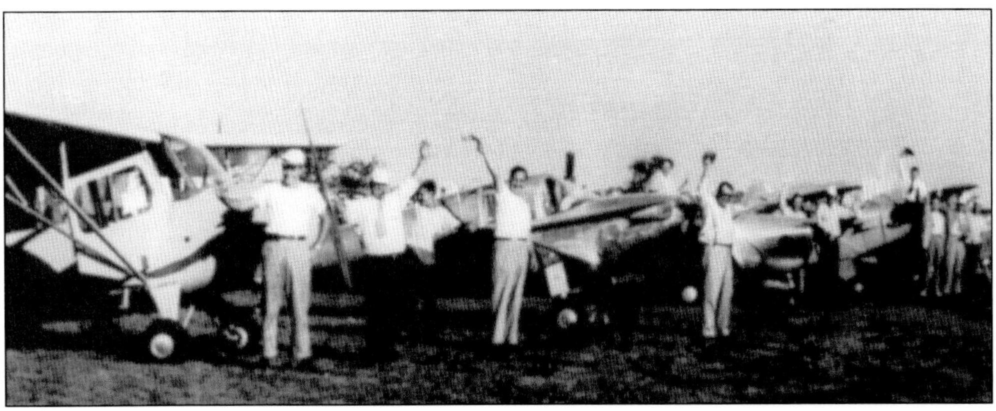

Taken in 1944 at Liberal's first official airport, this image shows the Liberal Chamber of Commerce Goodwill Air Tour in front of their planes. The first plane shown is an Aeronca 65CA Super Chief.

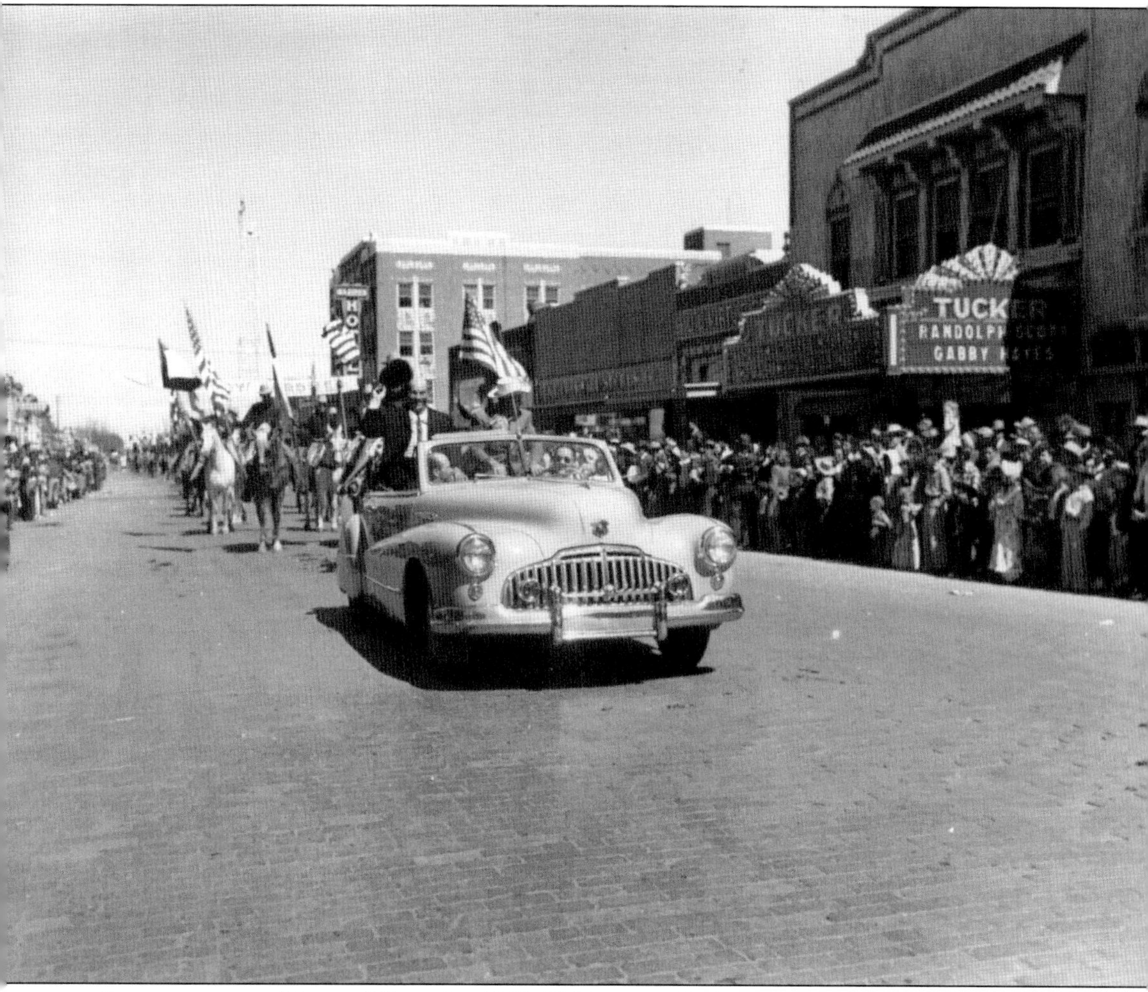

It was time to celebrate. When the 1947 RKO movie *Trail Street* premiered in Liberal, 30,000 people attended the festivities. Free barbeque, free showings of the movie, and Hollywood stars drew happy throngs of people dressed in their Western best. This image shows Billy House, one of the stars of the movie. (Courtesy of the Jean Randall family.)

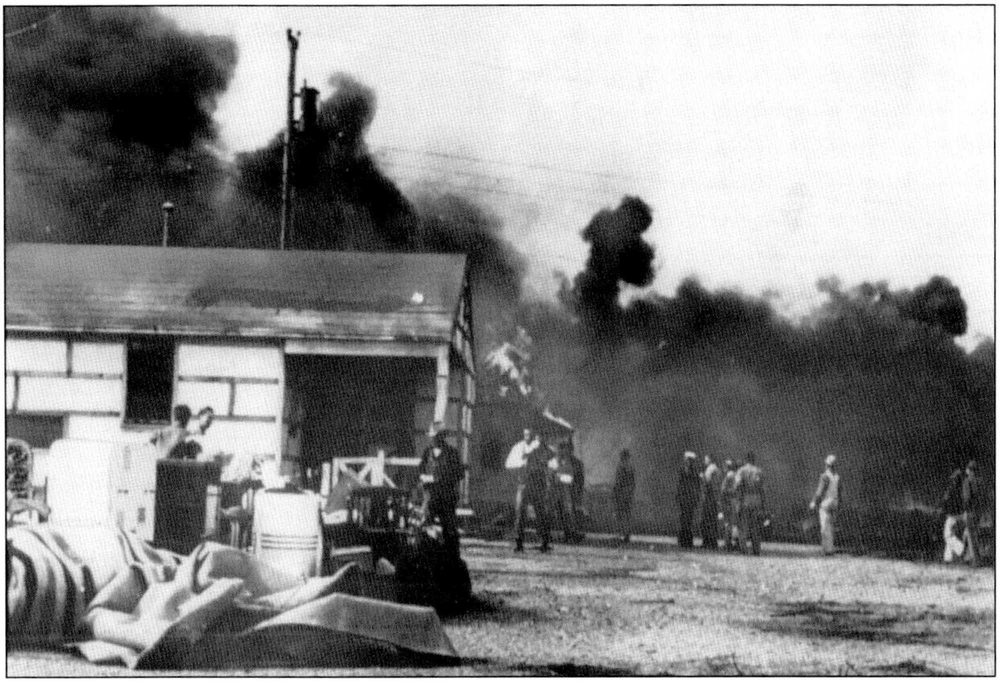

On February 3, 1950, a grassfire pushed by a stiff wind destroyed several unoccupied buildings that had been used by the military on the airfield. The American Legion lost furnishings that had been stored in the vacant buildings. (Courtesy of Lidia Gray.)

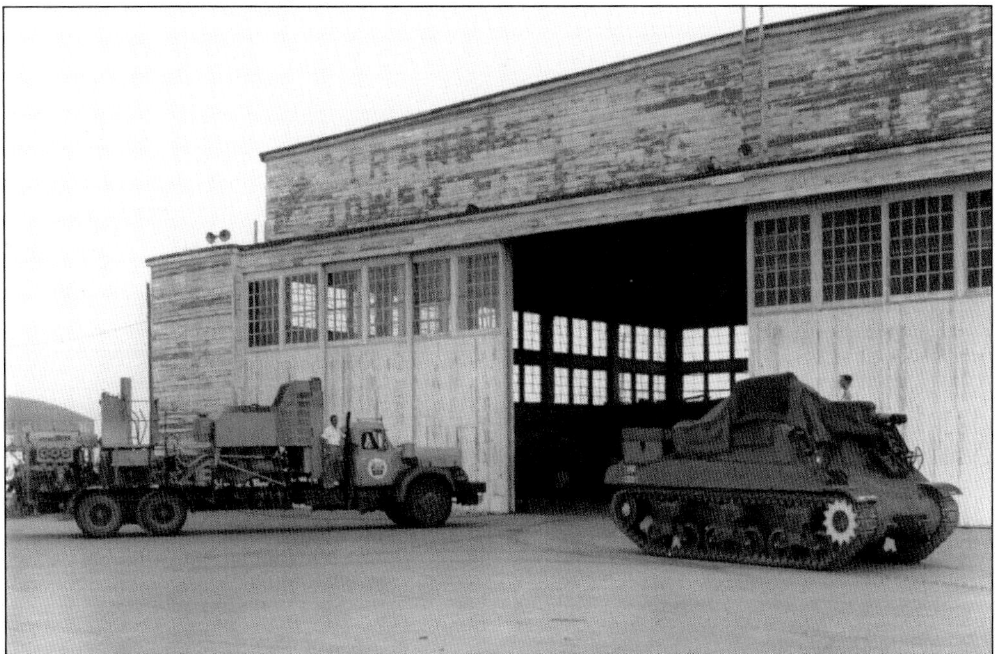

After vacating the B-24 hangars, the Kansas National Guard made good use of the sturdy buildings to house their equipment. Liberal's 161st Armored Field Artillery called this hangar home until the Guard built their new armory in 1958. (Courtesy of Lidia Gray.)

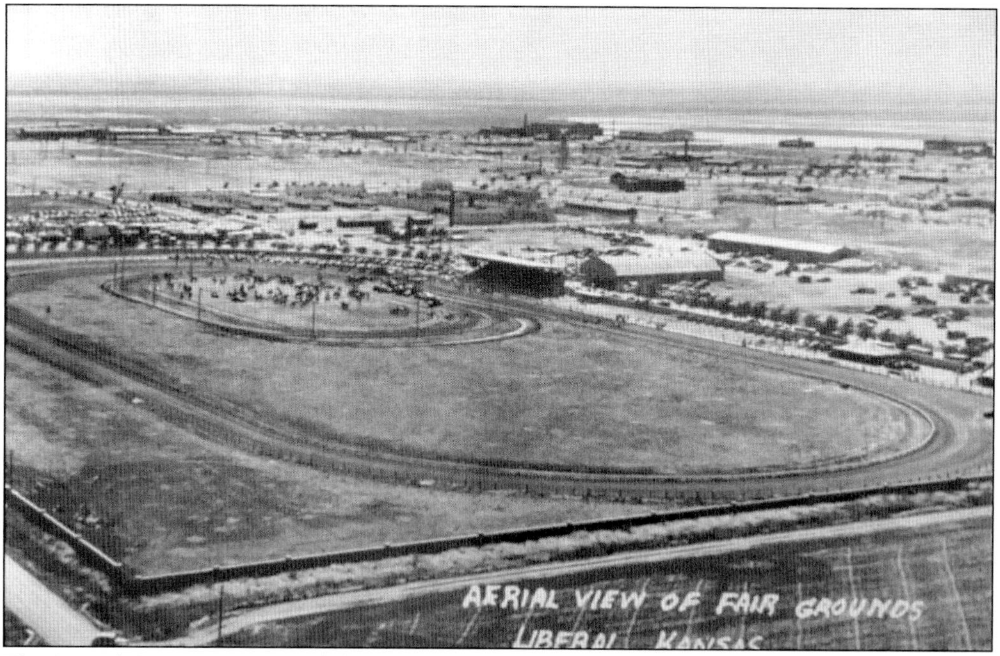

The Seward County Fairgrounds has been a familiar site in the Liberal area since 1912. The rock wall surrounding the fairgrounds was the result of a 1936 Works Progress Administration (WPA) project providing residents a place to play a ballgame, race a horse, or enter a quilt. The airfield is just beyond the fairgrounds in this 1950s image. (Courtesy of Lidia Gray.)

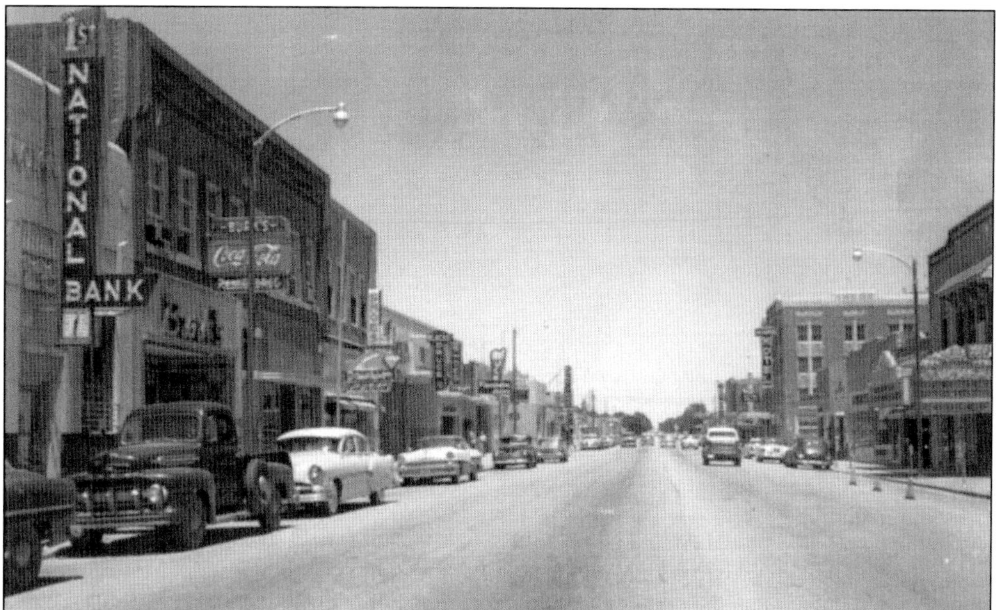

They left as fast as they came. The army airfield was only in Liberal for 27 months, but it meant a life-giving boost to the economy of Liberal leaving the town better off with new businesses, expanded businesses, and new people. (Courtesy of Lidia Gray.)

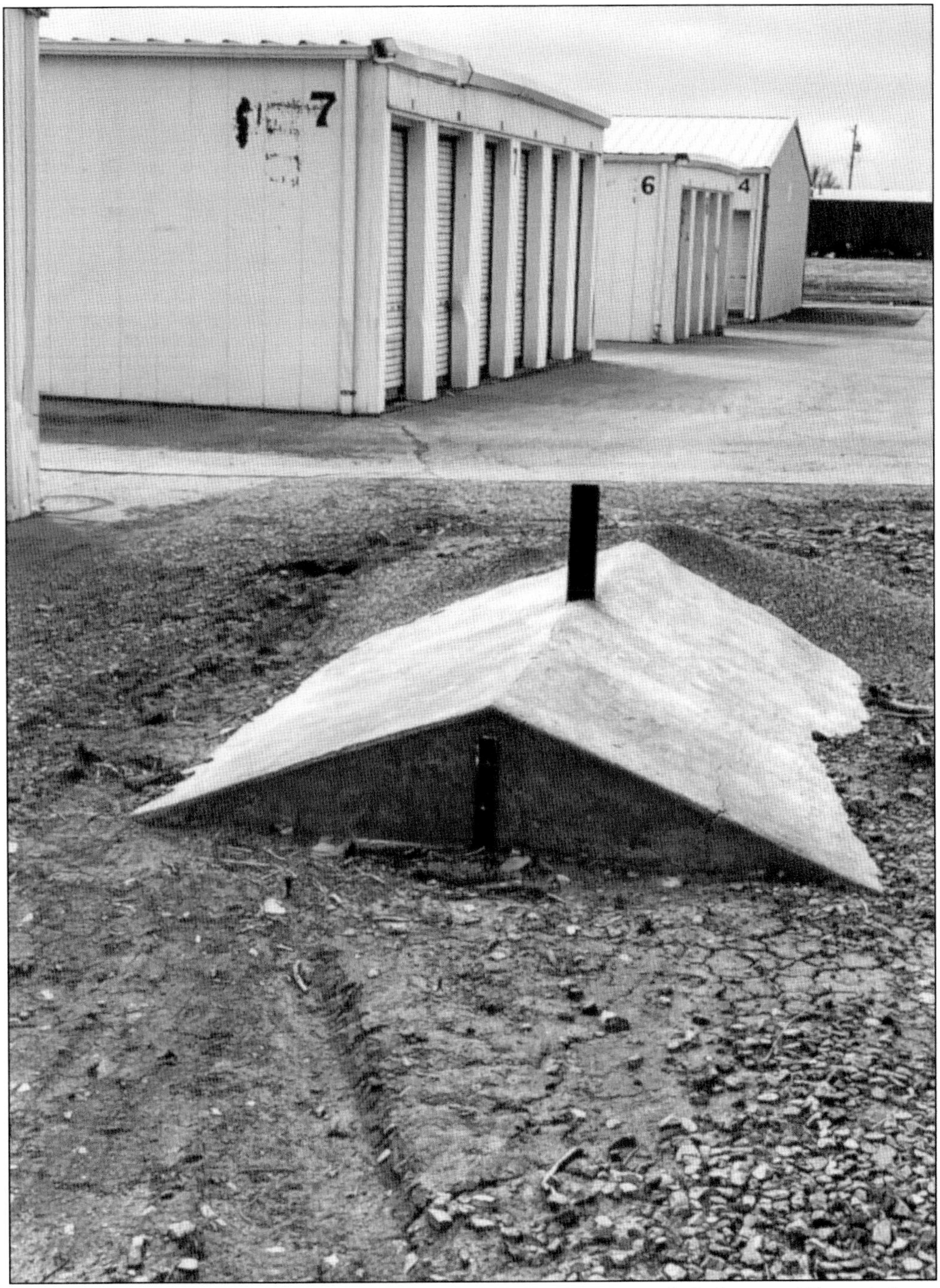

During World War II, many types of structures were used as air raid shelters or fallout shelters. These structures are completely sealed but the top can be seen on the airfield with a stovepipe rising out of concrete for ventilation. Shelters were installed on the base for the protection of soldiers during the event of bombs being dropped. Steep stairs down led to the entrance of a concrete buried structure the size of a living room. These were only provided with temporary supplies, and soldiers were expected to exit as soon as possible. (Courtesy of Connie Bowman.)

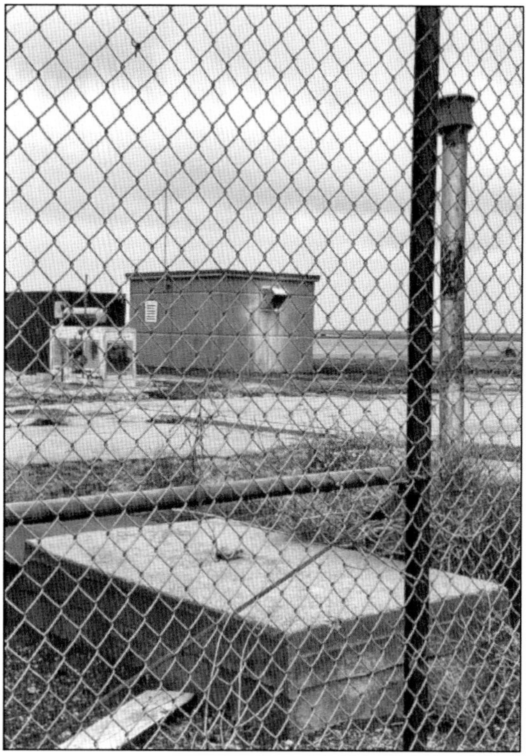

Among the more interesting initiatives of the Federal Civil Defense efforts was the creation of fallout shelters to protect people from deadly radiation. Looking through the fence of the restrictive part of the airport today, there is a sealed concrete slab that covers one such fallout shelter. A photograph of the interior shows much of what a typical shelter looked like. Some of the items recommended for a two-week period were water, dehydrated or canned food, cooking utensils, bedding, sanitation and medical supplies, clothing, and lanterns with extra fuel. Fortunately, these shelters were never put to the test.

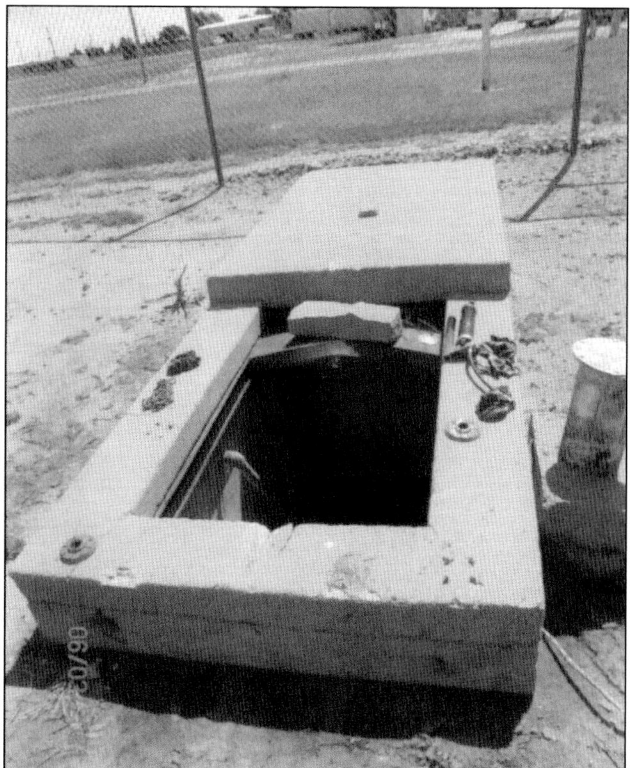

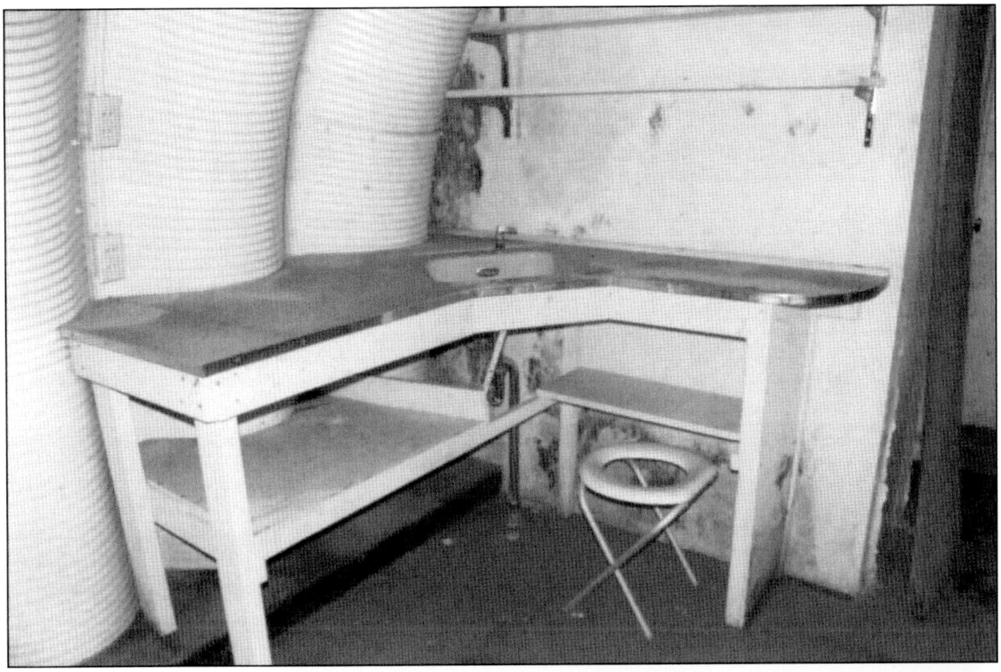

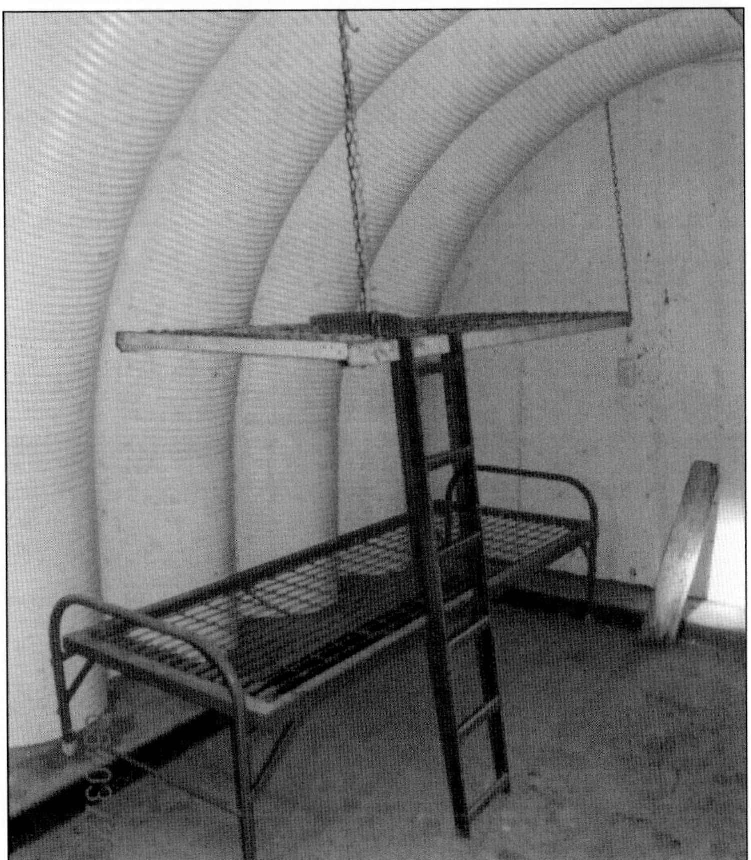

The underground shelter, installed during the Cold War era, is designed for installation completely or partially underground. It provides a living area of 80 square feet and an entrance and storage area of 36 square feet. Although this shelter is not called a blast shelter, it does provide considerable protection from blast heat and immediate nuclear weapon effects in the range of three to ten miles from ground zero. The shelter is now completely sealed and remains behind a secure area.

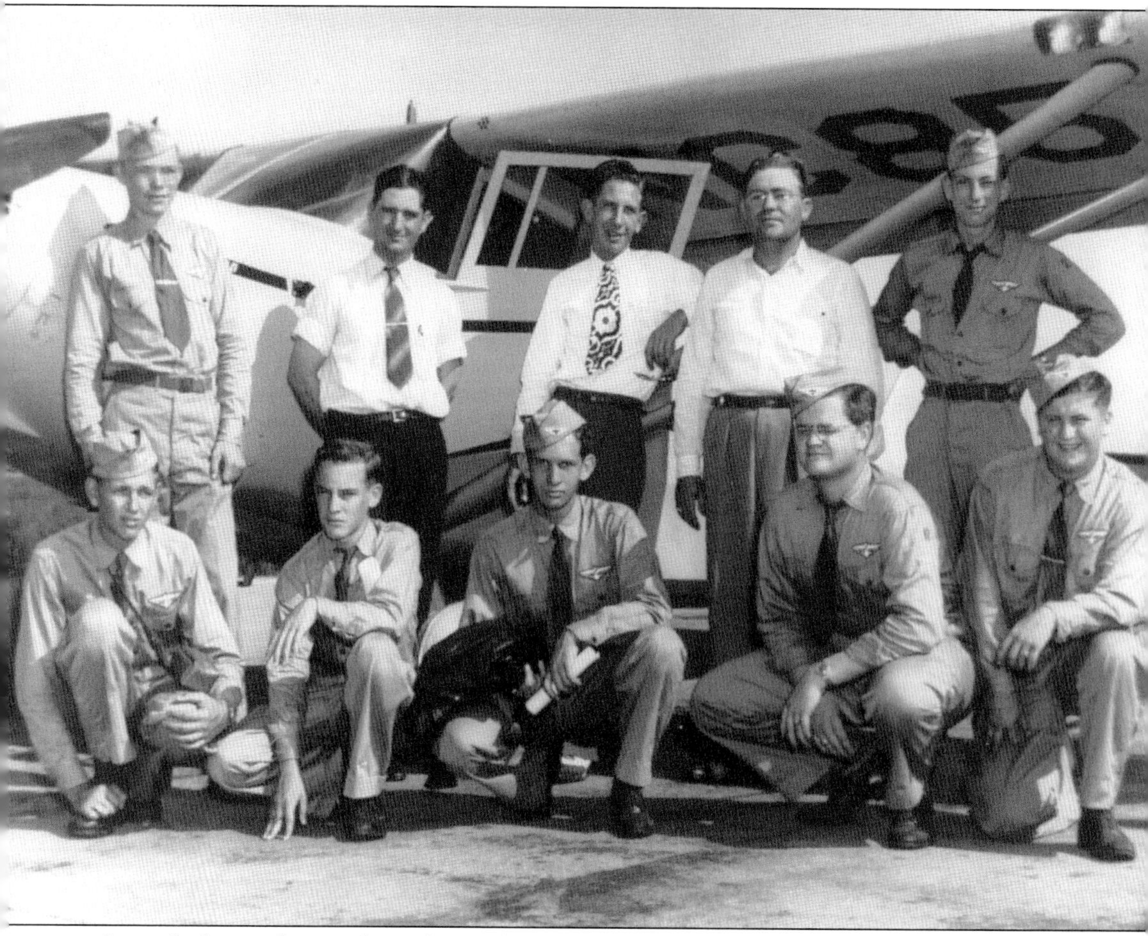

Instead of grounding civilian pilots and aircraft during the war, the War Department authorized the Civil Air Patrol (CAP) to provide training assistance, border patrols, courier service, and search and rescue missions. In case of a plane crash, CAP pilots could fly low and slow and knowing the terrain, could spot accidents in rural, remote areas, quickly getting help to the accident site. Posed in front of one of their planes is Liberal's CAP 1944–1945.

One of the remaining rows of base buildings is now being used as storage. These were the base Link Trainers, and one of the buildings was the War Room. The Link Trainers, or pilot trainers referred to as "flight simulators," were used by student pilots to give them additional instruction on the B-24. The War Room was a dedicated building next to the Link Trainers where military leaders discussed strategies, exchanged ideas, and talked about base activity.

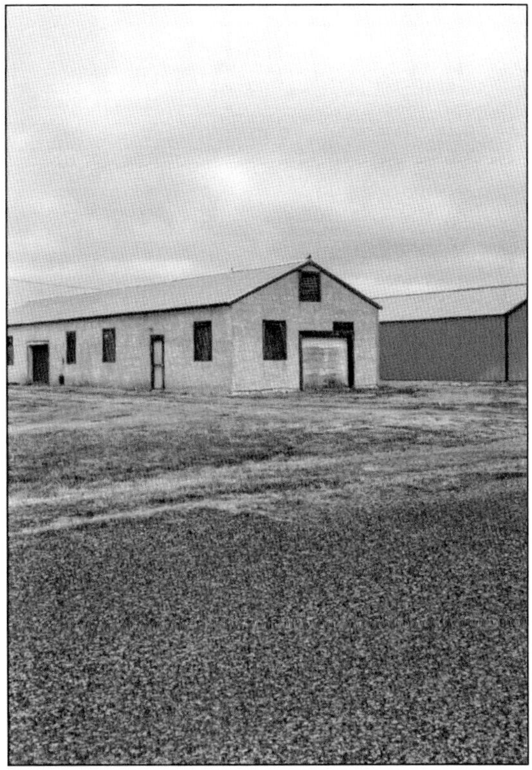

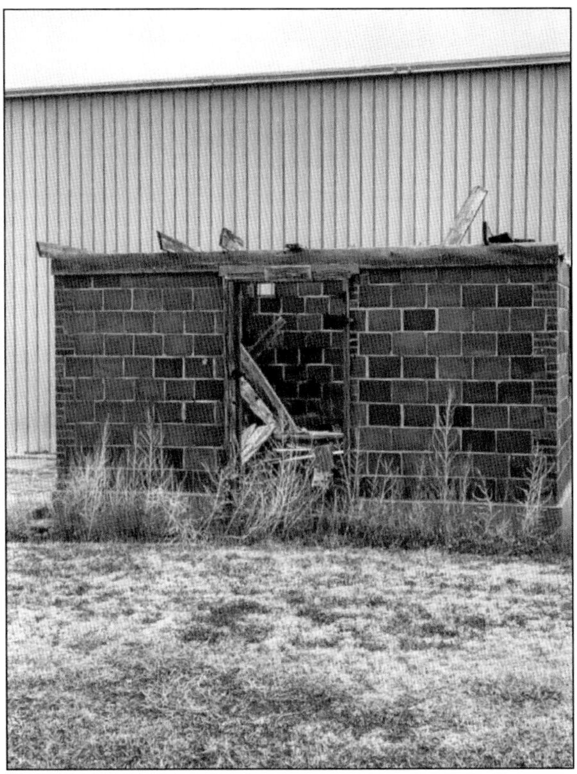

These remaining World War II cinderblock buildings were used to store highly flammable materials. They were used to store hydrogen, oxygen, oil, and paint. On the side of the building, there is lettering that warns, "Dope House, No Smoking Within Five Feet of this Building." Aircraft dope is a plasticized lacquer that is applied to polyester fabric, which tightens and stiffens when stretched. Due to the large size of a B-24, doping techniques were used to lighten the aircraft. (Courtesy of Connie Bowman.)

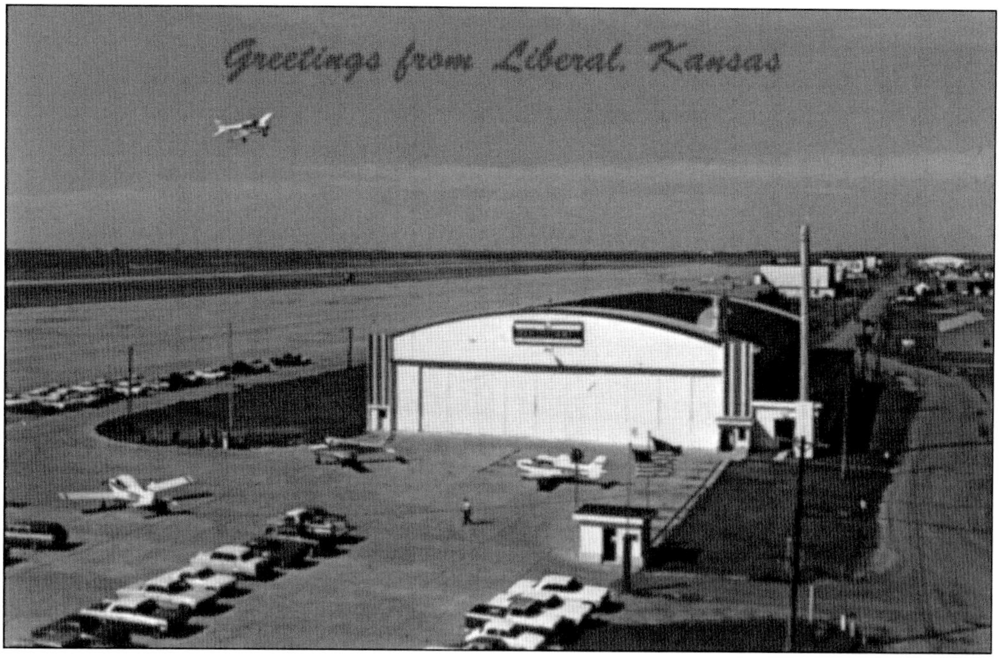

In 1951, the airbase came to life again. Beech Aircraft, headquartered in Wichita, Kansas, leased most of the hangars and began making components for Lockheed. Soon, the Liberal division began manufacturing private aircraft, proudly building the Musketeer, Sierra, Sundowner, the twin-engine Duchess, and the T-Tailed Skipper. The Liberal division employed more than 500 people. (Courtesy of Lidia Gray.)

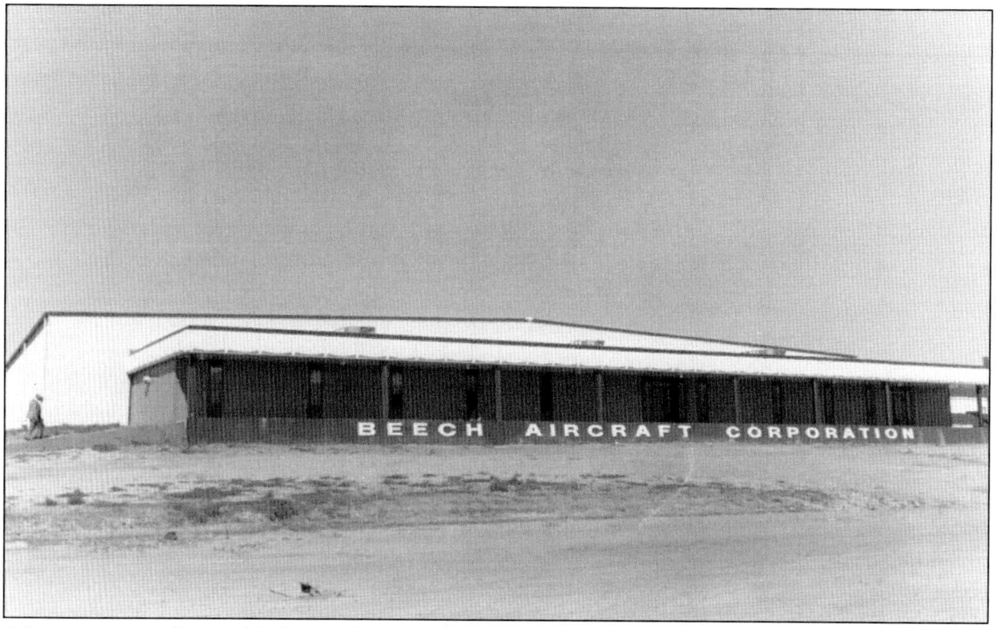

After a massive fire in 1965, Beech Aircraft made the decision to build this 86,000-square-foot building. The front portion included executive offices, sales offices, engineering, reception, and lobby. The main floor had open spans and huge doors to accommodate large machinery for aviation manufacturing. (Courtesy of Lidia Gray.)

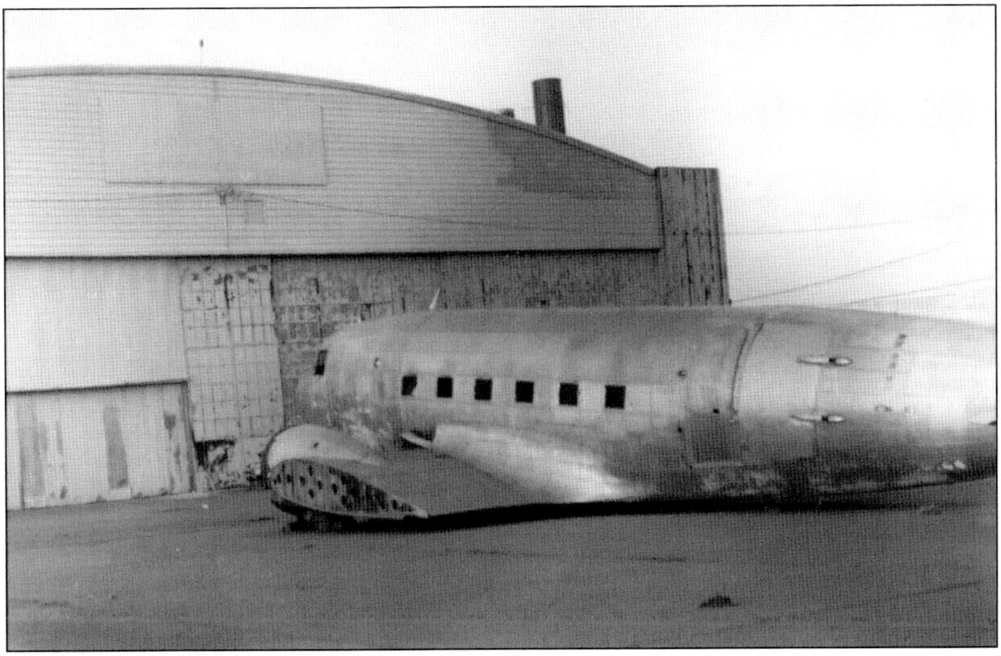

Both structures pictured here have seen better days. Bellied in front of one of the remaining steel hangars, this Douglas DC-3 seems to be waiting for the hangar doors to open.

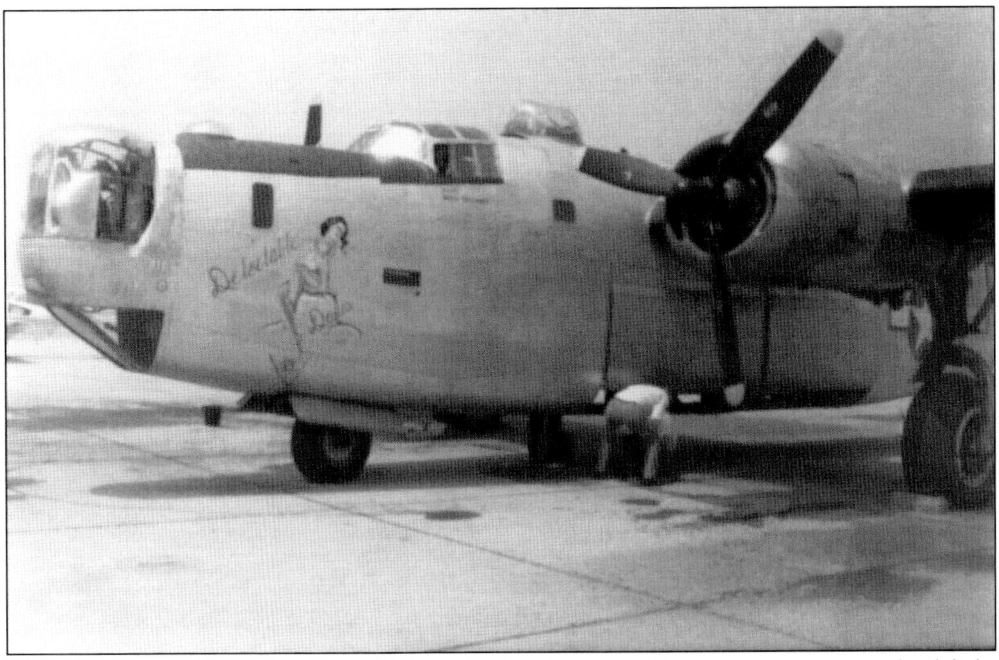

Coming in with only three engines, "Delectable Doris" touched down on the runway to the delight of the LAAF reunion attendees. Pilots, crews, and personnel who had trained at the airfield between 1943 and 1945 had come to reminisce about old times. Delectable Doris helped bring their stories to life. (Courtesy of Lidia Gray.)

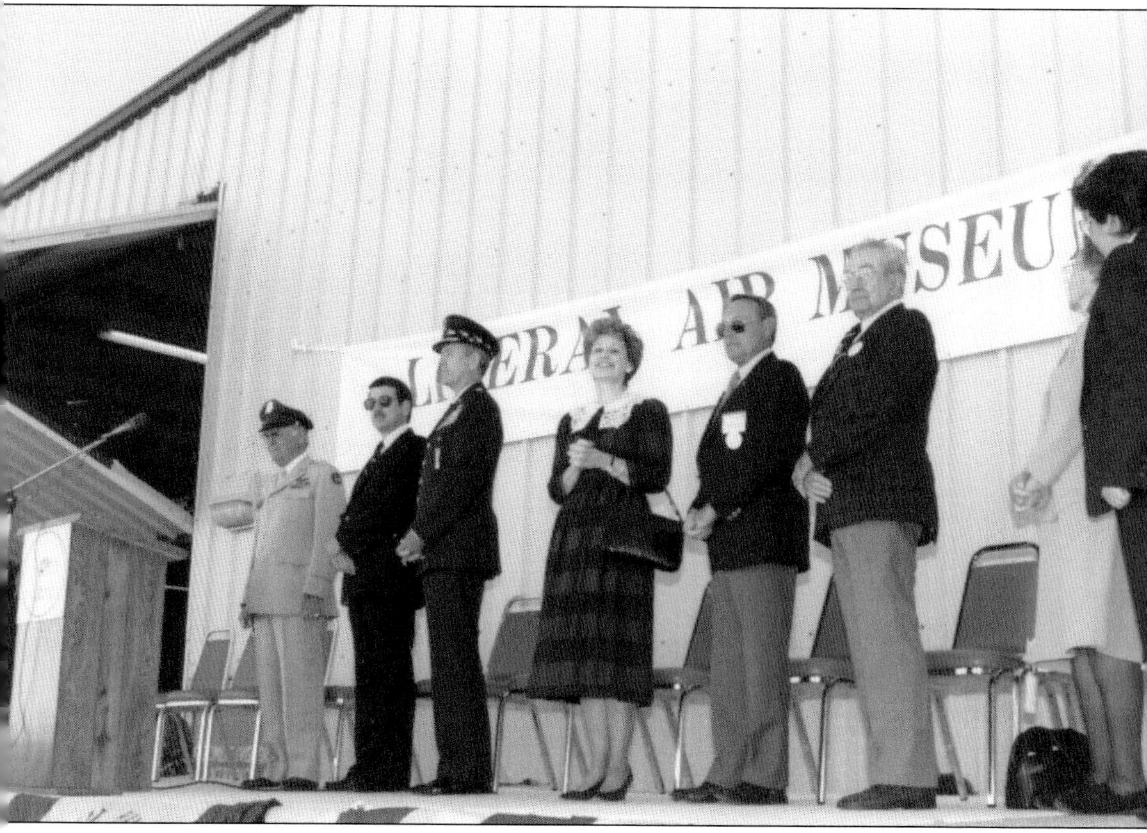

It was a great day on September 24, 1988, when the Liberal Air Museum had a dedication ceremony by opening the big hangar doors of the former Beech building. On hand were, from left to right, Col. Tom Thomas, World War II decorated fighter pilot and museum donor; John T. Smith, founding member; Gen. Larry Welch, USAF chief of staff; Eunice Welch, wife of General Welch; Don Rash, founding member; Oliver and Nina Katherine Welch, parents of General Welch; and Beth Koehn, mayor of Liberal. Not pictured are Keith Knos, Phyllis Windle, Max Zimmerman, Jim Thompson, and Kerry McQueen, also founding members. (Courtesy of John T. Smith.)

The Gage Auxiliary Airport was an important part of the LAAF training program. Through the years after 1945, the airport has been a lifesaver for a DC-6, a Grumman Albatross, and several incidents of blizzard emergencies. Gage was home to a National Weather Service Station and served as the Civil Aviation/ Federal Aviation Administration (FAA) Authority until the 1990s. Bill and Wanda Johnson (pictured below) operated Gage's station from the late 1950s to the early 1990s. (Courtesy of the Town of Gage, Oklahoma.)

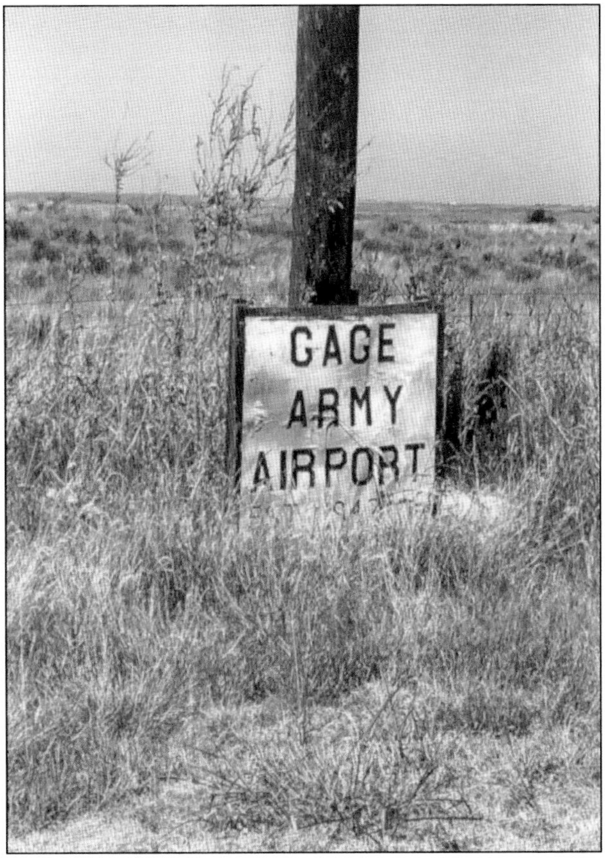

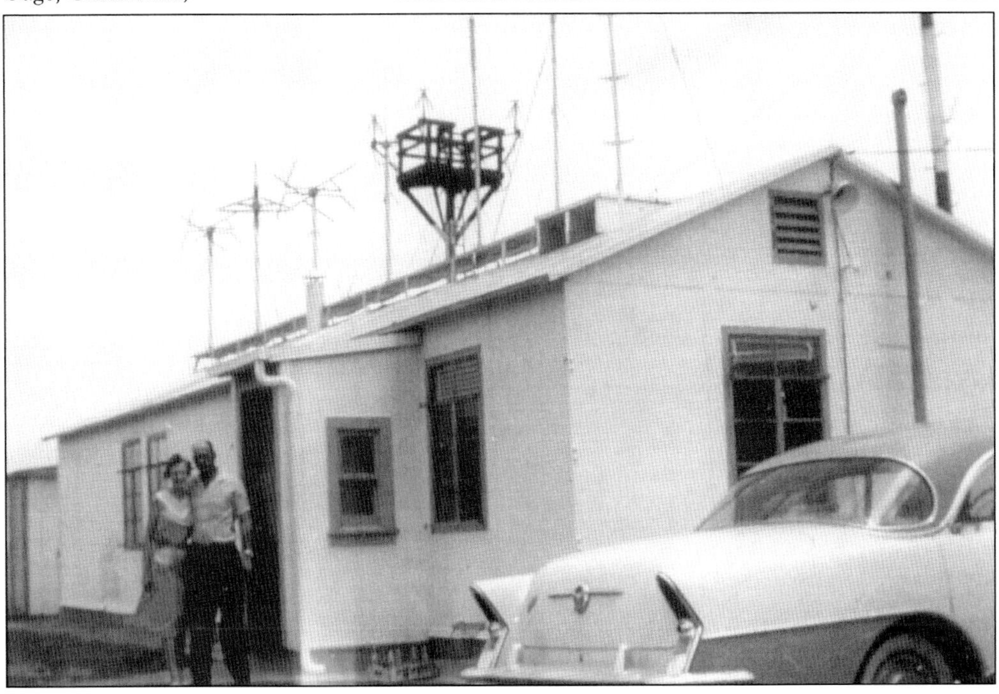

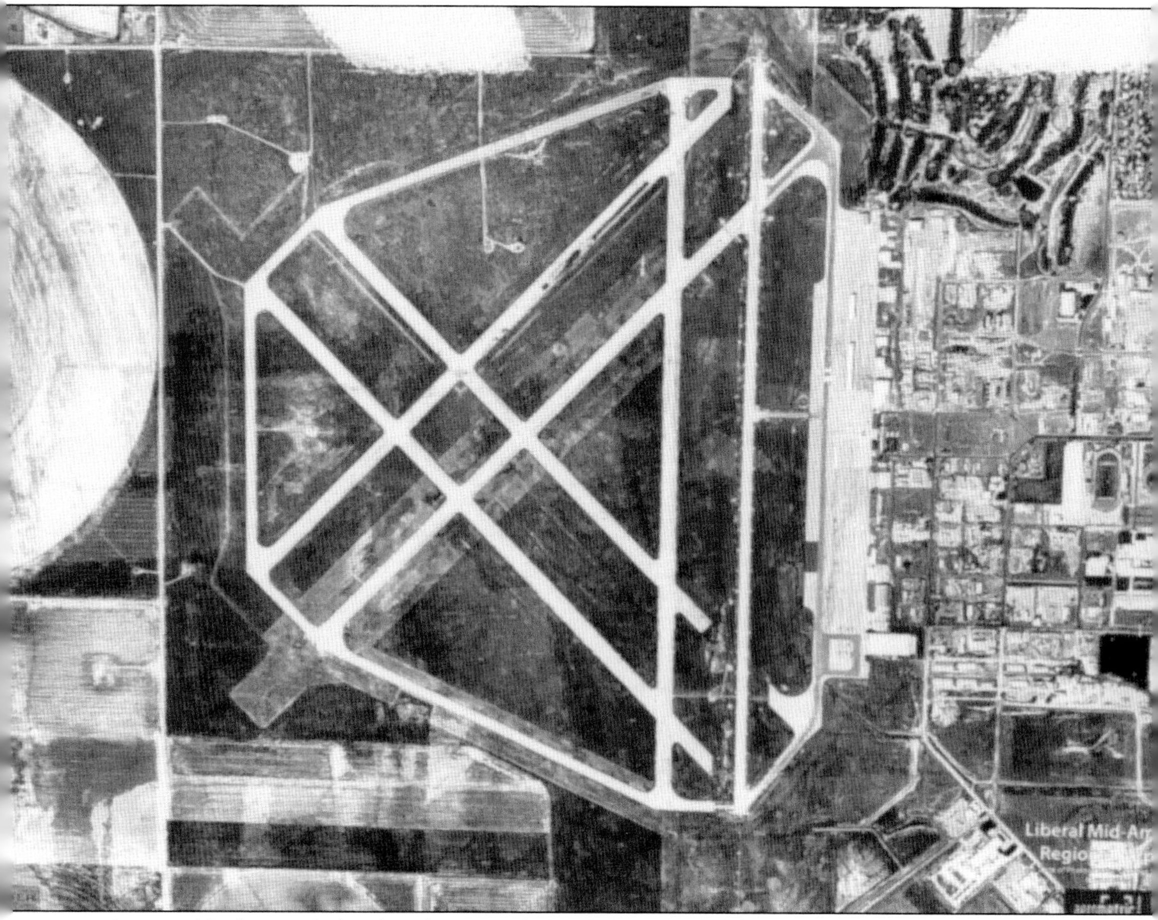

An aerial look at today's Liberal airport shows the former LAAF is now home to many industrial businesses, a fixed base operator, the air terminal, and the Mid-America Air Museum. Even though the airfield hangars, barracks, and warehouses are gone, their foundations remain. (Courtesy of the City of Liberal Airport Authority.)

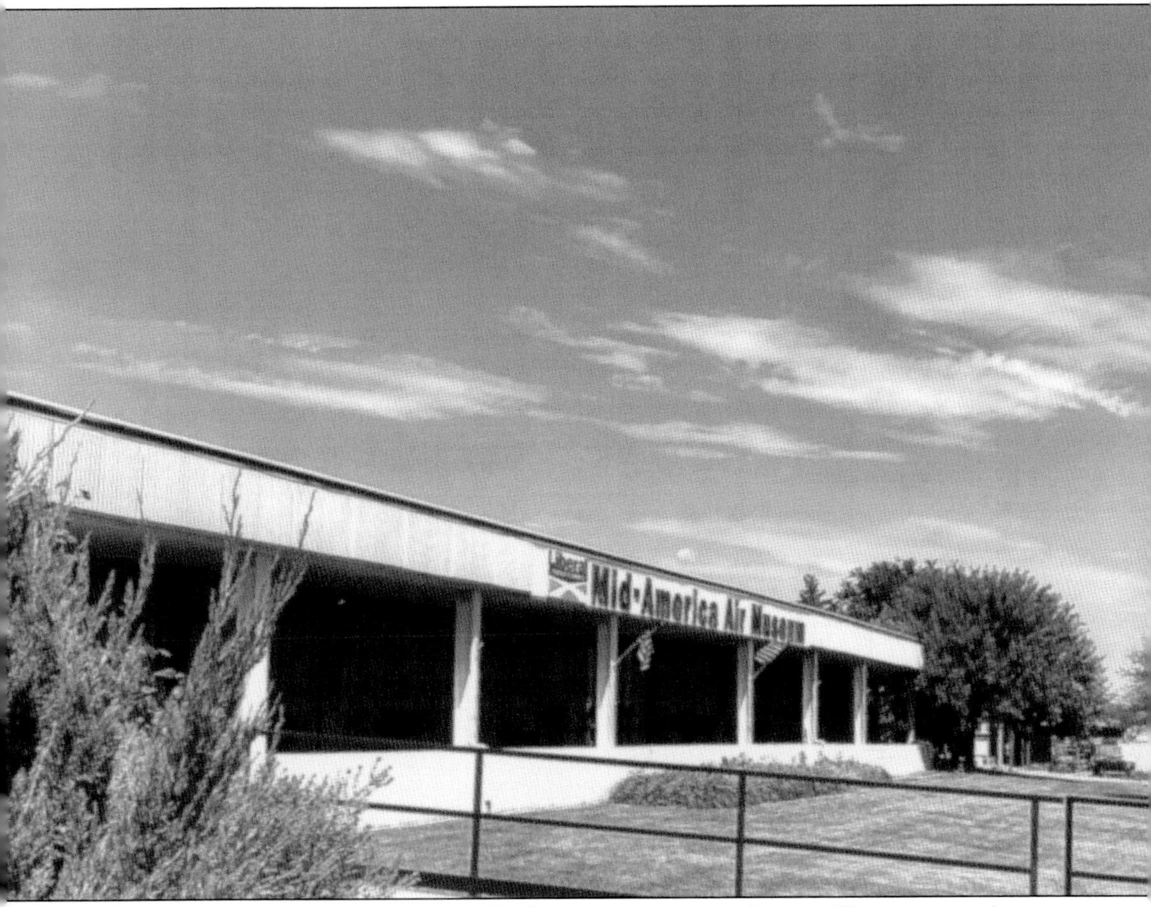

The Mid-America Air Museum was established to preserve aviation history. The museum is home to over 100 planes, all under an 80,000-square-foot roof. With everything from an ultralight to a B-25, to the futuristic Beech Starship, the museum has something for all aviation enthusiasts.

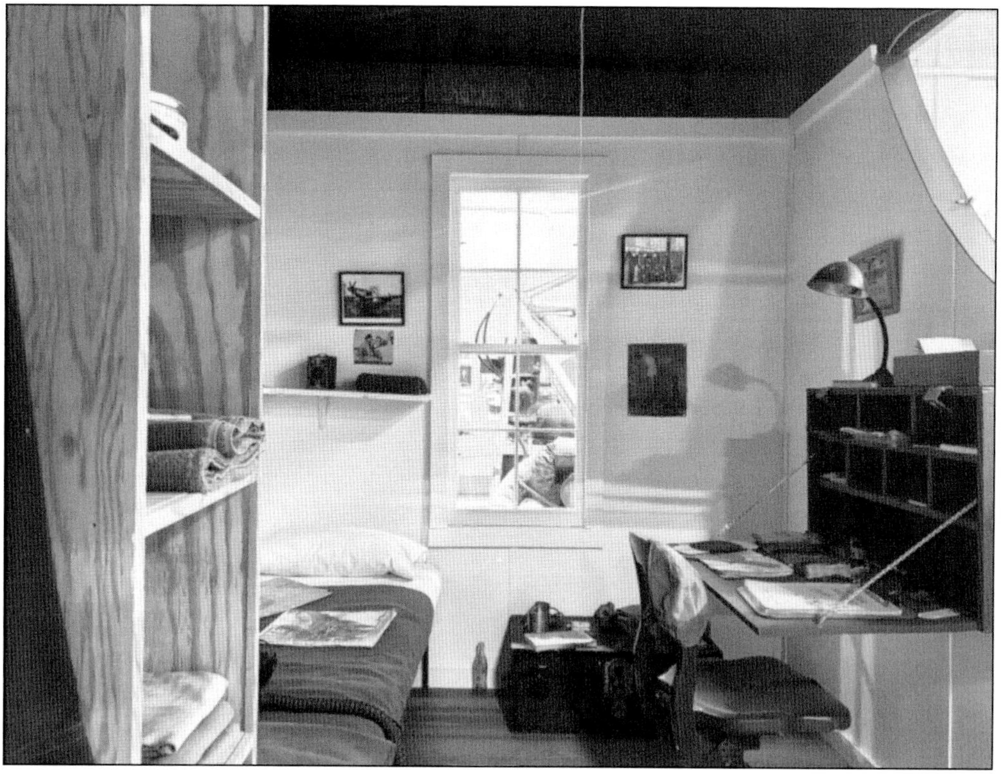

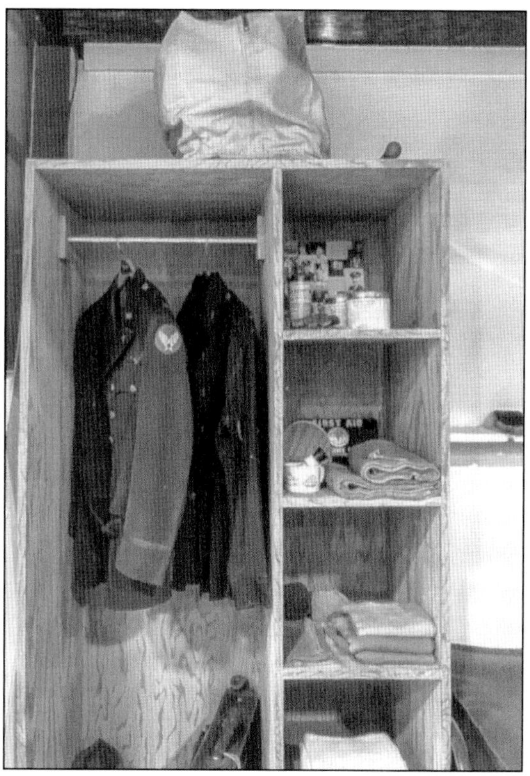

A portion of the Mid-America Air Museum is dedicated to the LAAF, featuring photographs, artifacts, dioramas, and even a nose wheel from a B-24. One of the exhibits here is an example of an officer's quarters while living on base.

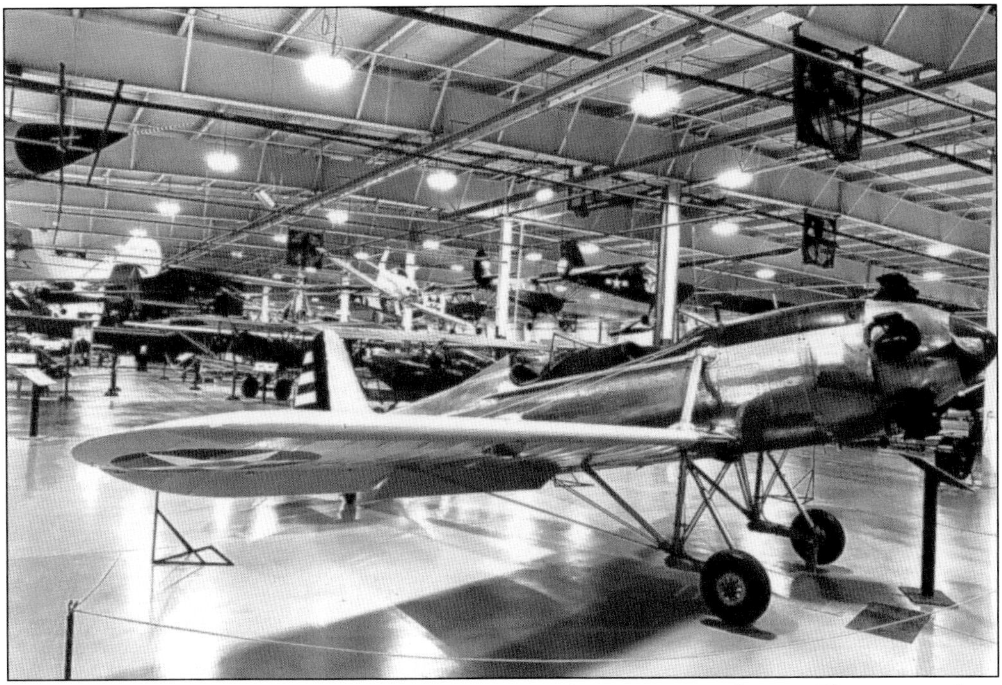

The Mid-American Air Museum is a dream come true for any aviation devotee. Planes range from Dwane Wallace's Cessna C-165, Max Conrad's Piper Comanche, and Ken Johnson's Glassair III to local crop duster Jim Floyd's Grumman Ag Cat. Revolving exhibits and events keep the museum and aviation alive.

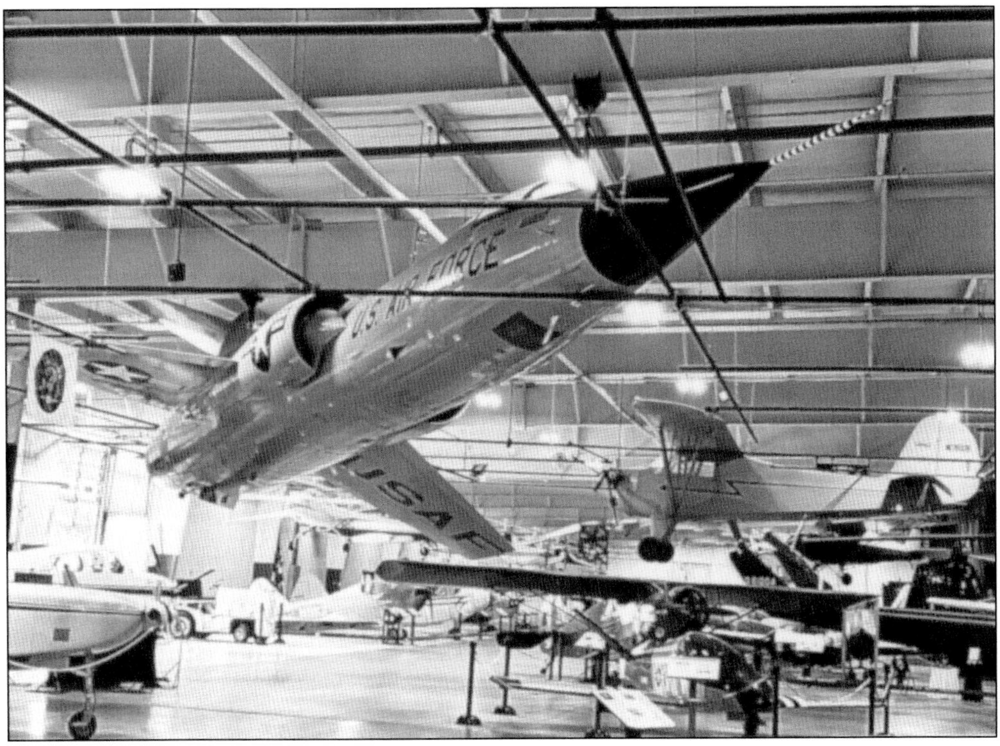

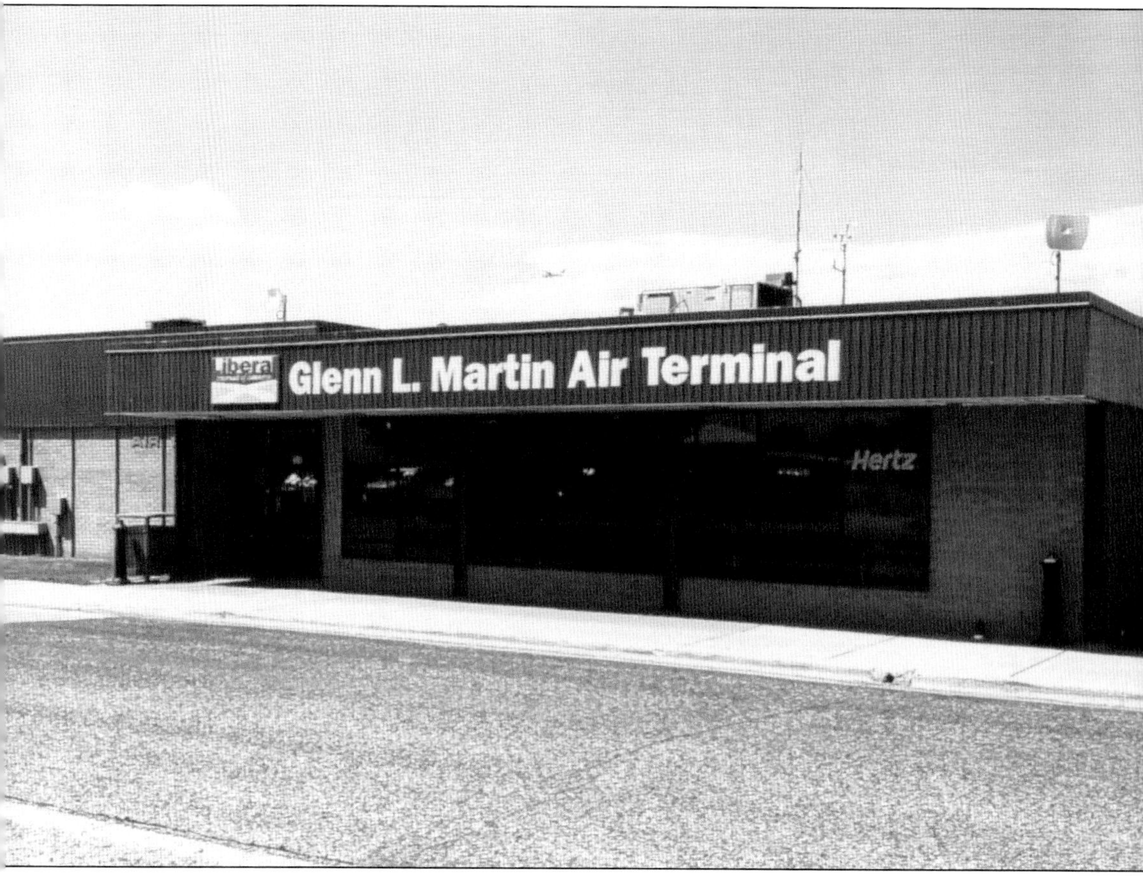

Named after Liberal's aviator, the Glenn L. Martin terminal presently serves the tristate area with daily flights. A flagpole and garden area in front of the terminal is maintained by the Liberal Rotary Club and dedicated to the men and women who served the LAAF. (Courtesy of Lidia Gray.)

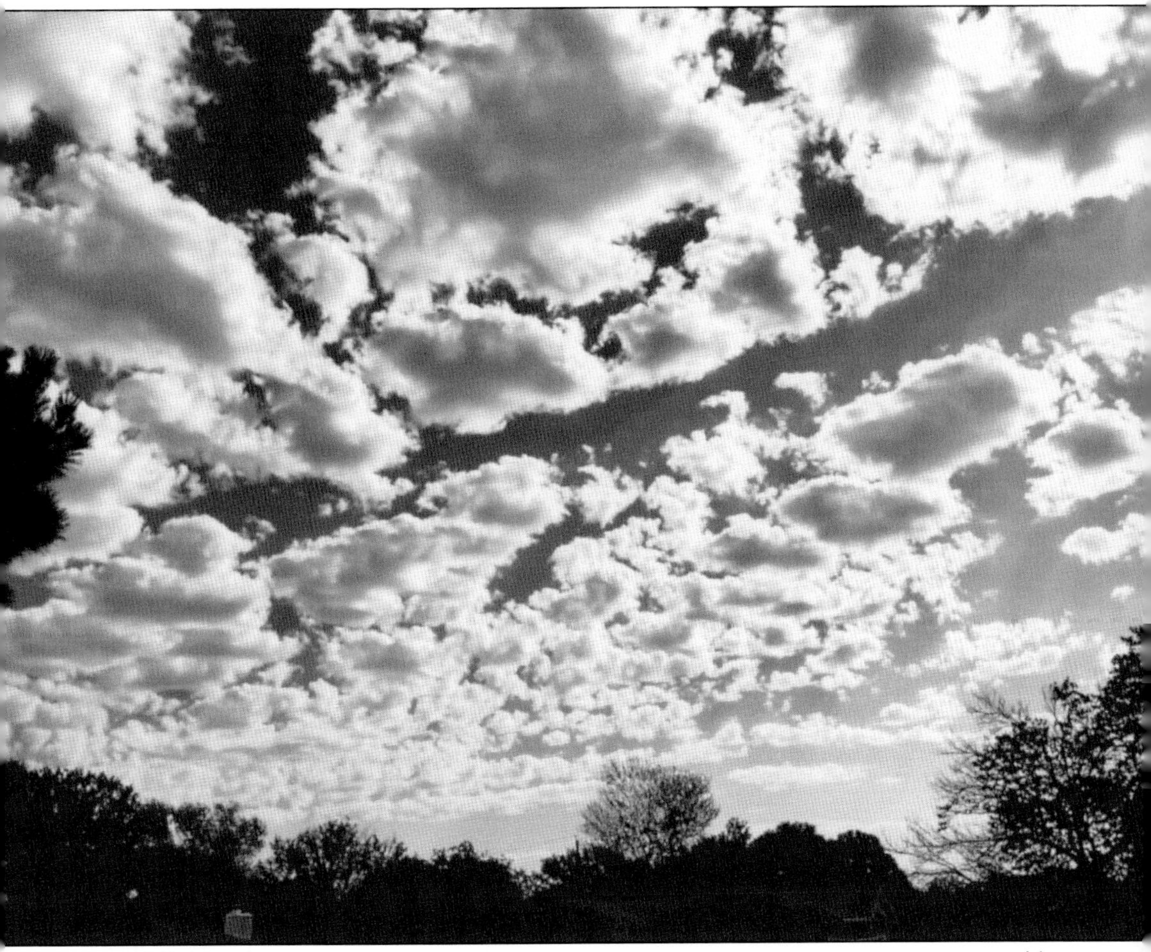

A beautiful sunset over Liberal and the Mid-America Air Museum, where once everyone would have seen those big, clumsy but beautiful B-24s punch their way through the clouds. It has been 81 years since Liberal has heard those loud engines overhead and the traffic making its way onto and out of the base. The base was here for just 27 months but will remain in Liberal's history books forever. Thank you to the Army Air Corps and all the branches of service for everyone's yesterdays and tomorrows. "Let Us Never Forget," and may we remember the sacrifice of so many. (Courtesy of Connie Bowman.)

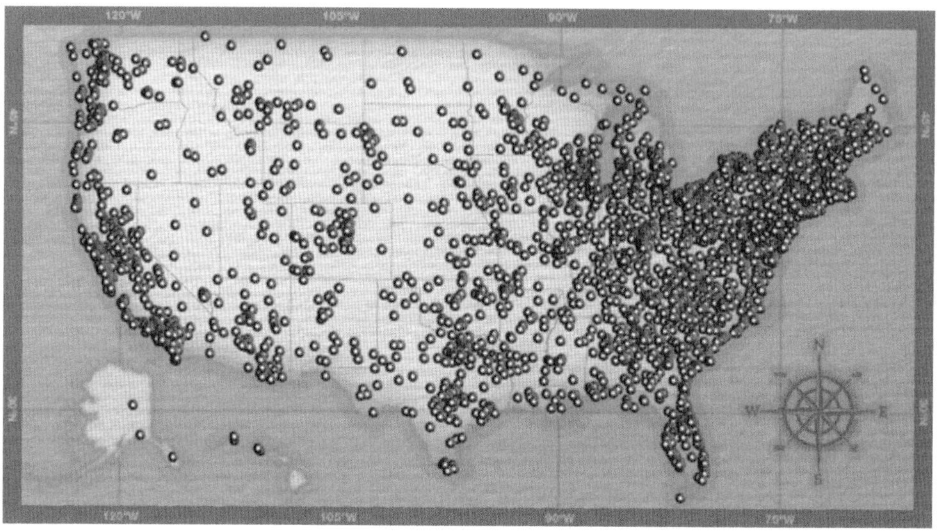